APPROACH TO FINAL VICTORY

APPROACH TO FINAL VICTORY

America's Rainbow Division in the Saint Mihiel and Meuse-Argonne Offensives

ROBERT THOMPSON

WESTHOLME
Yardley

Facing title page: Soldiers of the 166th Infantry outside Cheveuges, France, November 1918. (*National Archives*)

© 2023 Robert Thompson
Maps by Robert Thompson

All rights reserved under International and Pan-American Copyright Conventions. No part of this book may be reproduced in any form or by any electronic or mechanical means, including information storage and retrieval systems, without permission in writing from the publisher, except by a reviewer who may quote brief passages in a review.

Westholme Publishing, LLC
904 Edgewood Road
Yardley, Pennsylvania 19067
Visit our Web site at www.westholmepublishing.com

ISBN: 978-1-59416-409-5

Also available as an eBook.

Printed in the United States of America.

In loving memory of my father, Harold Thompson, who passed away as I was completing this book. He lived to see his 100th birthday, was married for 70 years, and was a combat veteran of both World War II and Vietnam. Thoughtful, stoic, and wise, he was the greatest man I ever knew.

CONTENTS

List of Maps — viii
Preface — ix

1. A New American Division in France — 1
2. From the Trenches to the Aisne-Marne — 17
3. The Calm Before the Storm — 45
4. Preparing for the Saint Mihiel Offensive — 61
5. Into the Salient — 76
6. Taking and Holding the Salient — 101
7. To the Meuse-Argonne — 119
8. The Assault on the Kriemhilde Stellung Begins — 138
9. Taking Hill 288 and Hill 242 — 160
10. The Côte de Châtillon — 172
11. Exploiting the Breakthrough — 187
12. The Race to Sedan — 198
13. Armistice — 215

Afterword — 221
Notes — 229
Bibliography — 251
Index — 259

MAPS

1. *The Rainbow Division's deployment in the Baccarat Sector, May 13, 1918*   *25*
2. *The Rainbow Division's positions in the Champagne Defensive, July 15, 1918*   *31*
3. *The Rainbow Division's campaign during the Aisne-Marne Offensive*   *41*
4. *The plan for the Saint Mihiel offensive with German defensive lines*   *71*
5. *The Rainbow Division's advance on September 12, 1918*   *83*
6. *The Rainbow Division's advance on September 13, 1918*   *104*
7. *The Rainbow Division's final positions in the Saint Benoît Sector*   *113*
8. *The Rainbow Division's attack on October 14, 1918*   *147*
9. *The Rainbow Division's attack on October 15, 1918*   *165*
10. *The Rainbow Division's attack against the Côte de Châtillon on October 16, 1918*   *177*
11. *The Rainbow Division's final positions opposite Sedan on November 8, 1918*   *208*

PREFACE

In late 2019, I began research for a book on the Ohio National Guard's 166th Infantry Regiment, which served in France during World War I as part of the 42nd Division. That legendary unit became known popularly as the "Rainbow Division" because the War Department created it from the National Guard units of twenty-six states and territories. Because I found the story of the 42nd so compelling, I wrote a second book about the division's service during the Aisne-Marne Offensive. Therefore, this book marks my third step in documenting the role of Rainbow Division in what the world then called the "Great War." As I was working on those two previous books, *Suddenly Soldiers: The 166th Infantry Regiment in World War I* and *Nine Desperate Days: America's Rainbow Division in the Aisne-Marne Offensive*, I began to sense a growing and deep connection to the ordinary yet remarkable men of the Rainbow Division, these citizen-soldiers who went to France in 1917.

I was poised to begin the final chapter of this book just before November 11, 2021, Veteran's Day. We originally called that date Armistice Day to commemorate the end of the Great War. It occurred to me that the change from Armistice Day to Veteran's Day, though clearly well intended, was unfortunate. Altering the day's name and purpose further diluted the nation's diminishing collective memory of the sacrifices made by the men of the Rainbow Division and all the other Americans who went to France in 1917 and 1918. The change was another step toward making a massive human catastrophe that forever changed the world into a forgotten war. If I had one hope for my books on the Rainbow Division, it would be that in some small way they help people remember these men and the war in which they fought.

This leg of my journey with the men of the Rainbow Division chronicles their participation in the final Allied offensives of the war at Saint Mihiel and in the Meuse-Argonne. The division's experiences in these two campaigns differed markedly. Saint Mihiel showed how much the American Expeditionary Forces, or AEF, had evolved. This first offensive planned and led by American forces for the most part was well-conceived and well-executed, resulting in a rapid advance and quick victory. However, as events in the Meuse-Argonne later proved, in terms of the AEF's ability to conduct a massive offensive, the Saint Mihiel Offensive was something of an outlier.

The Meuse-Argonne—at the time the largest operation ever undertaken by the U.S. Army—was more than the army's leadership and organization in France was capable of handling. Five of the nine American divisions assigned to make the initial attack had not been sufficiently trained and had no combat experience. Their orders required them to fight on some of the most challenging terrain in France against formidable German defenses. Worse, perhaps, AEF leadership set unrealistic objectives for American forces, then pushed those men to greater effort that led to ever more casualties incurred gaining little ground. Eighteen days after the offensive began, the Rainbow Division found itself rushed into battle in the Meuse-Argonne, a replay of the poor planning and leadership that had plagued the men in the Aisne-Marne. As in that fight, the division achieved success only through the leadership, courage, and valor of those at the front lines.

Since beginning my first book on the Rainbow Division, I have been struck by the quality of leadership demonstrated by the unit's officers and noncommissioned officers, or NCOs, at the battalion, company, and platoon levels. Even young, inexperienced officers hurried into service from the Citizen's Military Training Corps learned quickly and rose to the occasion at seemingly every turn. Conversely, Regular Army officers at the higher echelons of command varied in their leadership but, for the most part, their performance was mediocre at best. Among more senior officers, this mediocrity was clearly a product of pre-war U.S. Army culture. The army's doctrine and weapons were outdated, and while a reform movement had begun in the early twentieth century, the farther one went up the chain of command, the less the impact achieved by particular reforms.

Perhaps the best example of this phenomenon was the AEF commander. In many ways, Lieutenant General John J. Pershing performed admirably as overall commander of American forces in France. He effectively balanced diplomacy and confrontation in his dealings with the British and French. This duality enabled Pershing to achieve President Woodrow Wilson's objective of creating an independent U.S. Army organization in France despite intense opposition from some in the Allied leadership. But when Pershing attempted to assume command of the new U.S. 1st Army, he faltered. He had never truly embraced the type of warfare demanded by modern weapons, especially the effective use of heavy artillery, believing instead in the primacy of the infantryman and his rifle. As a result, he sometimes opposed the proper use of artillery, and, in the Meuse-Argonne, he set objectives to be achieved in three to four days that actually took forty-seven days to accomplish at a cost of over 120,000 casualties. And when Pershing did not get the results he desired, he blamed his field commanders, fired competent officers, and pushed subordinates to gain ground no matter the losses they might suffer.

Some upper echelon AEF officers stand out as solid professionals. One was Colonel George C. Marshall. Marshall, a captain when the United States entered the war in April 1917, was one of the few men in the army who had attended the Command and Staff College at Fort Leavenworth. Initially assigned to serve as chief AEF planner, he later moved into that role at 1st Army Headquarters when it came into being. Marshall employed all he had learned at Fort Leavenworth to lead his staff in devising the offensive at Saint Mihiel. The eventual plan was masterful, a comprehensive document with annexes for every possible support contingency that served as a model for the U.S. Army going into World War II.

General Douglas MacArthur began the war as a major. He became the Rainbow Division's Chief of Staff, commanding the division's 84th Brigade at the time of the offensives at Saint Mihiel and in the Meuse-Argonne. Intellectually brilliant, MacArthur seems to have had a well-balanced perspective on tactical success and his troops' welfare. But he was vain and ambitious and at times hungry for favor, success, promotion, and fame. This hunger sometimes led him to propose plans that, had they been implemented, not only would have failed but would have done so at the cost of thousands of lives. Following the war, his quirks impelled him into a curious relationship with accuracy and truth, a tension that only worsened with the years. Stories and recollections from MacArthur often do not pass muster when compared to official records and other officers' accounts. Historians must exercise great caution in weighing whether to use anything MacArthur said afterwards about the war.

In my research, what stood out the most about leadership in the Rainbow Division was the fact that, in several cases, despite orders issued by headquarters based on inadequate, faulty planning, the division's men nonetheless achieved tactical success because officers at the regiment or battalion level developed and followed a better plan. The best examples are the operations to seize the infamous Côte de Châtillon at a critical moment in the Meuse-Argonne Offensive. The Côte de Châtillon was a high, steep, forest-covered hill that dominated the final German line of defense. Unless they took that ground, American forces would not be able to advance and break German resistance. Plans and orders from higher headquarters had been utterly inadequate to the task, but two of the division's battalion commanders, Major Ravee Norris from Alabama's 167th Infantry and Major Lloyd Ross from Iowa's 168th Infantry, planned and led an attack that enabled their men to take the Côte de Châtillon, setting the stage for the final German collapse in the Meuse-Argonne. Norris and Ross were National Guardsmen; neither had attended West Point or spent a day in the Regular Army. But Norris and Ross were able to use all they had seen and experienced on the Western Front, plus common sense, to achieve victory—a trait that seems to have been common among the Rainbow Division's National Guard leadership.

It is probably not surprising that I have come to admire and respect the courage and tenacity demonstrated by the men of the Rainbow Division. I also have found myself wondering how they survived such profound horror and terror. In total, the division spent 164 days in combat, ranking those men third among American divisions in the war. Besides living under the constant threat of death or terrible wounds from enemy artillery, poison gas, and machine gun fire, they lived with filth, mud, rain, cold, rats, and infestations of "cooties," or body lice. They often subsisted on canned beef and hard crackers for days, even weeks at a time.

Remember that these men were not military professionals. At the outset, they were mostly National Guardsmen, ordinary fellows who as citizen-soldiers had never imagined they would be fighting in Europe in what at the time was the most costly and horrific war in history. Many had enlisted in peacetime hometown units for the social opportunities Guard membership provided. At monthly drill sessions they got to wear uniforms, practice close-order drill, and sometimes fire rifles. Most went to summer camps in their home states for two weeks of additional drill. Rank and file enlisted men were paid $1 per month, not an insignificant sum in pre-war times. The businessmen and attorneys who populated the officer corps could use the Guard context to foster enterprises and form and maintain political connections.

All Guardsmen knew Federal mobilization had been a possibility since the Militia Act of 1903 and the National Defense Act of 1916, but none dreamed that this might mean going to France to fight the Germans. In 1917, the concept of the National Guard as the U.S. Army's primary reserve force was a relatively new one. Still, most Guardsmen seemed to go to France not just willingly but with an enthusiasm that flared after the declaration of war in April 1917, leading to a flood of enlistments in Guard units across the country.

My own research and writing benefited from marvelous histories of the Rainbow Division and its regiments written by veterans of that unit: Henry Reilly, a colonel of artillery in the division, who later became an infantry brigade commander; Raymond Cheseldine, a captain in Ohio's 166th Infantry Regiment; and John Taber, a lieutenant in Iowa's 168th Infantry. But perhaps the most compelling and human of the witnesses was Father Francis P. Duffy, chaplain of New York's 165th Infantry. Duffy was not only an eloquent and thoughtful writer, but a great humanitarian and a model military chaplain, serving his regiment with both courage and love.

In my research, I found differing, even contradictory accounts by participants describing the same event. This is not surprising since almost all the stories were written or recorded many years later, and memory is an unreliable witness. Seeking a common thread, I evaluated and analyzed contrasting narratives, then did my best to piece together an account that seemed the most reliable as well as the most probable.

I am very grateful to Major William Carraway, a historian with the Georgia Army National Guard. As he had done previously, Major Carraway gave me access to photos he took during a 2018 visit to Rainbow Division battlefields in France. I was also able to use some of the thousands of wartime photos and films taken by members of the U.S. Army Signal Corps. I discovered that in 1919 the government had published a catalog identifying every photo taken by the Signal Corps during the war. Using those serial numbers, I was able to get digital copies from the online collections of the National Archives and Records Administration. I hope that these photos and those by Major Carraway enhance readers' experience by providing an important visual context for this final stage of the Rainbow Division story.

I must once again thank my publisher, Bruce H. Franklin, and his very able and helpful staff at Westholme Publishing. Without their professionalism and skills, this book would not exist. They continue to be an absolute joy to work with.

In this book, I have striven to hew to the narrative style I employed in my previous works, setting forth the facts and documenting their sources while also telling a rich and colorful story. While this is a history, it is primarily a story of people, their experiences, their successes, and their tragic failures. I hope reading this passage in the saga of the Rainbow Division during the Great War will mean as much to you as it did to me in writing it.

1

A NEW AMERICAN DIVISION IN FRANCE

"I fear very much that the Kaiser has a surprise coming when this outfit is turned loose, for I never saw a more determined set of men."
—Lieutenant Leon Miesse, 166th Infantry,
in a letter to his wife, February 2, 1918

It had been four months since President Woodrow Wilson had declared war on Germany. Now, in early August 1917, Major Douglas MacArthur stood with crisp solemnity at his desk in the War Department's Mobile Army Section, at 1650 17th Street NW in Washington, D.C. His stance always matched his somewhat imperious and dramatic language. MacArthur's desk, set in a corner of the section's small office, seemed utterly inadequate as a place for important and dramatic announcements. However, MacArthur had called reporters to that little corner to deliver what he said was interesting news.

Once the newsmen were in place, MacArthur said, "We have organized on paper at least, the first National Guard division and the first division other than the First Division of the Regular Army, to be designated for service in France." While the army had not numbered the new division, the idea was to make the division "as representative as possible of the whole union,"[1] he added.

He explained that Secretary of War Newton Baker had asked Major General William Mann, head of the U.S. Army's Militia Bureau, and MacArthur to study the idea of forming a division made up of National Guard units from as many states and territories as possible. Two Guard divisions, one from New York and one from Pennsylvania, already existed, but Baker wanted to avoid implying that the burden of mobilizing for the war in Europe was falling entirely on two states. Nor did he want residents of other states to feel shortchanged when it came to supporting the war effort.[2]

As MacArthur finished characterizing the new unit, he uttered what would be prophetic words. "In the makeup and promise of the future of this division, it resembles a rainbow,"[3] he said. "Rainbow, there's the name for the division," a newsman remarked. "I shall call it the Rainbow in my dispatch." Fellow reporters nodded. As newspapers across the country published articles about the unit on August 14, 1917, Americans first learned of the Rainbow Division.[4] Within just over two months, this new division of National Guardsmen from twenty-six states and territories, numbering almost 30,000 citizen-soldiers, would be sailing to France.

Many would never return.

In April 1917, as the United States was beginning its buildup for the conflict that had been raging in Europe since August 1914, no one in the War Department knew exactly how to respond to the Allies' desperate need for men and firepower. America's Regular Army was pitifully small and ill-equipped for an industrial-age war in terms of doctrine, training, and organization. The National Defense Act of 1916 had authorized the Regular Army to double its strength, but as of April 1917, the army still only had 5,800 officers and just over 120,000 men. More revealing of the service's overall weakness was the fact that the army had no units above the regimental level—not a single brigade, division, corps, or army organization existed.[5] In terms of doctrine and culture, the U.S. Army had not changed since the Spanish-American War of 1898.

The War Department's first act was to mobilize the bulk of the Regular Army's infantry and support units into a single division. The 1st Division would deploy to France in June 1917. Once that transit occurred, the question became which unit would go next. Readying more Regular Army divisions would require enrolling men via enlistment and conscription and then training them, a process that would take time the Allies did not

Workers rush to complete the new training facility at Camp Mills on Long Island, New York, in August 1917. (*National Archives*)

have. The only alternative was to mobilize and deploy existing National Guard units.

At first, most of the army's General Staff opposed sending Guard units to France. Even before the United States declared war, the General Staff's twenty-one members had debated the issue, with the majority resistant. But a vocal minority led by Major MacArthur insisted that the National Guard would be critical to America's ability to fight in Europe, should that come to pass.[6] With the nation now at war, everyone on the General Staff agreed that the MacArthur faction had it right. Nonetheless, many officers in the War Department and in the headquarters of the new American Expeditionary Forces, or AEF, believed National Guardsmen to be fit for nothing more than service as replacement troops for Regular Army units, and that their regiments would never be able to fight as frontline units.

But in late September 1917, a National Guard division—the second American division to go to France—sailed from New York. The 26th Division included Guard units from the New England states. Owing to geographical proximity and an East Coast locale, the "Yankee Division," as it came to be known, was faster to organize and deploy than other new National Guard divisions. The Rainbow Division, officially designated as the 42nd Division, was gathering at Camp Mills on Long Island, New York.

Because Mann and MacArthur had led the process that created the 42nd Division, Secretary Baker had named Mann division commander and MacArthur, now a colonel, division chief of staff. The units they would command were required to meet the stipulations set forth in a new table of organization and equipment for an American infantry division. The division would need a total of 991 officers and 27,114 enlisted men. Its four infantry regiments, each with 3,600 men, would be organized into two infantry brigades of two regiments each. The artillery brigade would consist of three regiments with twenty-four 155mm howitzers, forty-eight 75mm guns, and a trench mortar battery. Each infantry brigade had its own machine gun battalion, with another machine gun battalion assigned to each regiment's headquarters company, giving the division 260 machine guns.[7]

The units Mann and MacArthur selected to make up their division included Maryland's 117th Trench Mortar Battery and, to provide light artillery support, the Illinois 149th Field Artillery and the Minnesota 151st Field Artillery. Indiana's 150th Field Artillery would supply the division's heavier 6-inch artillery.[8] Also incorporated were the 117th Engineering Regiment, composed of South Carolina and California units, along with the 117th Engineering Train, which came from North Carolina. The 117th Field Signal Battalion hailed from Missouri, and there were Military Police companies from Virginia and a Headquarters Troop from the Louisiana 2nd Cavalry. There was also the 117th Ammunition Train from Kansas, the 117th Supply Train from Texas, the 165th Ambulance Company from New Jersey, the 166th Ambulance Company from Tennessee, the 167th Ambulance Company from Oklahoma, the 168th Ambulance Company from Michigan, the 165th Field Hospital from the District of Columbia, the 166th Field Hospital from Nebraska, the 167th Field Hospital from Oregon, and the 168th Field Hospital from Colorado.[9]

The core of the division's combat capability was its four infantry regiments, organized into two infantry brigades—the 83rd and the 84th. The 83rd Infantry Brigade was to be commanded by Brigadier General Michael J. Lenihan, an 1887 graduate of West Point who had served on the American frontier, in the Philippines, on the General Staff in the War Department, and at the Army War College. Lenihan's brigade included the 165th Infantry Regiment from the New York National Guard and the 166th Infantry Regiment from the Ohio National Guard. Command of the 84th Infantry Brigade went to General Robert A. Brown, an 1885 West Point graduate. Like Lenihan, Brown had served along the frontier, in

Left, Major General William Mann, commander of the Rainbow Division, and Colonel Douglas MacArthur, the division chief of staff, at Camp Mills in September 1917. Right, Brigadier General Michael Lenihan, commander of the 83rd Brigade, seen here in France. (*National Archives*)

Cuba during the Spanish-American War, and in the Philippines, as well as studying at the Army War College.[10] His new brigade was composed of the Alabama National Guard's 167th Infantry Regiment and the Iowa National Guard's 168th Infantry Regiment.[11]

As the division assembled at Camp Mills in late August and early September 1917, the New Yorkers of the 165th Infantry clearly displayed the most esprit de corps and organizational maturity. That regiment's history stretched back to the famous "Fighting 69th" of the Civil War. Further unity flowed from the fact that all the regiment's companies drew their men from New York City, and that those men were overwhelmingly of Irish American descent. These natural bonds held firm even as new recruits and transfers arrived. When the regiment began recruiting in May 1917, the campaign played to the tight-knit nature of Gotham's Hibernian community. Rather than use garish advertising and stage boisterous town hall meetings in the mode of other Guard regiments, the 165th relied on connections provided by current members and Catholic clerics. Word went out among these unofficial "recruiters" that the regiment wanted special men, men who would join for the right reasons and "who would be worthy successors of those unforgotten patriots who at Bloody Ford and on Marye's Heights earned the title of 'The Fighting Irish.'"[12] Veteran members sought out friends they deemed reliable, and priests sent good men from parish athletic clubs.[13] When it came time to admit transfers, all new men came from other New York City Guard regiments.

The 165th Infantry's sister unit in the 83rd Brigade was the Ohio National Guard's 166th Infantry Regiment. The 166th, formerly the 4th Ohio Infantry, traced its roots to the Mexican War. The companies comprising the Ohio regiment, from ten cities and towns in central Ohio, were steeped in the Guard routine, accustomed to conducting monthly drill sessions at local armories and traveling to an annual summer encampment by the entire regiment at Camp Perry on the banks of Lake Erie.[14] Like all the other units mustered into the new division, the 166th had been mobilized into Federal service in 1916 and deployed to the Mexican border, returning home in March 1917, less than a month before the declaration of war.[15]

Regarding new recruits, the Ohio regiment got a leg up on other units by starting its recruiting campaign in April. Within days of America's entry into the war, the Ohio Adjutant General had issued an order saying, "You will at once recruit your company to War Strength of 152 enlisted men for each letter company, 37 enlisted men for Supply Company, and 74 enlisted men for Machine Gun Company."[16] As with other National Guard infantry regiments in the Rainbow Division, unit strength requirements soon increased, and each of the regiment's ten companies accelerated efforts to attract men. The regiment mobilized all its companies at their home armories across central Ohio on July 15, and recruitment continued until the regiment formally mustered into Federal service on August 5, 1917.[17] On August 13, the regiment's companies each received a secret order to assemble at Camp Perry.[18]

At camp, the regiment learned it had a new commanding officer. Born and raised in Delaware, Ohio, Colonel Benson W. Hough was forty-two years old, a graduate of Ohio State University, and a successful attorney.[19] Only he and one other regiment commander in the Rainbow Division held their jobs throughout the war, primarily because Hough proved to be a superb military leader and, in many ways, a perfect fit for the role of commanding citizen-soldiers. He was tough and demanding but also uncompromising in defending his men and seeing to their welfare. Quiet, thoughtful, and, as one of his officers put it, "intensely human," Hough approached his job with great seriousness, and his judgment of men was "uncanny." Alison Reppy, a captain in the regiment, graduate of the University of Missouri, and former high school coach from Hillsboro, Missouri, wrote that Hough was a "big man physically and intellectually, who

Left, Brigadier General Robert Brown, commander of the 84th Brigade. Center, Colonel Benson Hough, commander of Ohio's 166th Infantry Regiment. Right, Colonel William Screws, commander of Alabama's 167th Infantry Regiment. (*National Archives*)

hates formality and shuns publicity; a man who is reserved, yet friendly; a man who is ordinarily quiet and has but little to say, but who, when occasion demands, becomes a veritable volcano of action, sweeping aside all immaterial considerations and speaking directly and briefly on the real point at issue. It is this combination of qualities which binds men to him."[20]

The other two infantry regiments, the 167th and the 168th, made up the division's 84th Brigade. The 167th, created from the old 4th Alabama, was an oddity among the division's four infantry regiments, being the only regiment to have flown the Confederate battle flag. In fact, during the Civil War the regiment had fought against the 69th New York.[21]

The Alabama regiment was also distinctive because of commanding officer Colonel William P. Screws. Screws led the regiment from its deployment to the Mexican border through the end of World War I. Besides being a lieutenant colonel in the Alabama National Guard, he was also a captain in the Regular Army, serving simultaneously as regiment commander and Federal mobilization officer when the regiment was called to service. Screws was the only regiment commander whose men elected him to that post; Alabama maintained the militia tradition of having the men choose their officers.[22]

The fourth infantry regiment was the 168th, originally formed in Council Bluffs, Iowa, in 1859 to defend settlements from Sioux, Sac, and

Fox raiders and bandit gangs. That unit was the foundation for the 3rd and 5th Iowa Infantry Regiments, merged as the 3rd Iowa in 1888.[23] The Iowans served in the Spanish-American War and fought in seventeen battles during the Philippine insurrection before returning home in September 1899.[24] This experience served the regiment well. Mobilizing to fight Germany in June 1917, the commanding officer, his deputy, the three battalion commanders, the Medical Detachment chief, five company officers, and a number of NCOs and enlisted men had served in combat in the Philippines.[25]

The Iowa Adjutant General ordered the companies making up the new 168th Infantry to report to the State Fair Grounds in Des Moines on August 17. Quickly arriving, the companies made camp on a hill just east of the exhibition grounds.[26] Owing to a belated start at mobilization, the 168th was the last regiment to leave for Camp Mills, departing the fairgrounds on September 9. Thousands gathered to cheer the men as they marched to the train station. Not surprisingly, the departure proved emotional. Major Winfred Robb, the regimental chaplain, later wrote, "With something gripping our throats, which we could not swallow, struggling to hold back the teardrops from our eyes, we stood upon the back of the train and watched the crowd of folks who came to see us off, become a blur and then indistinct in the distance. Our journey had begun."[27]

One young officer described the process of leaving for war as both heartbreaking and bitter:

> It was not until the first trains backed into the terminal at the Fair Grounds that the members of the 168th learned what leaving home was to mean to them. War, until then, had seemed such a remote and nebulous possibility that few had ever thought of themselves as actually in it. But now they realized, as did their friends and families, that every move was a step nearer to the uncertainty of the battle line. The fear that this might be the final parting, that this might be the last embrace, made more bitter the ordeal of farewell. It was amid smiles forced through tears, and stifled sobs from breaking hearts, that the crowded trains moved slowly out and disappeared in the distance.[28]

As each regiment arrived on Long Island, the camp's tempo accelerated, with soldiers pitching tents, setting up kitchens, and readying garbage dumps while organizing themselves for a stay of indefinite length. The men soon had to cope with outbreaks of measles and meningitis as the army did its best to make sure they had clothing and supplies. "While the line companies were sweating out on the drill fields," wrote John Taber, a lieutenant in the 168th, "the Supply Company was working at full speed to procure and distribute supplies and equipment." Eventually, every man would get a woolen uniform and a short trench coat to replace his longer coat, but some outfitting was going on the night before the division embarked for France.[29]

The major activity at Camp Mills was training, and the daily regimen was relentless. On the first day that the division assembled in camp, Mann and MacArthur issued a training program and schedule with three straightforward objectives. The first was to build discipline and unit cohesion; the second, to develop a high degree of physical fitness. Finally, the troops had to learn from the school of the soldier how to drill, maintain personal hygiene, and care for personal combat equipment. Mann and MacArthur ordered all company officers to learn the required drill, be ready to lead both the drill and physical exercise, and ensure they instructed NCOs prior to each training day while the men were eating and preparing for the day's activities.[30]

Availability of officers to lead each company's platoons and squads presented a challenge. As the division began to organize, Mann and MacArthur had to transfer talented company- and field-grade officers up the chain of command at the division and brigade levels. This created vacancies down the chain, typically filled by young officers fresh from training at Plattsburgh, New York, under the aegis of the Citizen's Military Training Corps, a forerunner of today's Reserve Officer Training Corps and Officer Candidate School programs. Integrating these new lieutenants into companies was problematic. They were outsiders thrust upon very insular units. Men transferring into state regiments were one thing, but at least they came from that state. The Plattsburgh graduates came from all over, and almost all, in a term usually muttered derisorily all around the country were "college-bred men."[31]

Rumors about the impending arrival of inexperienced officers stirred loud grumbling in the 166th, and this grumbling was not confined to the rank and file. The initial contingent of new officers did not impress Lieutenant Leon Miesse, who had recently left Company L for a position at 83rd Brigade Headquarters. "The new Officers came to-day that have been assigned to the Regiment, Co. L got three new ones," Miesse wrote to his wife. "One of them is all O.K., but the other two I can't give very much."[32] Later, as the new officers tried to figure out their responsibilities, Miesse told his wife, "The boys in the Company call them the 'Sears and Roebuck

Officers.' Most of them are not much good, but you can't say anything except to sit tight with your mouth closed."[33]

In the 167th, enlisted men from Alabama resented the fact that most new officers were "Yankees"—and, unlike the usual home-grown officer, the newcomers were college graduates or former undergraduates. These new lieutenants' lack of experience complicated training; they and their men, themselves greenhorns, were equally at sea when it came to military culture. Still, the new officers were welcome; the regiment, like all others in the Rainbow Division, desperately needed them.

With officers in place, training quickened. The men drilled incessantly in the new manual for the bayonet, which many believed pointless. After all, some said, this was a modern war where you kill your enemy at long range using a rifle, machine gun, or artillery. Experience proved bayonet training to have been anything but a waste of time.

Shortly after training at Camp Mills began, Lieutenant General John J. Pershing, commander of the AEF, issued guidance on pre-embarkation training. Pershing still clung to pre-war American military doctrine that stressed the rifleman's primacy. Despite all that Pershing and other American military leaders had observed of war on the Western Front, they had not embraced, and never really would embrace, the importance of mass artillery and machine gun fire. This intransigence would cost the doughboys of the AEF dearly. Pershing's guidance came in the form of a small booklet, distributed to every officer, stressing the need for riflery practice and marksmanship training before troops embarked for France.[34]

But Camp Mills had no rifle range. Men underwent no shooting or marksmanship training. Instead, the emphasis was on rapidly developing a physically fit, cohesive organization. The real training was to come in France, where French Army instructors awaited. No one in the Regular Army or National Guard was schooled in trench warfare or, more importantly, many of the weapons American troopers would be using in combat. No one in the division had seen a hand grenade, much less used one. The U.S. Army of 1917 had no trench mortars or automatic rifles; training in their use would have to wait until they reached France.

On October 17, the division received orders to begin breaking camp and moving to points of embarkation in Hoboken, New Jersey, and New York City, as well as Montreal, Canada. The first transports carrying men of the division left Hoboken on October 18. Other vessels departed Montreal on October 27 and New York City on November 3. The initial convoy from Hoboken dropped anchor at Saint Nazaire, France, on October 29.

But the army had to use such suitable vessels as were available, no matter where they were located. As a result, subsequent troopships departed from New York and even Montreal. And, with some French ports overcrowded, certain troop transports paused at Liverpool, U.K., before finally docking at Le Havre in late November and early December.[35]

As each convoy arrived, the men aboard offloaded to stay at nearby camps for a few days before boarding trains bound for training areas in the French interior. Most of the division's soldiers were crammed mercilessly into boxcars one soldier sarcastically termed "the pride of the French National Railway system."[36] Many men had ridden the American rails in boxcars at home, but those accommodations were palatial compared to the French version. French boxcars were tiny, only about eight feet wide and ten to sixteen feet long.[37] On each car's side a painted message read, "40 Hommes-8 Chevaux"—"forty men or eight horses"—and, as one soldier pointed out, "the change from men to horses or vice versa, was often only a matter of a few moments."[38] Carrying all their equipment on their backs, men could not sit, and the boxcars were unheated, making their transit across France cold and brutally uncomfortable.

Lieutenant General John Pershing, commander of the American Expeditionary Force. (*National Archives*)

By early December, the bulk of the division had encamped in small villages adjoining the First Training Area, near Morlaincourt, and the Fifth Training Area, near Vaucouleurs. Only a few miles south, near Tours, were the front lines. The ominous rumble of artillery duels between French and German artillery batteries constantly reminded the newcomers of the war's intensity—and proximity.

As the top brass were beginning to prepare the division for combat, an issue arose that would determine how the National Guard units were to serve—a point of contention that would shake the division's chain of command. Within days of the division's arrival in France, AEF Headquarters redesignated the 42nd Division as the 1st Replacement Division. This meant the men of the Rainbow Division would constitute nothing more than a

Members of the Rainbow Division march through Saint Nazaire, France, shortly after their arrival in November 1917. (*National Archives*)

pool of doughboys to be siphoned off as replacements to replenish depleted American divisions. General Mann vigorously protested this move to General Pershing to no avail. Pershing, who earlier had staunchly opposed using the Guard, still harbored strong disdain for citizen-soldier units.

Seeking to change Pershing's mind, General Mann and Colonel MacArthur marshalled political influence. The two reached out to officials who each and sometimes both knew in the twenty-six states and territories represented by the Rainbow Division, asking them to mount a campaign of persuasion. Letters and telegrams of protest inundated the War Department and even the White House. At first, Pershing and his staff resisted. But when Army Chief of Staff General Tasker Bliss told Pershing that President Wilson and Secretary of War Baker also thought the replacement redesignation a very bad idea, the general relented. He had his revenge on Mann for the younger man's upstart ways, on December 15, 1917, relieving him as commander of the Rainbow Division. Mann's successor was Major General Charles T. Menoher, West Point '86 and a man Pershing knew and trusted.[39] His choice of Menoher reflected Pershing's desire to have the Rainbow Division commanded by someone who would not challenge decisions by AEF Headquarters. Menoher's wiry, athletic physique made him look the part of a general, but in personality and command style he was no field commander. One label given him was "inoffensive." Pershing found him "easygoing and without initiative." A career spent mostly in the army's small-unit culture had habituated him to indecision; he elevated waffling into an art form. Amid the peacetime army's chronic internecine bickering, he strove to avoid confrontation by simply avoiding decisions that might cause conflict. The higher he rose in rank, the less he decided, in Pershing's eyes making him the perfect man to pacify a rebellious Rainbow Division staff.[40]

At lower echelons, Rainbow Division soldiers spent the first half of December learning how to fight on the Western Front. Their French Army instructors sought to inculcate in them everything the Allies had learned since 1914. Officers and men assigned to use unfamiliar gear attended schools and drilled daily under watchful French eyes. For the four infantry regiments, the first weeks of training focused on weapons.

Major General Charles Menoher, who replaced General Mann as commander of the Rainbow Division in December 1917. (*National Archives*)

Many experienced Guardsmen were very proficient in the use and care of their M1903 Springfields, officially United States Rifle, Caliber .30-06, Model 1903. But none had ever used the hand grenade, the Stokes mortar, or other standbys of the fighting in France. The British 3-inch Stokes mortar that the AEF received in France was a simple but ingenious invention. The Stokes, like all mortars during the war, provided organic support fire for infantrymen by lobbing shells into enemy trenches and shell holes. Essentially, the muzzle-loading Stokes was a portable steel pipe that fired a high-explosive round. The propellant was a shotgun charge (without pellets) inserted in the projectile's base. Dropped into the barrel, a round slid down the tube, at whose base a fixed firing pin detonated the charge. The resulting explosion forced the shell out of the tube and sent it on its way to the target.[41] Mortarmen aimed their weapon by adjusting the angle of the firing tube.

Rainbow Division machine gunners had used American weapons systems, but not the French-made Hotchkiss machine gun standard in France. Another key Allied weapon on the Western Front was the

The 117th Field Signal Battalion on the march during the infamous Valley Forge Hike, December 27, 1917. (*National Archives*)

Chauchat automatic rifle. The air-cooled 19-lb. Chauchat was light, with a firing rate of 240 rounds per minute, and fed by a twenty-round magazine. But the Chauchat was shoddily made, notorious for misaligned sights and shabby assembly. Spare parts were scarce. No American equivalent existed. American armorer John Browning had provided a prototype automatic rifle to the army just prior to America's entry into the war, but that weapon was more than a year away from practical field use. The only "trench broom" available was the Chauchat, which the French had developed in 1915.[42]

As Guard units were learning new skills, few in the division knew the AEF and the French Army had never intended them to be in the First and Fifth Training Areas. The original plan had been for them to train in the Seventh Training Area near Rolampont, sixty-five miles south. That locale had not been ready when they debarked, hence their deployment to the First and Fifth Training Areas.[43]

Rumor that December had it that the Germans were planning a winter offensive in the vicinity of Toul, spurring a shift of French Army units into the area occupied by the 42nd Division. On December 11, orders came to move to Rolampont. As the move to the Seventh Training Area was starting, transport was scarce. Locomotives and boxcars were in short supply, and the division had only enough trucks to carry rations for the

Men from the Rainbow Division performing bayonet drills in the Seventh Training Area, January 1918. (*National Archives*)

men and forage for the thousands of mules shipped across the Atlantic to France. For lack of trucks and trains, mules would have to pull hundreds of wagons and carts carrying the division's equipment to Rolampont. The soldiers had to march to Rolampont. On December 12, 1917, as the division was forming up to begin that sixty-five-mile trek, there came heavy snowfalls and subzero temperatures. What would have been a challenging march came to be an endurance test known as the "Valley Forge Hike."[44]

Some men had no overcoats; they were wearing summer weight gear, including light boots issued at Camp Mills, and much of that was worn out. On icy roads south to Rolampont, thousands of bleeding feet marked their progress in red, stark against the snow. At times, winds created white-out conditions, but the division kept moving.

The soldiers of the division met the challenge. In later years, General Pershing hailed their gumption. "I recall your courage and your fortitude under all of these trying circumstances, with poor billets and bitter cold nights," he told a division reunion in 1923. "But I also felt at the time, and can say now, that the experience prepared you as nothing else could have done perhaps for that trial of courage that came to you on many a battlefield.... I felt that nothing could have been more fortunate than that you had that experience."[45]

The division paused and made camp from December 16 to December 26, resuming their march in even worse weather and reaching the Seventh Training Area on December 29, 1917. At the new bivouac, the men rested until New Year's Day. Two battalions of the 32nd French Regiment arrived to train the Americans in trench warfare with grenade and riflery practice, along with firing the Stokes mortar and the Hotchkiss gun.[46] After six weeks, trainers pronounced the division combat ready. On February 16, 1918, the Rainbow Division boarded trains at Rolampont, bound north to a part of the Lorraine front known as the Lunéville, Saint Clement, and Baccarat Sectors. From then until the Armistice, except for a brief interlude in August 1918, the division served almost continually on the front lines.

For the men of the Rainbow Division, life would never be the same.

2

FROM THE TRENCHES TO THE AISNE-MARNE

"It was savage and there was no quarter asked or given. It seemed to be endless. Bitterly, brutally, the action seesawed back and forth. A point would be taken, and then would come a sudden fire from some unsuspected direction and the deadly counterattack. Positions changed hands time and again. There was neither rest nor mercy."
—General Douglas MacArthur on the Aisne-Marne Offensive in his memoir, *Reminiscences*

British soldiers of the Great War called trench warfare "damned dull, damned damp, and damned dangerous."[1] On the frigid night of March 1-2, 1918, all three elements, especially danger, enveloped a regiment of the Rainbow Division. On this night, the men of the 166th Infantry's 1st Battalion, waiting for the 3rd Battalion to relieve them in a trench complex near Lunéville, were stamping their feet in deep mud, trying to summon feeling back into wet, cold toes. Impatient to end their latest ten-day turn in the trenches, known as a "trick," they stared into the forbidding "no man's land" between them and German trenches several thousand yards away. No man's land was a desperate tangle of barbed wire, smashed trees, thousands of shell holes, and here and there decaying corpses of soldiers who had not made it back from a patrol. The gruesome panorama was terrifying to behold, especially on a night as gloomy as this one.

About 100 yards forward of the main trenches were listening posts manned by soldiers assigned to peer into no man's land, watching and listening for signs of German patrols or full-bore attacks. Field telephones connected some listening posts to the main trenches, but many did not have this luxury. To signal an alert, soldiers manning unconnected posts would have to send up a rocket-propelled red flare before running back to the main line. The flares floated to earth under parachutes. Watchers' imaginations often took flight. "Wire posts," wrote Raymond Cheseldine of the 166th, "looked like Germans and many an unoffending stick of wood was made the target of a shower of rifle bullets and hand grenades." Uncertain of what he might or might not be hearing or seeing, many a nervous man sent up a warning flare. After a while, nervousness subsided into workaday vigilance, and war in the trenches receded mostly into tedium.[2]

On this night, the ears and eyes at one listening post belonged to a man from D Company of the 166th, Private Dyer Bird. Bird, who had grown up in Broadway, Ohio, had turned eighteen on January 5. His mother had died when he was three months old; his grandparents had raised him. He lived most of his life in Broadway but was working in Marion, Ohio, when war was declared, and within weeks he enlisted in the Ohio National Guard.[3]

Struggling against boredom and anxiety, Bird stared, trying to be ready to warn his comrades on the main line that something was afoot. Suddenly, he saw movement near a stretch of barbed wire. Probably concerned that his eyes might be playing tricks, he looked again and this time clearly saw a German raiding party emerging from a nearby trench. He reached down, grabbed two hand grenades, and hurled them at the enemy. As the grenades exploded among the Germans, Bird turned to run back to the regiment's trenches and warn his comrades. He leaped from the listening post trench, heading toward the main line, shouting.

The Germans opened fire. The young private fell forward. "The Germans are coming in the form of a wedge!" he shouted before he died. "Boys, I'm dying. . . ."[4] The 166th Infantry, the Rainbow Division, and the people of Union County, Ohio, had lost their first man in combat.

When first ordered to Lorraine, the men of the division were told they were in for ten days of training. But ominous signs abounded. The men were ordered to pack excess baggage for storage, to be retrieved after train-

Private Dyer Bird of the 166th Infantry is buried with full military honors. (*National Archives*)

ing ended—seemingly extreme, given the training session's brevity. And division headquarters directed that the soldiers should bring along only a thirty-day supply of field equipment such as clothing, mess kits, and entrenching shovels. "Feverish preparation" began, but no one was quite sure what constituted thirty days' worth of field equipment. Lest they take too much, men cut their stock of gear and clothing to the bone, a sensible approach—except that they were not to see their stowed belongings again until March 1919.[5]

On February 16, 1918, the division began to move by train toward Lorraine, where the troops were assigned duties in the trenches of what the French and the AEF considered a "quiet sector." The Germans had briefly overrun the area around the Lunéville, Saint Clement, and Baccarat Sectors of the front in 1914. The foe then withdrew to a line running roughly from Reillon southeast to Domèvre-sur-Vezouze. The situation stabilized. Both sides dug elaborate networks of trenches, strung barbed wire, and seemed to agree tacitly not to intrude upon one another. Neither side had used gas along these lines, and "in the daytime, a shot was seldom heard."[6] All that was about to change.

In terms of military planning, the move to Lorraine was relatively simple but nonetheless a severe challenge. The AEF staff was struggling to produce cogent, coordinated, and sensible orders while plagued by a prewar Regular Army short on well-trained staff officers to meet wartime demands in France. The reforms of the early 1900s had led to creation of command and staff courses at Fort Leavenworth and the Army War College in Washington, D.C., but as of April 1917 only 379 officers had graduated from those institutions.[7] Most graduates were majors and lieutenant colonels. Their training helped make the best of a bad situation, but they were reporting to senior officers in command and chiefs of headquarters staff divisions who were completely out of their depth.

General Pershing later acknowledged the magnitude of this problem, which left the service "confronted with the task of building up an army of millions that would require as many trained staff officers as we had officers in the whole Regular Army at the beginning of the war."[8] To succeed in the context of modern war on the Western Front, the AEF Headquarters needed G1 (Personnel), G2 (Intelligence), G3 (Operations), and G4 (Logistics) divisions capable of functioning smoothly and developing plans that effectively met operational demands. Such was not the case. Plans developed by the AEF were often severely flawed. Orders sometimes came too late or defied comprehension. Worse, perhaps, many plans and orders reflected an ill-informed or inadequate thought process. Matters improved somewhat as the war continued, but even at war's end, the AEF was still ordering units to achieve impossible objectives, and operations often lacked needed fire and logistics support. This pattern worsened at the corps and division levels, where green staffs struggled to analyze and implement orders received from a higher headquarters, American or French.

Deploying to Lorraine, the Rainbow Division was ready to move units to the front lines on February 21, 1918. Initially, the deployment was treated as training, with French units supervising the Americans as they encountered a real enemy firing live ammunition. The infantry regiments spread along the line from Lunéville to Saint Clement and then Baccarat, where they reported directly to officers of the 164th, 14th, and 128th French Divisions. The division's other combat units also took up posts along the line. The 150th Field Artillery was placed to the far left with the 41st French Division in the Dombasle Sector, while elements of the 149th Field Artillery supported the 164th French Division and the 165th Infantry. The rest of the 149th was assigned to the 14th French Division and the 166th Infantry, and the 151st Field Artillery and the 117th Trench Mortar Battery supported the 128th French Division, the 167th Infantry, and the 168th Infantry.[9]

At first, only half a platoon of about 30 men from each regiment deployed to the trenches, serving man for man with French *poilus* for a few days of instruction. Next, full companies moved forward, and, finally, full battalions took over each regiment's front.[10] As men advanced toward the front lines, many seemed to understand the importance of what was happening. John Taber of the 168th later wrote that the men felt that this was a "testing period." "Every one of them now realized that in a few days, at least, he was to be put on trial," he recalled, "tested as a man and as a soldier, tested for personal courage, and tested for military efficiency before the eyes of his comrades, which to him were the eyes of the world."[11]

The division's four infantry regiments quietly moved into the trenches overnight on February 21-22, 1918, beginning a process that would continue for four months. A battalion from each regiment would take its place in the trenches for a ten-day "trick," while a second battalion stood by as support, with a third farther to the rear as a strategic reserve. When the first battalion completed its trick, the second clambered into the trenches. The third would come forward as the supporting battalion, while the first battalion went to the rear in reserve.[12]

Soldiers found the reality of life in actual trenches to differ dramatically from what they had seen in training trenches. Even in the cold and the mud, rats infested the trenches. The mud left a particularly strong impression. After the war, Louis Collins of the 151st Field Artillery wrote about the misery that men and horses pulling big guns endured.

> Never will the men of the 42nd Division forget the mud of Lorraine. Comrades may be forgotten, details of fighting go glimmering, marches and campaigns become hazy, but that awful February–March battle with the mud of Lorraine will stand out in their memories until final taps are sounded over the last surviving member of the division. For ten days the men of the 151st ate in mud, worked in mud, slept in mud, and dreamed of mud—when the mud would let them sleep. The picket lines in the echelons were in the mud; the men had to wallow through mud to get to the horses; and the horses had to wallow through mud to get to water. Every day it rained or snowed and the already villainous character of the mud became ever more villainous. ... There is no mud like that of Lorraine.[13]

But mud and rats were a mere sideshow. Nights jittered with flashes and bursts of machine gun and rifle fire. Rockets arced across the dark sky, signaling what men did not know. And in every mind was the thought that a few thousand yards away in the blackness hordes of Germans were waiting to kill you—with a measly bullet or a shell from one of the heavy artillery batteries hammering the Allies from just behind the enemy trench lines. The first such barrage came twenty-four hours after the untried Americans arrived in their trenches. The Germans had apparently decided that with interlopers from across the Atlantic now in the line, the Kaiser's troops no longer had to observe the unofficial understanding that this was to be a quiet sector, and they rained high explosive and gas shells on the Rainbow Division. The roaring and crashing were unnerving. "The earth around us boiled and churned and heaved and groaned and shivered," young Martin Hogan, a private in the 165th Infantry, wrote. "The air above us hissed and roared and snapped. The steady streaming rush of the messages of the guns withered our hearts as they smote and smote our trench."[14]

Starting with Dyer Bird's death on March 2, the casualty list grew slowly but steadily. Many deaths and wounds came from enemy artillery, but others resulted from the nightly game of sending patrols into no man's land. Both sides did so, the Americans usually detailing three to ten men and an officer to creep and scuttle through the wire toward the German lines. For an hour or two, a patrol would roam, sometimes assigned to take prisoners, others to check incursions by German patrols believed headed for the American side of the wire.[15] Any patrol was a dangerous exercise; in hindsight, the ritual's potential for gain seems not to have offset very real losses in life and limb that it inevitably cost.

On the night of March 5, the Germans at Lorraine upped the ante. Seeking to penetrate the American lines and cause considerable damage, at around 4:30 a.m. they opened a massive barrage on an area defended by the Iowans of the 168th Infantry. High-explosive rounds chewed up Allied trenches, collapsing dugouts, trapping men underneath tons of earth, and turning the whole area "into a hecatomb of horror and confusion."[16]

As German gunners gradually walked fire to the Allied rear, the German infantry attacked. But as the attackers came within range, the Iowans brought to bear a withering retort with rifles, Chauchats, Stokes mortars, and Hotchkiss machine guns. Few Germans reached the Allied trenches, and those who did were killed within seconds. Surviving Germans limped back to their trenches, leaving dozens of corpses sprawled across the American wire. Major Walter Wolf later reported that "for a month thereafter, we were picking his dead from our wire and our portion of No Man's Land."[17]

The Rainbow Division had passed its first major test under fire.

In late March, the entire division was shifted into the Baccarat Sector and given responsibility for that sector's defense. For the first time in the

Men from New York's 165th Infantry in their trenches in the Saint Clement Sector, March 1918. (*National Archives*)

war, an American division was being entrusted with an entire divisional, two brigade-in-the line sector. On April 1, 1918, the Rainbow relieved the French in the Baccarat Sector. Day-to-day operations at Baccarat continued as they had for three months with a notable exception. In early April, just after the division had relieved the French, the division received its first replacements, all of them freshly conscripted and tragically undertrained draftees. Rushing to get replacements to the front, the army had not sent these young soldiers for training under seasoned French instructors. Nor had the army put these men through even the basic training that division veterans had received at hometown National Guard armories. Of replacements sent to the 166th, most had been in the army less than thirty days and in France less than nine days. Three had never fired their Springfields. This situation persisted and worsened as the war progressed; casualties among replacements were always extremely high. Raymond Cheseldine of the 166th wrote that their deaths in combat were "little short of murder."[18]

The division remained at Baccarat until June 18, when French infantry relieved them. The men were supposed to receive a rest after 120 days at the front. However, in what would become a permanent pattern, that rest period was scotched. Less than forty-eight hours after pulling out of the Baccarat Sector, the division received orders to march to nearby rail stations to board trains for an unknown location.[19] They had proven themselves by enduring the trench warfare routine of the "quiet" sectors in Lorraine, where they conducted nighttime patrols, dodged artillery shells, and fought rats and mud. Now the division was moving 130 miles west to the area around Châlons-en-Champagne in the Marne region to join an Allied effort to stop what would be the final great German offensive of the war.

The trains left June 21 and moved via four different routes to the Marne River Valley on June 22. After the regiments offloaded from their trains, the division was to advance to the area around Châlons-en-Champagne. The weather, warm and sunny, belied the war raging only miles away. Leon Miesse of the 166th found time for a swim in the Marne Canal.[20] Despite years of war, the Marne River Valley remained relatively unscarred. Here Marshal Joffre had turned back the first great German assault of the war in September 1914. Since then, the Marne had been relatively quiet. One British soldier wrote that the area presented "a pleasant well cultivated scene, unmarred by the shell holes, trenches, and barbed wire to which we had become so accustomed on the static front."[21]

The division was here to counter an offensive meant to end the war on Germany's terms. Starting in late March 1918, the Germans had unleashed four major attacks that continued into June. The first had succeeded, driving the British and French back twenty-five miles over a fifty-mile front, but each of the next three had achieved far less than planned.[22] To compensate, General Erich Ludendorff, nominal deputy to chief of the general staff Paul von Hindenburg, planned a fifth attack that he called *Friedensturm* ("Peace Offensive"). The name reflected Ludendorff's intention of enveloping and capturing the ancient French city of Rheims, threatening Paris, and so depleting Allied forces that the French would have to propose peace talks. The initial target was French forces at Champagne. German planning and preparation were meticulous. Three German armies totaling fifty-two divisions spent more than five weeks planning an attack to occur across a thirty-five-mile-wide front.[23]

Ludendorff meant for his 500,000-man force to sweep past General Henri Gouraud's French Fourth Army, whose ranks numbered less than 100,000. In the crucial front-line area east of Rheims, this hope was especially well-founded; Gouraud had only 40,000 men to face 300,000 of Ludendorff's troops.[24] This was where the Rainbow Division was to deploy.

Gouraud knew from intelligence reports that an attack was coming. From their planes Allied reconnaissance pilots had observed German

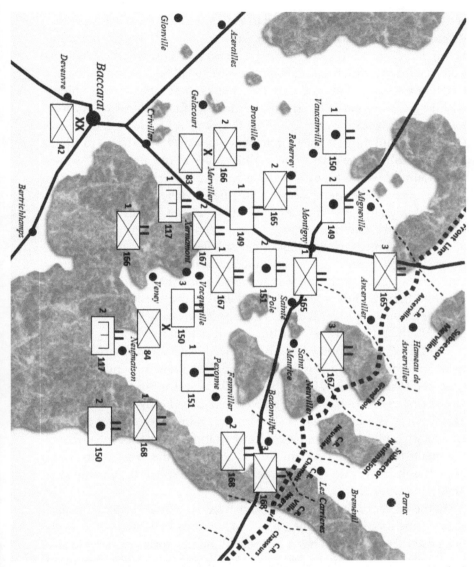

Map 1. The Rainbow Division's deployment in the Baccarat Sector, May 13, 1918. (*Author*)

forces massing opposite the French lines along the Py River east of Rheims. Knowing he faced a severe challenge, Gouraud planned a defense in depth that would confuse the Germans, then subject them to murderous artillery fire as they advanced across open ground toward two successive lines of defense. He planned to leave a skeleton force in his current defensive line south of the Py River with just enough men to make the Germans believe the bulk of his army still occupied the trenches. As soon as the German attack began, these men were to fall back as well, allowing German rounds to fall on empty trenches as the French troops quietly withdrew to a second or intermediate line and a final defensive line, both incorporating positions the Rainbow Division would occupy. Once the Germans found the first line of trenches empty, they would have to attack the intermediate line across one to three miles of open ground. As they did, Gouraud would let fly a massive barrage by French and American artillery. Should the enemy overrun the intermediate line, the bulk of the Fourth Army's forces would stand fast at a final line of resistance about a mile behind the intermediate line.[25]

The last element of the French general's defense in depth was to be a series of signal posts about a half-mile forward of the intermediate line. Personnel at these positions were to signal when the Germans began to advance, then hold their ground until killed or captured, inflicting such damage as they could on the foe. These positions were termed "sacrifice posts,"[26] which proved a terrible but appropriate name.

On July 2, the Rainbow Division received orders to move to the area near Suippes and join the forces of the 21st French Army Corps of Gouraud's Fourth Army. Here, the 21st Corps sector ran for eight miles, and at first the National Guardsmen were assigned only to the final line of resistance. However, the French seemed to gain some confidence in the Americans' abilities and moved select battalions from all four infantry regiments into the intermediate line, likely to take the brunt of the German assault.[27] The men dug into the chalky white soil of the Champagne plains and waited.

In the center of the no man's land between the Py River trenches and the intermediate line were the 21st French Army Corps area's four sacrifice posts. Three were manned by French infantry forces ranging in size from a platoon to a small battalion of three companies.[28] The remaining sacrifice post was assigned to the 166th Infantry's 3rd Battalion. Battalion commander Captain Roger Haubrich chose I Company to man the post. Men staffing sacrifice posts were being asked to fight until annihilated, wounded, or captured, so Haubrich felt he could not morally order men onto the assignment. He told I Company commander Captain Henry Grave to ask for twenty-five volunteers as well as an officer to command the position. When Grave made the request, Lieutenant Clyde Vaughn, a

Top, camp of the 168th Infantry near Suippes, France, July 8, 1918. (*National Archives*) Bottom, left, General Henri Gouraud, commander of the French Fourth Army. (*Library of Congress*) Right, Captain Henry Grave (on the left), the tough, resolute commander of I Company of Ohio's 166th Infantry. (*National Archives*)

"Sears and Roebuck" officer and twenty-three-year-old schoolteacher from Liberty Hill, Texas, stepped forward to lead the detachment. Also stepping forward were twenty-five soldiers volunteering to man the position and its supporting anti-tank gun.[29] Vaughn and his men were to await orders to move out once Gouraud was sure an enemy attack was imminent. Vaughn was to send up red flares when he saw Germans coming, then open fire with his detachment's rifles, machine guns, Chauchats, and anti-tank gun. The idea was to break up and slow the German advance until almost certainly overwhelmed and "submerged by it—just as the rocks break up the advancing wave."[30]

The one ingredient Gouraud needed to complete his defense in depth recipe was reliable intelligence pinpointing exactly when the Germans would strike. He got that ingredient, in two doses. In the evening hours of July 13, a solitary German officer crossed the Py to scout French positions he and his men were to assault. He quickly found the French positions, but the skeleton crew of French soldiers guarding the line captured him before he could recross the river. The *poilus* took him prisoner, finding on his person a complete copy of the German attack orders. A few hours later, a French lieutenant led a patrol across the river that captured twenty-seven German soldiers, including an officer who told his interrogators the time to the minute for the German artillery barrage and subsequent infantry attack. Enemy gunners would open fire at 12:10 a.m. on July 15 and their infantry would cross the Py at 4:00 a.m.[31]

Forewarned, Gouraud alerted his command and ordered an Allied bombardment starting at 11:45 p.m., twenty-five minutes before the planned German barrage.[32] That night, when the French and American guns opened fire with a crash that "fairly lifted men from their feet,"[33] their shells caught the German infantry in the open as they were moving to their jump-off positions. As the Germans scrambled for cover, their casualties mounted, and several units were unable to advance.

But at 12:10 a.m., the Germans, as planned, lit up an awe-inspiring display of firepower. Ludendorff had assembled more than 2,000 artillery pieces—one gun for every twenty yards of the forty-mile front, the largest concentration of artillery to that moment. The German plan was to begin by shelling the first line trenches, which they did not realize had been abandoned. Once the Germany infantry secured those trenches, a rolling barrage was to support the infantry as it advanced further. Rolling barrages preceded attacking infantry in a carefully choreographed process that adjusted supporting fire so shells fell just ahead of the men advancing on the ground. Both sides used this technique, and barrage methods differed. But they all proceeded in measured steps, focusing artillery fire on one line before moving forward to the next set of targets at a designated time. A successful rolling barrage allowed infantry to progress through areas cleared of enemy defenses. The speed and timing of rolling barrages varied with the terrain and the strength of the enemy's position, but they

The desolate, chalky plains of Champagne across which the Germans advanced on July 15, 1918. (*National Archives*)

typically stayed just ahead of the infantry's pace of about 800 feet in ten minutes.[34]

As the timed barrage of the Champagne front was taking place, heavier long-range German guns sent shells toward the final line of Allied resistance and, beyond that, supply areas at the rear. By the time the barrage ended, German shells had struck as far as twenty miles away in Châlons-en-Champagne. The fire was so terrifying that it became the basis for comparison in every subsequent German barrage, and none ever matched it. One soldier from the 167th Infantry said that, for him, that night's barrage was when the "real war began."[35]

After four hours of unabated shelling, the German infantry crossed the river to find the French trenches empty. The attackers quickly recovered from this surprise to press on. The first wave included six first-class units: a Guard Cavalry Division along with the 2nd, the 88th, the 1st, the 5th, and the 7th Bavarian Divisions. These men were fresh from two weeks' rest in the rear. In front of them were a few battalions of French and American infantry at sacrifice posts and on the intermediate line. Three divisions attacked the French at the center. Two divisions assaulted positions on the Allied right manned by Alabama's 167th and Iowa's 168th. A full division made its way against the left, where Ohio's 166th and New York's 165th waited.[36]

The sacrifice posts functioned as Gouraud had planned. The 166th's post held out until every man was dead or wounded. Survivors, out of ammunition, surrendered. A German bullet had torn away part of Lieutenant Vaughn's jaw and chin, but he and his detachment had held up the German assault until almost 8:00 a.m. Hundreds of enemy dead lay in piles in front of the sacrifice post.[37] French and American troops at the sacrifice posts had bought the Allies precious time; the enemy attack against the intermediate line would have to take place in broad daylight.

From emplacements just behind the intermediate line, Allied artillery blasted the attackers, who at some spots managed to get within yards of the American and French trenches and penetrated lines held by the 165th Infantry on the far left of the sector. There, the New Yorkers fought hand-to-hand, mainly with rifle butts and bayonets. "Clubbed rifles were splintered against skulls and shoulder bone," Martin Hogan wrote. "Bayonets were plunged home" over and over and withdrawn covered in gore, "a gruesome mess" that seared the sight of his trench in Hogan's memory.[38] But there and all along the Allied line, defenders turned back the Germans in disarray and with heavy losses.

In hindsight, the fight on the plains of Champagne marked a turning point. The Germans suffered tremendous losses while utterly failing to achieve their objectives. Rheims remained in Allied hands, and Paris was safe from German attack.

With the failure of the German Peace Offensive, the conflict changed drastically. Static trench warfare became a thing of the past as the Allies aggressively pursued offensive operations fought in the open, severely taxing the AEF's ability to command and control its forces. Smoke from the fighting at Champagne had barely cleared when on July 21, 1918, the first units from the 42nd Division entrained at St. Hilaire-au-Temple, heading north to Château-Thierry, where they would prepare to go on the offensive.

For months, Marshal Ferdinand Foch, Supreme Commander of the Allied Armies, had been hoping for an opportunity to go on the attack. Defeat at Champagne had sunk German morale to an all-time low; in addition, the numbers now swung in the Allies' favor. Wrote Pershing, "Thanks to this unprecedented movement, Allied inferiority in March [1918] had been within three months transformed into Allied superiority of over 200,000 men."[39] From this moment on, the Allies never again fought on the defensive.

As his target, Foch chose the Marne Salient, a protrusion formed by German gains made during offensives in March 1918. From about seven

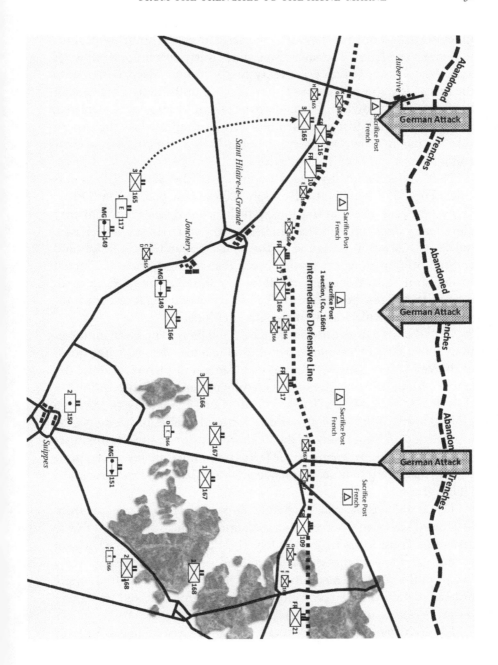

Map 2. The Rainbow Division's positions in the Champagne Defensive, July 15, 1918. (*Author*)

miles northwest of Soissons east to the Vesle River at a point about three miles west of Rheims, the salient was about thirty-five miles wide. At its apex the enemy-held area was twenty-five or so miles deep, centered on the Marne River near Château-Thierry. Four months of fighting had left the forty German divisions defending the salient "disorganized, depleted, and exhausted."[40] Most of those units were concentrated on the eastern side, leaving the salient's western portion held by a small force from General Johannes von Eben's Ninth Army.

That underdefended western boundary of the Marne Salient was where Foch launched his attack on July 18, using the French Tenth Army as his spearhead. The attacking force, which included nine French infantry and cavalry divisions plus the AEF's 1st and 2nd Divisions, struck east, quickly capturing Soissons and cutting vital German lines of supply and communication along the road between that city and Château-Thierry. At the same time, General Jean Marie Joseph Degoutte's French Sixth Army attacked northeast toward Château-Thierry using four French divisions and the American 4th and 26th Divisions.

With the road from Soissons to Château-Thierry cut, German forces in the salient began a strategic withdrawal to a new defensive line north of the Vesle River. This withdrawal included a well-planned, skillful delaying action, using artillery and carefully placed fortified positions to slow any Allied advance. The area from Château-Thierry to the high ground north of the Ourcq River now featured a series of strong points. Capitalizing on the terrain and the locale's profusion of stone farmhouses and outbuildings, the enemy made farms into miniature fortresses, positioning machine gun units that made every structure and clearing into a killing ground.[41]

The 26th Division, New England's Yankee Division, advancing from Château-Thierry, met fierce resistance, almost immediately taking severe casualties. Those losses triggered a July 21 order for the Rainbow Division to move east toward the Marne Salient and join the French Sixth Army as part of the newly formed American I Corps. Initially, Degoutte simply ordered that the division be stationed in the I Corps zone and "remain in the army reserve until new orders employing it elsewhere."[42]

The 26th Division's struggle to overcome the German defensive array was complicated by two factors related to the upper command echelons. The first particularly affected the American I Corps and National Guard units like the 26th and 42nd Divisions. So far, Americans had fought defensively from fixed positions. Now, however, they had to fight a war of maneuver characterized by fluid, dynamic situations. Such operations were far more challenging to execute than a static defense because troops and commanders had to react to changing terrain and the countermoves of an enemy using that terrain to his advantage. American unit commanders, especially above the battalion level, had little experience with this sort of attack. Few, if any, had working knowledge of how to conduct a maneuver-based operation. Learning on the job, as they had to, these novices made many mistakes.[43]

In addition, General Degoutte and his French Sixth Army staff were working from their own seriously flawed analysis. Degoutte seemed convinced that the Germans were a broken foe desperately trying to escape and therefore could be easily stampeded into a panicked retreat. As a result, he repeatedly ordered headlong pursuits of the enemy. On July 21, he decreed, "All units will push straight ahead," ordering French cavalry to advance and be ready to pursue German troops when they broke for the rear. In these same orders, he declared that "only a relatively small, but well-equipped, force of artillery" was needed.[44]

General Jean Degoutte (right), commander of the French Sixth Army, pictured with General Omar Bundy, commander of the U.S. 2nd Division. (*National Archives*)

The scenario had played out before. When the Germans were stopped in the First Battle of the Marne in 1914, the Allies made the same mistake. The French and British assumed the Germans, withdrawing in long columns along every available road, to be a beaten enemy who could be pushed into a mad dash to the rear. Allied forces undertook a vigorous pursuit, but found not a fleeing enemy army, but one that had carefully selected and manned positions along the Aisne River, where the Germans conducted a highly disciplined defense-in-depth to cover their army as it withdrew to a new line.[45]

Now, throughout what became known as the Aisne-Marne Offensive, the French Sixth Army issued similar bullheaded orders for frontal assaults. These operations reflected little planning or knowledge of tactical realities and seeming inattention to reports from troops in the fray of a stiff, disciplined, and determined German resistance. Rainbow Division historian Henry Reilly[46] later wrote, "In other words, it was not a case for pell-mell determined pursuit of a defeated retreating enemy, but was one for careful reconnaissance and patrolling followed by a first-class plan of attack and a carefully arranged coordinated assault in accordance with that plan."[47] The division paid dearly for this pattern of ordering poorly planned infantry attacks with almost no artillery support, a pattern that continued through the offensive.

On July 21, 1918, the Rainbow Division departed for the Aisne-Marne. Boarding trains at two stations, the men again had no idea where they were headed. Many apparently were hoping for a long-awaited rest in a rear area. Instead, they detrained near Château-Thierry at stations in Trilport and La Ferté-sous-Jouarre, with the infantry regiments arriving July 22-24. The regiments immediately marched to villages to be billeted while they awaited orders.

Degoutte may have intended to use the 42nd Division as a strategic reserve, but events made that impossible. As the Rainbow Division was traveling to the Aisne-Marne, fellow National Guardsmen of the Yankee Division were fighting their way into the Marne Salient from its southwest corner. When they moved forward on July 21, encountering minimal German resistance, the New Englanders reached the vital highway linking Soissons and Château-Thierry in less than eight hours. After a brief rest, they marched on, meeting fierce resistance near Épieds and Trugny.[48]

Here, General Degoutte's misplaced assumptions about the likelihood of a general German retreat collided with reality, but no one at the command level seemed to notice. The American I Corps Headquarters, believing adjacent German positions to be lightly defended rear guard outposts, ordered the 26th Division to attack that evening with no artillery support. After several unsuccessful attempts, the 26th briefly gained entry to both towns before furious German resistance pushed them out. The next morning, July 22, the Yankee Division tried again, but withering German machine gun fire and a counterattack by the German 201st Division drove the Americans back.[49]

Repeated attacks with only minimal artillery support were stopped cold by murderous German machine gun fire and heavy artillery barrages. As tactical commanders begged for help, those at the brigade, division, and corps levels failed to realize that the encounter was no minor rearguard action. New England Guardsmen paid a terrible price for this blind stupidity.

As the Yankee Division was attempting to push forward, the remaining German forces withdrew, some toward their next defensive line, above the Ourcq River, others farther to the rear and a new front line of resistance on the Vesle River. The 26th Division took Épieds and Trugny on July 23 only to discover that Germans there had withdrawn to the north and northeast. The Americans now moved a short distance forward to the edge of a dense woodlands, the Forêt-de-Fère, site of the Château-de-Forêt. Here, they dug in. The division's men were exhausted and had suffered terrible casualties. In the ten days since the German offensive began on July 15, the 26th Division counted more than 4,000 casualties, over 3,000 of those lost July 18-23.[50] To relieve the battered Yankee Division, the French Sixth Army ordered the Rainbow Division forward.

The 167th and 168th Infantry of the 84th Brigade were the first to get started on July 24, with the 168th reaching a shattered Épieds by truck around 6:00 a.m. on July 25. Seized only hours before by the 26th Division, which moved on toward the Forêt-de-Fère, the ruined city was still smoking beneath steady rain. The Iowans lined up and began to march forward as German shells hammered a field a few hundred yards ahead. The column soon passed a large overturned German artillery piece and a group of German dead. John Taber of the 168th Infantry wrote in his diary that the scene suggested "an exaggerated chromo of a civil war battle." A few minutes later, entering a wheat field, they found the ripe yellow crop disarrayed by the bodies of men from the Yankee Division's 101st Infantry Regiment. German machine gunners firing from concealment in the nearby woods had cut them down, but there had not been time to bury them. It was a most dispiriting sight.[51]

The Alabamians of the 167th arrived about an hour later, unloading from trucks at Courpoil, approximately a mile and a half northeast of Épieds. They paused for what would be their last hot meal for several days, then headed northeast through the wheat toward the Bois de Fary and the positions occupied by the 26th Division in the Forêt-de-Fère, five miles away. The regiment's mules were lagging, so the men were deputized as beasts of burden. The sanitary detachments hauled stretchers and boxes of medical supplies; individual infantrymen lugged rations, full canteens, and 250 rounds of ammunition. Machine gun companies used hand carts to roll heavy Hotchkiss guns and ammunition through muddy wheat fields.[52]

Reaching the southern portion of the forbidding woods of the Forêt-de-Fère, the 168th passed carnage inflicted only hours earlier, as chronicled by John Taber:

But if there were any illusions as to the nature of the task that was in store for the regiment, all that was necessary to dispel them was a glance at the fields round about. Shell holes, twisted rifles, crusted bayonets, machine guns with half-emptied cartridge belts, and Germans—dead Germans—beside them, littered the trampled wheat. And every few yards, in the open stretch or before the hedges that had screened an enemy nest, were crumpled khaki forms pitched on their faces their hands gripping rifle stocks in the vise of death. This was the sight that greeted the men of the 168th as they moved forward to battle. In making a relief there is nothing so destructive to morale as to come upon the bodies of dead comrades: it makes one think; and thinking is bad, even for soldiers who have schooled themselves to look upon death as the common fate of all.[53]

The advance into the forest and the relief of the Yankee Division infantry did not go smoothly. The New Englanders had barely enough men to establish a formal line of defense, with the 102nd Infantry having fewer men than one battalion of the 167th or 168th. Nor did the men have a clear idea of the Germans' strength or location.[54] Amid heavy German artillery fire, the 167th and 168th moved into the woods as night fell and formed a line as best they could.

The long night of July 25-26 was one of the worst of the war, and one indelible for those who spent it in the Forêt-de-Fère. Lawrence Stewart recalled darkness "black as ink, drenched with ghostly mists and pierced with the eerie whine of falling explosives."[55] All night, the Germans blasted the woods where the 167th and 168th lay with anti-personnel and high explosive rounds. Shelling caused numerous casualties. Those trying to treat the wounded could not see without flashlights that had to be shielded and used carefully lest Germans see the gleam and level even more murderous fire. John Taber wrote, "The roaring guns, the flashing bursts, the frequent gas alarms, intermittent showers, a chilling wind, and lack of shelter combined to make it a night of pure misery.... Never was daybreak more anxiously awaited."[56]

With dawn on July 26 came disquieting news. Scouts on the forward skirmish line reported seeing far across an expanse of open fields what seemed to be stone farm buildings surrounding a huge walled structure "medieval in style and fortress like in effect." This complex and environs seemed to be teeming with Germans.[57] The Americans were getting their first look at La Croix Rouge Farm.

The scouts had been able to ascertain very little about the strongpoint. Every foray closer by scouts or reconnaissance patrols drew machine gun fire directed by German lookouts that impelled American patrols to retreat. The Americans remained essentially ignorant of the location and extent of the enemy's defenses.[58]

The situation should have dictated a cautious well-crafted plan of attack, but the pressure was on to continue pursuing German forces that higher headquarters still insisted were running away. Though initial French and American advances had encountered stiff resistance and taken heavy casualties in the Aisne-Marne, the French Sixth Army remained convinced that the enemy was in full retreat, except for small rear-guard units. The American I Corps situation report for the period ending at 8:00 p.m. on July 25 noted La Croix Rouge Farm to be part of the enemy line, merely saying, "La Croix Rouge Farm (machine-gun nest here)."[59] Orders for July 25 from General Degoutte's headquarters reflected the optimism of a staff certain that the enemy was fleeing. These orders gave the American I Corps until the morning of July 26 to seize the Ourcq River crossings and the town of Sergy. This, headquarters staff said, would allow French cavalry to chase the retreating Germans.[60]

Sergy and the river crossings were more than four miles northeast of La Croix Rouge Farm, where the 167th and 168th were positioned on the morning of July 26. That anyone believed those units should have advanced as far as the Ourcq by this time clearly demonstrates delusion or ignorance at a headquarters wallowing in wishful thinking.

The Germans had turned the farm complex into a citadel bristling with dozens of heavy 7.92mm Maxim machine guns placed to sweep adjoining fields in every direction. These guns were well camouflaged and set in trenches forming a V with the farmhouse at its apex and its arms spreading toward the forest. Each arm stretched about 200 yards southwest and northwest toward the Americans. Other machine gun nests were dug in north and south along the road to Le Charmel that lay at the back of the farm.[61]

As the day passed, the Germans awaited an assault by Americans they knew to be opposite them in the woods. Those Americans waited to attack an enemy position about which they knew virtually nothing. Late in the afternoon, orders to attack came, and in a manner embodying American forces' leadership and command problems during the offensive. About 3:00 p.m., the commanders of the 167th and 168th Infantry, Colonel William Screws and Colonel Ernest Bennett, were called to a meeting at the 84th Brigade Post of Command, or P.C. When they arrived, they found brigade commander General Robert Brown and two artillery regiment commanders waiting for them. Brown informed Screws and Bennett that they were to attack the farm complex at 4:50 p.m.—that is, attack in broad daylight an enemy of unknown strength deployed in unknown positions. Screws later said he listened to the orders being read in "utter amazement." "I protested as far as a Colonel could and still save his head," he recalled. Screws reminded Brown of what he believed was in his front and told the general that a better plan would be to "fall back out of the woods and bring as much artillery down on the enemy line as possible." Screws pleaded with Brown for at least some artillery preparation, but the general replied that there would be nothing more than a rolling barrage during the attack.[62]

By the time the meeting ended, the time for the attack was only twenty minutes away. Screws and Bennett informed their battalion commanders with dispatches that arrived late and at different times, scrambling the assault from the very start. Not only did the separate infantry assaults begin fifteen minutes apart, but the promised rolling barrage did not materialize. Absent or poorly coordinated artillery support characterized the rest of the offensive.

The Alabamians of the 167th's 1st Battalion started the attack, advancing from the woods into open fields toward La Croix Rouge Farm. German gunners aimed traversing fire from the V-shaped trenches with twenty-seven machine guns. Dozens of men fell almost immediately, and survivors took whatever cover they could about 100 yards into the clearing where they were trapped for over an hour. The 1st Battalion's attack had lasted only fifteen minutes.[63]

The Alabama regiment's 3rd Battalion fared no better. Taking heavy losses as soon as they emerged, they took cover behind trees, rocks, and even ricks of firewood left in the fields. From hiding, battalion riflemen spotted enemy machine guns and opened fire, downing several German gun crews. But while the 3rd Battalion had been taking cover, Germans infiltrated the woods to their left and rear from where they opened fire on the Americans. Private John Hayes later wrote that, in those critical moments, he thought he and his buddies "were trapped between two German forces and would in a matter of minutes all be killed or captured."[64]

The 3rd Battalion was saved moments later. Lieutenant Edward "Shorty" Wren, a former Auburn University football star, came forward leading a small detail armed with a 37mm one-pounder[65] gun. Wren and his men blasted the machine guns to the battalion's front, quickly silencing them. At the same time, a small detachment of infantry led by 1st Lieutenant Robert Espy of B Company attacked and drove back infiltrating Germans.[66]

As this action was occurring on the left of the American assault, the Iowans of the 168th were moving to attack on the right with the intent of taking the road to Charmel. When these men stepped into the open, German artillerists began a vicious bombardment of the woods and the fields beyond. This was followed by fire from what some men later said were as many as fifty German machine guns. The opening fusillade tore "great gaps" in the Iowans' ranks, and men immediately hit the ground. They formed a skirmish line and began to return fire, although, as had been true of the Alabamians to their left, the Iowans had trouble pinpointing German positions. John Taber wrote, "The air was a tumult of shell crashes, shouted commands, snapping bullets, crackle of machine guns, and calls for stretcher-bearers." As more men were hit, the Iowans slowly crawled forward, continuing the advance on the Le Charmel road.[67]

Around 7:00 p.m., the 167th's 1st Battalion began a second assault, sending in men who had survived the first attempt at a sortie augmented with men from companies that had not participated in the first attack. The second attack began when Lieutenant Ernest Bell led two platoons from D Company forward while Lieutenant Espy attacked with two B Company platoons. From the start, this attack achieved success, albeit at the price of heavy casualties. Within minutes, about 100 of Bell's and Espy's men were leaping into German trenches, savagely fighting enemy gunners hand-to-hand, killing foes "with rifle, pistol, and bayonet."[68]

Seeing Americans taking those forward trenches, German units began to withdraw, sealing the fate of the Germans on the farm's north and west sides. Those Germans quickly fled for a woods to the east, leaving "their guns, rifles and hundreds of boxes of ammunition." The 1st Battalion seized the bastion and most of the compound, and the farm fell into American hands.[69] On the right, Germans along the road, seeing the complex change hands, fell back, allowing the Iowans to advance and capture their objective.

The Americans held the farm that night amid driving rain, constant German shelling, and a failed German counterattack. But success had carried an unnecessarily high price. One Alabama officer described the ground around the farm as "covered with killed and wounded, both American and German. For some distance you could actually walk on dead men."[70] Poor leadership and command at higher headquarters had led to a near-disaster prevented only by the courage and determination of the soldiers who made the assault.

Americans who survived the fight for La Croix Rouge Farm enjoyed no respite. They and the rest of the Rainbow Division were dispatched to continue the pursuit of the Germans, who had fallen back to prepared defensive positions on the high ground north of the Ourcq River.

The next morning the division was ordered to continue advancing to the Ourcq. I Corps issued a field order at 1:10 a.m. July 27 informing its units that an attack across the Ourcq was anticipated for the night of July 27-28 using elements of the Rainbow Division. Once the 83rd Brigade moved into place to relieve the French 164th Division, the Rainbow Division would be assuming responsibility for the entire front of I Corps. In issuing the order, staff at I Corps was operating in the belief the main axis of attack would be by American columns moving both to the east and to the west of the Château-de-Forêt and the Forêt-de-Fère.[71]

A bit more than eight hours later, corps headquarters issued General Order 51, based on guidance from the French Sixth Army and providing a more detailed plan of attack. That plan directed the Rainbow Division to be prepared to attack "under cover of darkness on the night of July 27/28" at an hour to be communicated. The objective was an area north of the Ourcq River from the Meurcy Farm southeast to Hill 212, a distance of about two miles.[72] The hill's name, like all hills on the Western Front, reflected its elevation in meters.

The 84th Brigade, with the battered survivors of the fight at La Croix Rouge Farm, moved northeast toward the area just south of Hill 212 and the village of Sergy, while the 83rd Brigade slowly advanced to the area south of the river near the Meurcy Farm and the village of Seringes-et-Nesles. Progress to the river was not without incident. The Germans had a commanding view of the approaches to the Ourcq from high ground north of the river. Artillery observers all along the line directed highly effective barrages at the Americans as they moved forward, especially hitting the 84th Brigade on the right of the division's sector. As the 168th was approaching the river's edge to affect a crossing, intense artillery and machine gun fire from atop Hill 212 drove them back. They and the other infantry regiments of the Rainbow Division would have to wait until the next day to cross the Ourcq.

To cross the river and take the high ground, the division had to overcome multiple challenges. Hills confronted the Americans on the north

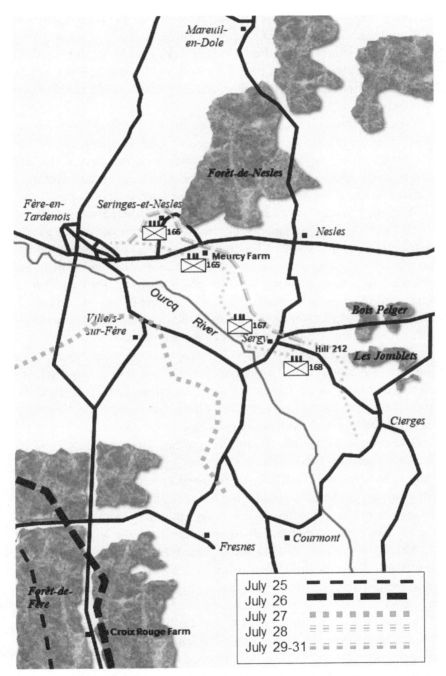

Map 3. The Rainbow Division's campaign during the Aisne-Marne Offensive. (*Author*)

side of the river from Hill 212 on the right to Hill 184 on the left. The hills and the defensive front dug in on them hugged the meandering Ourcq River, which changed course from running almost due north to practically due west downstream from Fère-en-Tardenois. The German defensive line similarly curved inward, causing the Rainbow Division two problems.

Given the terrain, German machine gunners could fire to their immediate front and flanks and engage targets at a considerable distance to their right or left. For example, enemy gunners on the crest of Hill 212 could fire on approaches to the town of Sergy and on American infantry moving south of the river well to the right or northwest of Sergy.[73]

And the Germans had carefully prepared their defensive positions. Their machine guns' placements reflected hard-fought knowledge gained in four years on the Western Front. Every weapon's position capitalized on the terrain to afford gunners unobstructed, elevated views down onto attacking American infantry, watching them approach for hundreds of yards. The defenders also nestled guns in wheat fields, woods, and on undulating ground, camouflaged with straw and tree branches. The arrangement constituted an almost perfect defensive position.

Fighting to seize the heights above the river from July 28-August 1, the Rainbow Division received artillery support of two sorts: completely ineffective or none at all. In one instance, American artillery shelled the 168th Infantry, not the Germans. The division endured almost constant German shelling with both high explosive and gas rounds.

The contest for the hills began early on the morning of July 28 when the 167th Infantry splashed across the river, no wider than a stream and only waist deep. The 168th Infantry followed, crossing the river in a dense fog bank to attack the Germans atop Hill 212 and in the village of Sergy to the left of the hill. After desperate fighting, the Iowans of the 168th took the crest of the hill and drove the Germans back but could go no farther. Soon, the New Yorkers of the 165th were attacking up the facing slopes and down the little valley toward the Meurcy Farm. They and the men from the 167th to their immediate right managed to move a few hundred yards upslope until devastating machine gun fire stopped them. The 166th made the final assault of the day in the late afternoon when one battalion crossed the river on the far left and tried to take the village of Seringes-et-Nesles. The Germans stopped the Ohioans cold using Maxims hidden among wheat fields covering the slopes between the river and

Dead soldiers from the from 167th Infantry and 150th Machine Gun Battalion lying in the fields above the Ourcq River. (*National Archives*)

the village, inflicting heavy losses and driving the Americans back to take cover just north of the river.

Over the next four days, Rainbow Division infantrymen courageously tried to advance but made little progress. They took Seringes-et-Nesles and Sergy on July 29, also driving the Germans out of the Meurcy Farm. But these were gains measured in yards, not the miles being demanded by the French Sixth Army and I Corps. Headquarters continued to press for aggressive action while providing no support whatsoever.

On the night of August 1, the Germans began withdrawing north of the Vesle River as they had figured to do all along. In fact, as early as July 27, the German Supreme Headquarters was planning a withdrawal for the night of August 1-2.[74] The positions along the Vesle had stopped Allied attacks before, particularly in the spring of 1917, when the French and British suffered more than 300,000 casualties there. When the Americans moved forward on the morning of August 2, the Germans were gone from their immediate front. The Rainbow Division was to have been relieved that night by the 4th Division but now received orders to pursue the enemy and regain contact. They did find isolated pockets of German troops, but by and large the foe was safely across the Vesle.

That night, the Rainbow Division began pulling out of the line and moving back to the Forêt-de-Fère. In nine days of combat, the division had suffered 903 men killed in action, 262 dead from wounds, and 4,311 wounded, a total of 5,467 casualties.[75]

For now, the survivors could get some rest and a hot meal.

3

THE CALM BEFORE THE STORM

"It is truly frightening to realize that you are in a place where you can get a bullet in your stomach, which is now sick and bottomless. The fear and terror that come then is an unreasoning and demoralizing panic that frantically attempts to blot out of the mind everything but the persistent thought of the job immediately at hand that must be done at once. In days or weeks, a fear like that becomes either grim determination or it festers into panic, hysteria, and collapse."
—Private John Hayes, 167th Infantry Regiment, from his memoir, *Heroes Among the Brave*

The rest that came after the terrors at La Croix Rouge Farm and along the Ourcq River was both blessed and cursed. Men who had not slept a full night in more than nine days could sleep, and those who for days had been subsisting on reserve rations of canned corned beef and hard crackers got a hot meal. Eventually all were able to launder or replace the dirty rags they had been wearing and bathe their tired aching bodies.

But rested muscles, full bellies, and clean socks could not erase what they had witnessed and experienced, and awful reminders abounded. Most of those killed along the Ourcq lay where they had fallen. The job of gathering and burying the unit's dead for burial was the official province of the 117th Engineering Regiment, but headquarters had mobilized the engineers as infantry and sent them chasing the Germans to the Vesle River. Graves registration duty fell to survivors of the battle. Father Francis P. Duffy, the much-loved chaplain of New York's 165th Infantry, later wrote that many of his regiment's men had toiled with him on "the heart breaking task of burying the dead." Father Duffy had known many of the men lost so well that he loved them as if they were younger brothers. "It has been the saddest day in my life," he wrote. "Well, it is the last act of love I can do for them and for the folks at home."[1]

Rest and quiet encouraged men to reflect, sometimes darkly. Private John Hayes, company clerk for I Company of the 167th, had been in the middle of the desperate

Father Francis Duffy, chaplain from New York's 165th Infantry. (*National Archives*)

fighting at La Croix Rouge Farm and on the slopes above the Ourcq. As he tried to recuperate from the stress of battle, Hayes's mind wandered to scenes he had witnessed at close hand:

> It is a fearful thing to advance into battle over a terrain littered and strewn with the wreckage and debris of military combat, and reeking with the odor of the dead combined with the smell of corrosive mustard and chlorine gas and the penetrating and acrid fumes of bursting shells charged with high explosives—past dead and swollen horses, their legs jutting stiffly in the air, and past human corpses blue and discolored and frozen in the grotesque positions assumed in sudden and violent death.[2]

Soon, men had to set aside musings light or dark to train for battles that would be on a scale unlike anything the U.S. Army had ever seen.

It would be hard to imagine any worse place for exhausted soldiers to try to rest than the northern portion of the Forêt-de-Fère. Located about a mile south of the Ourcq River, the hellish woodland's only attraction was that for now it was far out of German artillery range. John Hayes recalled a "damp, dirty, and inclement woods tainted with gas and rank with

A burial detail from the 165th Infantry moves out to find the bodies of their comrades following the Aisne-Marne offensive. (*National Archives*)

decay."[3] John Taber of the 168th Infantry wrote in his diary, "There are dead horses and other evil smelling things about us, the flies are abominable, and cooties bothersome. No way to get rid of them."[4] Father Duffy remembered a "dank, unwholesome spot and the daily rains make it daily more intolerable."[5] But I Corps, wanting the division close by in reserve, ordered the unit to stay there eight days, during which many men, weakened by nine days of continuous combat, became ill. "Sixty per cent of our men are sick with diarrhea and everybody is crawling with cooties," Father Duffy reported. "The men are sleeping in shelter tents or in holes in the ground in the woods and they are a sorry looking lot."[6]

It was an inexcusable way to treat survivors of the worst fighting any American unit had seen thus far. But the Guardsmen's performance had earned them respect. I Corps commander General Hunter Liggett called the 42nd "a first class division in every sense; swift in attack and tenacious in both attack and defense."[7] As the men and their field commanders took stock of the infantry regiments, though, what they saw was dispiriting.

"In this one battle nearly half our strength is gone," Father Duffy wrote of the 165th Infantry. "We have lost fifty-nine officers and thirteen hundred men and of these thirteen officers and about two hundred men have been killed outright."[8] The situation in Alabama's 167th was similar. An Alabama man later wrote that "the men had used up the last bit of energy they possessed," largely because during their nine days on the line the soldiers "received only one meal a day, and some days they had nothing to eat." That unit, too, had lost more than half its men.[9] In the 168th, Lieutenant John Taber wrote in his diary:

> On August 5th we are just learning how badly we've been hit. In our Battalion, Heath Noble and Bernard Van Hof have been killed, and today we got word that Tim has died of his wounds, Eric, Captain Dunn and GBN [Lieutenant George B. Noble] were wounded, and with Hupp, Lefferts, and Blake gassed, we are short of officers. But the 2nd Battalion is worse off than ours, and Brad has been transferred to F Company, and Teddy Jones to H. Rubel, a good officer, was killed early in the fight, and Douglas Greene (Lt. Douglas B., H) was sent back in dying condition. GBN was hit in the arm. Soon our outfit won't be recognizable.[10]

Father Duffy looked in on Villers-sur-Fère. About the time the Germans were falling back ten miles, the little village's residents had begun trickling home, checking on their shattered residences and retrieving what possessions they could find. Father Duffy was mapping potential grave locations when he encountered a group of French civilians. "Most of them were men who had been sent ahead by the family to see what was left," he recalled. "But occasionally we met a stout old peasant woman pulling a small cart behind her on which rested all her earthly substance, or a haycart drawn by oxen with the family possessions in it and two or three chubby youngsters with their mother perched on top." The chaplain followed one middle-aged farmer and his son into their badly damaged house near the church. Duffy noted, "All the plaster had been knocked off the walls and the glass from the windows, and there was a big hole in the roof, and altogether it looked like anything but a home." Looking the house over, the son turned to his father and said in a satisfied manner, "*Pas trop demoli*" ("Not too much damage."). The priest could only admire what he saw as "optimism and courage" in desperate conditions.[11]

A highlight of the division's stay in the dreary Forêt-de-Fère came in an appearance by what one man compared to "a goddess just stepping out of the clouds for a bit to see what it was all about down here below." On a sunny afternoon, the men were ushered out of the woods to a field where stood a wagon bed surrounded by musicians led by American singer Elsie Janis. Beginning what became a national tradition, Janis was touring the front performing for doughboys at her own expense. For a couple of hours, the tired, disheveled men of the Rainbow Division got to forget the war as Janis "danced and sang before a vast concourse of unwashed doughboys who suddenly remembered that there was such a thing in the world as a pretty American girl—and were somewhat awed and saddened at the remembrance."[12]

With over 5,000 casualties in the Aisne-Marne Offensive, the Rainbow Division needed a very large infusion of replacement personnel. Previous replacements had come in much smaller increments, and most were draftees. This time, given the numbers needed, new men would come from other units, joined by enlistees and draftees from all over the United States. John Taber's comment about his regiment no longer being recognizable would soon apply to the entire division, whose great losses were altering its very character. And before the rest period ended, the unit's leadership also underwent significant changes.

Elsie Janis, the popular American singer, performed for American doughboys all along the front at her own expense. (*Library of Congress*)

Major alteration came first for the 84th Brigade while the division was still fighting along the Ourcq. On the morning of July 30, as the 167th and 168th were preparing to resume an assault on the village of Sergy and the ridge beyond, I Corps commander Liggett arrived at the brigade P.C. With him were his aide-de-camp, Lieutenant Colonel Pierpont Stackpole, Major General Charles Menoher, commander of the Rainbow Division, and Colonel Douglas MacArthur, Menoher's chief of staff. The brass had come to address what they saw as the 84th Brigade's alleged lackluster performance and commanding General Robert Brown's unfitness for command.[13]

Brown seemed to sense that trouble was coming from the division's leadership and felt he needed to restore his bosses' confidence in him. Based on what he had observed of Colonel Ernest Bennett, commander of the 168th Infantry, at La Croix Rouge Farm and at the Ourcq, Brown believed Bennett had lost confidence in himself and his men. Bennett had been with his regiment since its days as the 3rd Iowa Infantry and then as the 51st Iowa Infantry fighting in the Philippines. When Wilson declared war on Germany, he was the obvious choice to command the regiment. He brought along his operations officer, Lieutenant Colonel Mathew A. Tinley, who had also served in the Philippines. Bennett was popular with his men, especially those who were native Iowans and had been with the regiment since its Iowa National Guard days. Brown knew that firing Bennett and removing him from the regiment would likely damage the unit's morale. So, on July 29 he decided to retain Bennett as regimental commander but restrict him to purely administrative duties and assign operational command to Lieutenant Colonel Tinley.[14]

Brown hoped this would satisfy Liggett and Menoher, but the change came too late and was not nearly strong enough to assuage their doubts. Menoher wanted Brown gone, and Liggett approved the recommendation, forwarding his decision to AEF Headquarters that night. The next day, July 31, General James McAndrew, AEF chief of staff, directed Liggett by telegram to relieve Brown of duty and replace him with Douglas MacArthur, who along with Brown's job received a brevet promotion to Brigadier General.[15]

The formal report by the AEF Inspector General that followed Brown's firing was a whitewash designed to blame Brown and justify his removal. The fifty-nine-page report indicated that Menoher's and Liggett's firing of Brown and his replacement by MacArthur were supported by six officers from 42nd Division Headquarters. However, those closest to Brown, including seven officers serving in the 167th and the 168th Infantry, testified that they saw nothing in Brown's performance to justify removal. They made statements supporting Brown despite what some of them felt was pressure from the Inspector General to say otherwise.[16]

The report stated that Brown constantly complained about the fitness of his command for combat. The report scorned these complaints as baseless because no such similar grievances were received from the 83rd Brigade commander, General Lenihan, and "the two brigades had practically the same hardships, practically the same amount of fighting and practically the same officers.... They [the soldiers in the 84th Brigade] had been subjected to exactly the same conditions as the rest of the Division."[17] This was patently false. The 84th Brigade had suffered numerous casualties in two days of brutal fighting at La Croix Rouge Farm while the 83rd Brigade was still moving into the area of operations. The report also stated bluntly that Brown was unfit for combat command. Brown's replacement, Douglas MacArthur, was the source of the allegations about unjustified complaints and being unfit for command.

At best, Brown's removal was an effort by staff at I Corps and 42nd Division Headquarters to absolve themselves of their miserable, almost criminal mismanagement of the Aisne-Marne campaign. At worst, the firing may have resulted from a carefully executed plan by Menoher and MacArthur to move MacArthur to brigade commander. A vain and ambitious officer who had strong support from General Menoher, MacArthur had been slated to return to the United States to take command of a new, untrained brigade that might not ever make it to combat in France. By removing Brown and replacing him in this way, Menoher would not lose someone he saw as an indispensable officer. MacArthur would not only get his wish for a brigade command, but also a position leading one of the AEF's best combat brigades. For anyone who has spent time at a major military headquarters and has had to maneuver its inevitable political labyrinth, Brown's firing clearly seems to have had someone's fingerprints all over it. Those fingerprints likely belonged to Douglas MacArthur.

Major William Donovan, commander of the 1st Battalion of the 165th Infantry. (*National Archives*)

In late August, the New Yorkers of the 165th Infantry experienced a similarly dramatic change in command. The 165th enjoyed the strongest unit cohesion in the division. Colonel Frank McCoy, a Regular Army officer, had taken over in April as the regiment's fourth commanding officer since mustering in July 1917; cohesion enabled the men to navigate conflicts arising from such volatility. McCoy was being promoted to brigadier general and reassigned.[18]

Learning of this, Father Duffy noted that, while McCoy had only been in command for four months, he felt like a friend of forty years' standing. Speaking with Major William "Wild Bill" Donovan, the 1st Battalion commander, Duffy asked who was to replace McCoy. Donovan replied that the entire command staff had recommended to McCoy that he request that Lieutenant Colonel Harry Mitchell, the regiment's operations officer, be named commander. Duffy expressed approval, observing that Donovan might be a suitable replacement. Donovan demurred, saying that he wanted to spend his days fighting, not talking on the telephone.[19] Colonel Hough of Ohio's 166th Infantry and Colonel Screws of Alabama's 167th Infantry were the division's only original regiment commanders, and held those posts for the balance of the war.

Late on the afternoon of August 9, the division received orders to march from the Forêt-de-Fère to a rest area at the rear—an occasion for joy. John Taber wrote that the unit's latest orders "definitely dispelled the persistent rumor that we were to be thrown into the fight again, and because it meant putting distance between us and this pestilential, fly infested swamp."[20] The 168th and the 167th departed the forest around noon on August 10, with the 166th and 165th following on August 11.

As the Iowans of the 168th emerged from the shadowy woods, they seemed to be leaving behind Aisne-Marne's terrors and deep losses. "Promptly at twelve o'clock, the column marched out into the intoxicating, splendid sunlight," John Taber wrote. "It seemed like another world." Within minutes, someone started singing a marching tune. The farther they got from the forest, the higher morale rose. With the 167th on their heels, the two regiments marched about eight miles, making camp at Verdilly, a small town north of Château-Thierry. The men pitched shelter tents for the night in a field beside a clear, rippling stream, and as they prepared to sleep, artillery flashed on the far northern horizon. For the first time in weeks, the night was quiet and undisturbed.[21]

Back in the Forêt-de-Fère, the 165th began Sunday morning August 11 forming up on the road leading away from the Ourcq. That morning's Mass was to be a memorial for those left behind along the river. The priest's traveling altar, per Colonel McCoy, stood in a field adjoining the route of march. Reaching that point, the men turned off the road to form a hollow square around the altar and Father Duffy. After Mass, he gave a homily based on the gospel of John 15:13. ("Greater love than this no man hath than that he lay down his life for his friends."). When he finished, the regiment resumed its march bracketed by the band in the lead and the supply wagon and ration carts at the rear, the Ohioans of the 166th close behind.[22]

An hour's marching brought the 165th to Beuvardes, where General Menoher and his division headquarters staff came out to watch them pass, prompting Colonel McCoy to have the band strike up the regimental air, "Garry Owen." The men "passed in review, heads up and chests out and stepping out with a martial gait as if they were parading at Camp Mills and not returning from a battlefield where half their number had been lost."[23]

From Beuvardes, the two regiments of the 83rd Brigade followed the route the 168th and 167th had the day before, moving through the ruin of Épieds to a spot north of Château-Thierry. As the 83rd strode down the road, the 168th and 167th, which were about twelve hours ahead, slowly moved through Château-Thierry, Vaux, and Le Thiolet amid "heavy traffic—great convoys of camions bringing up new forces to the line of battle, long lines of artillery, of supply wagons creaking with ammunition and food."[24]

The men noted terrible damage in Château-Thierry but soon realized Vaux and Le Thiolet had suffered more. "These two villages marked the supreme triumph of the gunner's art," John Taber wrote. "No two walls of the same building remained upright and there was not a habitable place left.... its jagged outline stood guard over a hopeless tangle of splintered beams, iron grilles and fences, and heavy blocks of stone." Beyond the village stretched shell-ravaged woods and fields stitched with "thick belts of barbed wire, and a system of trenches recently dug to stave off the once threatening drive on Paris."[25] Thanks in part to the Rainbow Division, Paris was never threatened again.

After covering another eight to ten miles, the 168th and 167th moved off the highway to Paris, dispersing to camp in five villages north and south of the highway. The following day, August 12, the 165th and the 166th did likewise, camping in three towns. Both the 166th and the 168th had elements camped in and around Coupru, about which opinions varied. Raymond Cheseldine of the 166th described Coupru as "a tiny village practically untouched by war, which was clean and neat compared to the awful desolation of the area just vacated."[26] John Taber of the 168th wrote, "Coupru is dirty, battered, and practically deserted."[27]

None of the towns encountered by the division were what the men had been hoping for in a rest area. The villages "were dirty, battered, and practically uninhabited, and there were no loud cheers when it was unofficially announced that these were to be our permanent rest stations," Taber wrote. "No cafés, no shops, no pretty mademoiselles, no fun."[28] Nonetheless, men could bathe, wash clothes (sometimes by boiling them), sleep, and eat three hot meals a day.

Much of the 166th Infantry ended up in Charly-sur-Marne on August 13. This small city was tucked into the Marne Valley behind hills that had protected it from German artillery. There was little damage in that peaceful, quiet place. Reclining that night in their billets, men went to sleep without hearing artillery and fearing enemy shells for the first time since coming onto the line at Baccarat in March. This was exactly the respite the men needed after their ordeal along the Ourcq.[29]

Charly-sur-Marne was too quiet for some men habituated to combat. That first night, an officer returning to his tent paused when he heard hushed voices coming from beneath a hedge. He counted fifteen of his men lounging in their underclothes, smoking and gabbing.

"Ain't it Hell? There ain't been a sound for three hours except that damned mule hee-hawin'," a man said. "If a battery don't cut loose somewhere pretty soon, I reckon I'll stay awake all night."

"This man's army don't know how to rest. We been fighting so long that we can't quit all of a sudden," a man replied. "It's just like cigarettes or booze—you got to quit slow, and here they stop us short after about five months. We'll get used to it in time, but this night sure is Hell. I can't sleep with that mule making such a racket."

The officer continued on his way. Back on the banks of the Ourcq he had struggled night upon night to keep his eyes open amid artillery and machine gun fire, but now when he tried to sleep he, too, found the quiet too loud.[30]

As the division was resting, its artillery finally caught up with its infantry. When the infantry had pulled back to the Forêt-de-Fère, the artillery brigade advanced, supporting the 4th Division's approach to the Germans along the Vesle River. On August 11, gun crews were directed to pull back and begin rejoining the Rainbow Division by marching about nineteen miles to Épieds, where they were ordered to bathe and clean up. The men stripped, handing over their wool clothing to be boiled in huge cauldrons to exterminate body lice. This killed cooties but also shrank uniform blouses and trousers, underwear, socks, and caps. Once the gear was dry and stacked by size, soldiers did their best to reclothe themselves, sometimes getting new socks or underwear from the supply company before undergoing mass fumigation and short, inspection-ready haircuts.[31]

Starting on August 14, regiments began to shift to villages near railways. On August 17, men began to entrain for towns in Bourmont, an area about 120 miles southwest of Château-Thierry, for a thirty-day rest period. Perhaps no setting in France could have been so conducive to rest and recovery, John Taber wrote:

> Untouched by war, situated in a country of wooded hills and valleys patched with well-cultivated fields and populated by very simple, very hospitable French peasants, they were ideal places in which to renew

The town of Bourmont, a place that seemed untouched by the war. (*National Archives*)

vitality, to laugh at the horror of war, and to forget its brutalities. Why, back this far one could have all the light he wanted at night—there wasn't even any danger from airplanes. There were comfortable billets for all, many in airy, well-constructed barracks, with a mess hall for each company, and one café to every twenty houses, at least. There were eggs and chickens and ducks to be bought—for a price, after the men started in to bid against each other. It was satisfying just to sit and look off into the distance, a blended vista of beckoning roads, fair orchards, neat farms, browsing cattle, blue sky, red roofs, and delicate spires.[32]

Given access to liquor, some men overindulged, led by the boys from Alabama, well known for testing army disciplinary limits. A military policeman, or M.P., from Virginia later recounted his experience with tipsy Alabamians. His detachment was arresting a member of the 167th who was drunk and found on him an envelope containing human hair. Questioned, he told the M.P. that it was the mustache he had cut from a German he had killed, adding proudly that he meant to send it to his sweetheart in "Alabam." This M.P. noted that men of the 167th referred to their state in two ways, depending on whether they had been drinking. A sober fellow would say "Alabam." But if he had been "courting Bacchus," the answer was always "Alagoddambam."[33]

Sex also reared its head. French authorities preferred that British and American soldiers use prostitutes, as had been army policy for garrisons in the American West, but the AEF, trying to curb venereal disease, prohibited soldiers from going to bordellos. The crowds of men in the 167th seeking treatment for "the drip" caused Colonel Screws to reinstate "short arm inspections" that quickly confirmed whores as the source. Doughboys' only alternative was to fraternize with female civilians who weren't sex workers. American officers did their best to discourage fraternization but were largely unsuccessful.[34]

Charles MacArthur of the 149th Field Artillery wrote that women in his unit's rest area "had big feet and looked like sausage balloons." Appearances did not stop many soldiers from initiating amorous campaigns. The "rigors of the front had materially affected any fixed ideals of our dreams," MacArthur wrote. Besides, he added, many of his comrades "had a very low boiling point" to begin with. A soldier in the 149th known as "the Greek" was the unit's cook. The unit's field kitchen was in the home of a local seamstress. Men believed the Greek to be trading her rations for sex. MacArthur said the Greek had "waxed his moustache" within ten minutes of setting up the kitchen, and from then on, he and his buddies "had to watch their rations like a hawk." Even the "slightest shortage of stew was attributed" to the Greek's "amorous designs, although he assured us fervently that he meant the lady no harm."[35]

During the rest period an AEF Inspector General investigated claims of atrocities by Rainbow Division men during the Aisne-Marne Offensive. Captured German communiques stated that the division did not take prisoners and that, during the fighting along the Ourcq, members of the division had shot Germans who were surrendering. Major Donovan of the 165th did little to dispel the rumors. "We took very few prisoners," he wrote later. "The men, when they saw the Germans serving machine guns against us, firing until the last minute, then throwing up their hands and crying 'Kamerad,' became just lustful for German blood. I do not blame them."[36]

Questioned by investigators about examples of atrocities, Major Ravee Norris of the 167th recounted incidents at La Croix Rouge Farm. In one, his men had located a German artillery piece in the woods north of the farm firing into the American rear. Without warning or requesting a surrender, Alabamians shot the gunners dead. In another, as his men were advancing toward the farm, they passed a German at a machine gun who seemed to be dead. As soon as they were past him the gunner, who had been playing possum, began firing at them. The doughboys shot him dead without offering him the opportunity for surrender.[37]

The headquarters of the Rainbow Division near Bourmont. (*National Archives*)

And during the intense fighting along the Ourcq, Norris said, he sent a corporal to the rear guarding seven or eight German prisoners. Once away from other Americans, the prisoners tried to jump their captor and escape. The corporal shot them all. At the same time, nine wounded prisoners were being delivered to Norris's P.C. for treatment. "They received the same attention as our own wounded men," Norris told the inspector. They then "were put on stretchers and carried to the rear, where they were evacuated to a field hospital."

"Now Colonel those are all the facts as I know them," Norris told his inquisitor. "You will have to judge for yourself as to the correctness of the charge."[38] After that, nothing more was heard about the charges.

Those thirty days of rest vanished in a blink when all units received a training schedule. Rumors were circulating at division headquarters of an offensive in which American forces would play a major role. The prescribed regimen emphasized the run-and-crawl tactic for attacking machine guns: advance in small separate groups, men were to crawl, then rise, run a few yards, and drop back to the ground, repeating that process until they were close enough to toss hand grenades into the enemy position. The elaborate four-week training schedule included several all-day and all-night exercises in which each entire regiment confronted and solved a tactical problem, down to using the wagons from support units. The first week focused on small-unit tactics: a platoon assaulting a machine gun emplacement, a company advancing through dense woods, a battalion making an assault over broken ground. Men rose at first light, set up exercises, performed close-order drill, and spent the afternoon attacking "imaginary machine gun nests, capturing and recapturing the high hills on the outskirts of the villages."[39]

Had the matter been open for discussion, the division's infantrymen probably would have argued that these were the tactics they had committed to heart along the Ourcq, and out of tragic necessity. They and their officers at the battalion and company levels had learned that the standard formation for an infantry attack prescribed in tactics manuals assumed proper artillery support that had been utterly absent at the Ourcq. Once, when the 165th was ordered to attack the Meurcy Farm, Major Donovan, the 1st Battalion commander, had found his men preparing to advance upright in waves. He immediately ordered them instead to employ the run-and-crawl tactic, "which is, one, two or three at a time, moving fast, and when they have advanced a few yards to flop."[40]

Flawed assault tactics originated at headquarters. After the war, Major Lloyd Ross of the 168th Infantry analyzed this issue. Ross had found that almost all young Rainbow Division infantry officers were bright and conscientious, but scarcely schooled in these sorts of tactics or the doctrine that guided fighting on the offensive in a war of maneuver. He aimed his biggest criticism at the senior staffs at the division, corps, army, and AEF levels, who had "an ever present tendency to rush troops forward and keep pushing them against enemy machine guns without adequate support from machine guns, howitzers, and artillery." Most American general officers "had never commanded troops in large bodies and against a first class well armed enemy," he said. In France top commanders were applying the same "driving tactics" used by smaller units in the Philippines during the Spanish-American War and the Philippine Insurrection. "They would not take the word of the officer in the front lines as to the opposing forces and weapons but kept driving troops forward inadequately supported by artillery," Ross said. Had a massive artillery barrage been ordered on day one at the Ourcq, "our infantry would have just walked over Hill 212, and the Germans would never have been able to organize along their next line."[41]

The latest training regimen might have been redundant for veterans, but its lessons were crucial for inexperienced and untrained replacements. What had been a trickle of new soldiers from February until June now became a flood. In August 1918 alone, the Rainbow Division welcomed over 5,600 replacements. For the most part, they came from divisions

Major Lloyd Ross (center), commander of the 1st Battalion of Iowa's 168th Infantry. (*National Archives*)

formed for that purpose at home and in France. Domestically, they came from the 41st Division, which consisted of men from Washington, Oregon, Montana, Idaho, and Wyoming; the 39th Division from Alabama, Mississippi, and Louisiana; and the 40th Division, from California, Colorado, Utah, Arizona, and New Mexico.[42] Some of these soldiers had undergone sufficient instruction and practice, but many had received only minimal military training.

Consider the 168th Infantry's experience. The first detachment of replacements reporting to the regiment in August consisted of 320 men from the Texas and Oklahoma National Guard. These men had put in months of service in their states and were well-trained, well-disciplined, and fully equipped. Not so the next two batches the Iowans received. These groups included 647 men, mostly draftees from eastern states. The vast majority were "far below the mental and physical standard of the original cadre." Many could not read, write, or speak English and most had never fired a rifle. "They had never heard of a skirmish line," wrote John Taber, "and couldn't have told the difference between a grenade and a platoon."[43]

An official report from the 168th's 2nd Battalion stated, "Investigation discloses the fact that not more than half of them have had over a month's training of any sort, and that few of them have had any instruction whatsoever in gas protection, or in the use of rifle, auto-rifle, and grenades." The commander of H Company reported that out of forty-three new men assigned to the company, one had received a week of training; four had received two weeks; twenty had received three weeks of training; and six had gone through four weeks of training. The rest had trained for one to three months. Taber later wrote, "It was criminal in the first place ever to permit them to leave the States in that condition." In his words, they were "cannon fodder, if there ever was any."[44]

During this period of rest and training, most of the men hoped to receive some small amount of leave, even if only a forty-eight-hour pass to see Paris. As training intensified, any hopes for a few days away from camp were dashed. Clearly the division was going to be moving back into the line very soon. The men heard rumors that military hospitals around Toul were being prepared to receive large numbers of casualties. General MacArthur, the new 84th Brigade commander, let slip the real situation. While he was observing the 168th as it trained, what he saw pleased him; he asked Iowa officers with him if the men were enjoying their rest. The Iowans replied frankly that "it was not their idea of rest and that the curtailment of the promised leaves had created tremendous dissatisfaction." A dramatic and forceful commander, MacArthur was also attentive to morale and believed in taking care of his men. He nodded in agreement. "I don't believe that we are going to get either leaves or rest," he said offhandedly. "They say that they need the 42nd to win this fight." The officers did not know what "fight" the general meant, but something big was apparently in the works.[45]

4

PREPARING FOR THE SAINT MIHIEL OFFENSIVE

"... some of the old men started the rumor that we were going into rest camp for the winter. The conjecture was that we had done our share through the summer, and that now the men of the National Army would carry on the winter's work. This conjecture, however, found little acceptance."

—Private Martin Hogan, 165th Infantry Regiment, from his book, *The Shamrock Battalion*

The 168th Infantry's march on the night of September 7 became legendary—but not in a good way. The objective was a forest about two miles south of Toul. The troops had to cover only five or six miles on foot.[1] But the men had marched six of the previous eight nights, often in torrential rain. It was raining again. They were wet, cold, and weary and this night proved particularly long.

En route to the night's campsite, the men turned off the main road onto a rough rural trail barely wide enough for four men to march abreast. As they were leaving the road, the rain intensified; men could see but a few yards. "It was like walking blindfolded,"[2] a soldier said. Confused, guides from one battalion mistakenly led the column off the trail and up a long, slippery hill. The error went undiscovered until wagoneers following the battalion had progressed so far that to turn around they needed to crest the hill. The soldiers ahead of the wagons could not turn back and get past them. Onward and upward the column snaked until it could correct its course.[3]

Many men openly cursed the fool who had caused this massive mess. But they grasped hands in the blinding rain and darkness and followed a leader "in whom they reposed a strange confidence." Winds were now whipping the rain sideways. Freshets gushed downhill. The beleaguered column finally got turned around and, with lightning showing the way, stumbled through underbrush and across ditches to their muddy campsite in the valley below.[4]

As the German offensives of the spring and summer of 1918 played out, Allied leaders were reviewing their options for seizing the initiative and ending the war in 1919. In conferences during the summer of 1918, Marshal Foch emphasized that both the French and British armies and people were exhausted and that, at minimum, Allied armies had to take back northern France and at least some of Belgium from the Kaiser's forces during 1919, if not earlier. To do so would require all available Allied divisions in a campaign of continuous attack.[5]

The debate was one of strategy—specifically, how to use the Yanks. By the end of August 1918, the United States would have over 61,000 officers and more than 1,300,000 enlisted men in France.[6] The question was how best to integrate them with the French and the British armies.

One option was to slam German forces hard enough to bring a victory so crushingly decisive that the Germans would have no choice but to admit for years to having been trounced and trounced utterly. This meant massively penetrating the German lines or driving the enemy back so far and so fast that a large part of his army could only escape destruction by surrendering unconditionally.[7]

The other, less ambitious option was to try to achieve peace without decisively defeating the German army. Some Allied planners had suggested a campaign to isolate a body of German troops, forcing the remaining German units out of France and Belgium and back onto home turf. This approach, seen as more practicable, risked leaving the German people feeling cheated of victory rather than compelled to accept defeat.[8]

Both endgames centered on the enemy's rail infrastructure. The German Army in France depended on three groups of rail lines crossing the

Rhine River to the French and Belgian borders and spreading in a network to the rear areas of the Germans' Western Front positions.

The northernmost rail group had two main lines running from Düsseldorf and Cologne to Brussels and Namur in Belgium.[9] The center group consisted of a rail line from Coblenz up the Moselle Valley to Trier, Germany, from which networked lines reached the French cities of Verdun, Metz, and Nancy.[10]

The third group's main line ran from Mainz, Germany, into the Saar Valley along with two other lines hugging both Rhine shorelines to Strasbourg, France. These three lines joined a network that supplied German forces in the Lorraine region. Connecting them were two main lines that ran parallel to the front. One went from Bruges, Belgium, through Hirson, Mézières-sur-Oise, Sedan, and Longuyon to Metz and then Strasbourg while the second line ran to the east of the first from Brussels to Namur, Luxembourg, Thionville, the Saar region, and then to the Rhine at Strasbourg.[11]

Since July 1917, when the AEF began arriving in France, Pershing had believed these rail lines might be the keys to a decisive Allied victory, and that the Saint Mihiel Salient offered the best path to that victory. The salient, which the French called *l'Hernie* ("the Hernia"), dated to October 1914, a bulge along the Western Front about twenty miles northwest of Nancy encompassing some 200 square miles. The salient had the town of Saint Mihiel as the apex of a right triangle, with a southern face crossing open, flat terrain toward the Moselle River. The salient was twenty-five miles wide at its base and protruded fifteen miles into the Allied lines. The base, which was the shorter leg of the triangle, ran east/west from Saint Mihiel to Pont-à-Mousson on the Moselle.[12]

The salient's northwest corner was near Les Éparges, a village on the reverse side of the Hauts de Meuse, a low ridge of hills on the northeast bank of the Meuse separating the plains of the Woëvre and the Meuse Valley. This side of the salient crossed the Meuse to a small bridgehead the Germans established around Chauvoncourt, a suburb of Saint Mihiel. The Chauvoncourt bridgehead was just large enough to cut the rail line between Verdun and Toul, a critical line of communication for the French. This line crossed the Meuse just above Saint Mihiel and ran east through the Hauts de Meuse and into the plains of the Woëvre at Apremont. From there, the line ran directly east to the Moselle north of Pont-à-Mousson.[13]

On the map, Pershing could clearly see that if the Allies could collapse the Saint Mihiel Salient, then drive to Metz and Thionville and down the

Moselle Valley, they could cut the German lateral railways running in general parallel to their line. This would threaten the path of retreat to the Rhine for all German troops to the left facing the French, British, and Belgians, leading to decisive victory. For this reason, Pershing always intended to place any new American army organization opposite the Saint Mihiel Salient.[14] But to do so Pershing had to persuade Foch to authorize him to create that American army.

Allied military leaders had been debating the notion of creating a separate American army organization since the first American division arrived in July 1917. The idea came to the fore at meetings of Allied leaders that began in July 1918. On July 10, when Foch hosted conferees at his headquarters in Bombon, Pershing argued on behalf of forming an American army as soon as possible. He spoke forcefully but in a unifying and diplomatic tone and offered a practical context. He stressed the necessity of using American forces to serve the common cause. So long as the Germans retained the initiative, he said, he was more than willing to deploy AEF units wherever needed to stop the Germans, even if that meant Americans served under French command. But he emphasized that if and when the Allies seized the initiative he wanted American troops assembled into a separate army organization used to inflict maximum damage on the enemy in a locale that would cause that damage to achieve decisive victory.[15]

Foch's reply to Pershing's arguments was lukewarm at best. The marshal "talked a great deal that day and went on to say that in order to bring victory to the Allies it would be necessary for them to have an incontestable numerical superiority," Pershing wrote later. "He laid particular stress on the view that the strength of the British and French divisions should be maintained, and the number of American divisions increased as rapidly as possible." Pershing's clear impression of Foch's opinion was that, while the French marshal had referred to an early date for creation of an American army, he did not believe that would be possible until September or October.[16]

When conferees met at Bombon again on July 21, circumstances had changed significantly. The Allies had stopped the Germans at Champagne in the opening of the Second Battle of the Marne with heavy losses, and French and American forces were driving into the Marne Salient as German forces withdrew. The initiative had changed hands at last. During the July 21 conference, Foch agreed to the rapid formation of the U.S. 1st Army using the 3rd, 4th, 26th, 32nd, and 42nd Divisions. These divisions were to be organized into two army corps deployed side by side with 1st Army Headquarters operating from either Coulommiers or Montmirail and with Pershing in command.[17]

It seemed sensible for the 1st Army's initial area of responsibility to be in the Marne Salient, but on August 10 Pershing moved his headquarters to Neufchâteau from which the 1st Army could continue planning for an operation against the Saint Mihiel Salient. Pershing's AEF staff had been scrutinizing the potential for such an offensive since June 1917 and had completed a first strategic study in September 1917. On July 24, 1918, Foch presented Allied leaders with his ideas for the overall offensive, assigning reduction of the Saint Mihiel Salient to the 1st Army.

At the time, the German defenses in the salient constituted a system of three defensive zones manned by eight full divisions and two separate brigades along the salient's forward face. The first component, four miles deep, was called the Wilhelm Zone. The Wilhelm Zone ran almost forty miles from Pont-à-Mousson in the east to the town of St. Mihiel, then north up the heights of the Meuse to Grimaucourt, southeast of Verdun. To the immediate rear of the Wilhelm Zone was the Schröeter Zone, the central interior line of defense. The innermost zone was the Michel Zone, which ran along the base of the salient's right triangle shape. The Michel Zone comprised three defensive lines. The first was the Hagen Stellung, or position, with the Volker Stellung to its rear. The final defensive line inside the Michel Zone was the Kriemhilde Stellung.[18]

German forces in the salient, known collectively as Army Detachment C, were led by General George Fuchs. Army Detachment C was organized in groups that defended specific geographic sections of the line. The Gorz Group, which included the 77th and the 10th Divisions of the I Bavarian Corps, was stationed along the German left flank. The Mihiel Group, which was composed of the 5th Landwehr Division and the 31st Division, also of the I Bavarian Corps, was assigned to the forward tip of the salient. The Combres Group, consisting of the 35th Austro-Hungarian and the 8th and the 13th Landwehr Divisions, was positioned along the German right flank. The Metz Group, placed in the rear, was assigned as a strategic reserve with the 195th Saxon and 123rd Divisions.[19]

Now that General Pershing had authorization to create the 1st Army, it was time for that army to plan, lead, and act as an independent force. Collapsing the Saint Mihiel Salient seemed a natural objective as the 1st Army's initial operation, but everyone knew the French had tried and failed repeatedly to reduce the salient. Pershing nonetheless believed the

1st Army might be able to take the salient and press on to the northeast to seize the strategic city of Metz. This, in turn, might threaten the Briey Iron Basin, an area critical to German war production, as well as the site of crucial rail networks serving the Saar coalfields.[20] From July into late August 1918, 1st Army staff toiled on a plan for an offensive that would accomplish all those objectives.

The elaborate plans for the Saint Mihiel Offensive sorely taxed the inexperienced AEF Headquarters and 1st Army staffs. As characterized, the undertaking would require over 500,000 American troops, more than 100,000 French soldiers, nearly 3,000 artillery pieces, 200,000 tons of supplies, and 50,000 tons of ammunition. Most men, guns, and matériel would have to reach the area using the few available roads, a daunting exercise in transport and logistics planning. Hardly less so were the issues of how many units to deploy and the timing of attacks and artillery support.[21]

The French and British believed Americans incapable of satisfactorily performing in high command and staff positions. Pershing's planners were out to prove them wrong, an effort that proved Herculean. "The more mechanical and complex war grows the greater importance the staff must take on," General Liggett said afterwards. "It is the nervous system and the brain center of the army." For Pershing, Liggett, and the other American generals, their "nervous system and the brain center" amounted to a cadre of graduates of the Fort Leavenworth Command and Staff College. At Fort Leavenworth, these relatively young officers had studied German textbooks, learned to recognize and analyze the important factors in a tactical situation, and how to prepare a proper comprehensive order—skills mandatory for planning operations like the one to take the Saint Mihiel Salient. More than that, a staff college education changed many students' thinking. George C. Marshall, a 1908 graduate, became the Chief of Operations of the 1st Army. Marshall said that, at Fort Leavenworth, "I learned how to learn."

Pershing's staff bustled relentlessly, unaware that General Fuchs was planning to quit the salient. Despite having thrown back multiple French attacks, the Germans in the salient knew their position was highly vulnerable to a pincer attack. The French had lacked the wherewithal for a multi-front operation, but Fuchs and the other German generals recognized that the massive infusion of American forces could win the day. Those spring and summer offensives in the Marne had cost the Germans dearly, and they needed to shorten their defensive line wherever possible.

Left, Marshal Ferdinand Foch (left) and Lieutenant General John Pershing, who differed over strategy and the creation of a separate American Army organization in August and September 1918. Right, Marshal Philippe Pétain (left) and Pershing, who met on August 31, 1918, to discuss Foch's proposed changes to the plan for the Saint Mihiel offensive. (*National Archives*)

In June 1918, they began planning Operation Loki, named for the shape-shifting god of Norse mythology. Under this plan, German forces were to stay in place so long as the sector remained quiet. At any signs of an Allied offensive, Fuchs would withdraw his forces to the Michel Zone along the base of the triangle and make a stand.[22]

The original American undertaking, which became known as the August Plan, was to seek to reduce the salient and provide a jumping-off point for a potential drive toward Metz and the Moselle Valley and a breakout into the Woëvre Plain. The plan emphasized gaining and maintaining momentum through surprise and speed that kept the Germans from counterattacking and breaching the Michel Zone before the foe could react effectively. If the Allies could achieve that, an attack toward Metz would be the logical next step.[23]

With fall and its wet weather on the horizon, Foch believed the offensive into the Saint Mihiel Salient should begin around September 1. The marshal proposed using fourteen American divisions supported by at least three French divisions. Pershing assigned the I, IV, and V Corps for the attack. I Corps was posted along the Vesle River, IV Corps was at Toul, and V Corps was still being organized. He increased I Corps to four divisions and moved the troops of III Corps to be adjacent to I Corps and so able quickly to replace them along the Vesle.[24]

The 1st Army staff began planning on August 13 by evaluating three options. They considered attacking the southern face of the salient, an attack on the southern face combined with one on the western face, and an assault directly against the nose of the salient. The direct assault was rejected as unfeasible but the concept of simultaneously attacking the southern and western faces received initial approval. This plan continued to evolve, and the Allies committed eleven American divisions and sixteen French divisions to the attack. Submitted to Foch on August 17, the proposal got his nod and then some. He offered to provide six additional French divisions.[25]

The plan called for a simultaneous attack on the salient's flanks with three or four American divisions moving against the western face supported by six divisions from the French Second Army on the French left. Seven American divisions would attack the southern face of the salient with three French divisions positioned to divert the enemy's attention at the nose of the salient. The objective was to reach the Marieulles Heights, south of a line from Gorz to Mars-la-Tour and Étain.[26]

As planning for the offensive continued, Marshal Foch suggested that the AEF undertake a misinformation campaign. The AEF staff cooked up a plausible yarn. Given the force's enormous size and with rumors of an impending attack toward Saint Mihiel rampant, there was no way to hide the fact that an offensive was in the offing. The misinformation effort strove to obscure the timing, location, and extent of the coming attack. Pershing directed his operations officer, General Fox Conner, to spread word of a fictitious plan to attack toward Mulhouse. Conner sent General Omar Bundy, commander of VI Corps, and some of his staff to Belfort ostensibly to plan this offensive—but did not let them in on the ruse, so they assumed they were working in earnest. Borrowing French radios, U.S. Army Signal Corps operators concocted decoy communications, sending thousands of coded messages intended for intercept by German monitoring stations. To lend the fake radio traffic credibility, they worked into messages the sorts of slang and profanity Germans expected American radio operators to use. German intelligence, falling for the increased but bogus message traffic, concluded that a new American corps was in the area, and that they knew its location.[27]

Conner dispatched one of his assistants, Major Arthur Conger, to check into an expensive hotel in Belfort known to be a den of German agents. Once in his room, Conger deliberately crumpled carbon paper filled with details of the supposed coming attack into the wastepaper basket. The carbon paper quickly disappeared and soon was in German intelligence agents' hands. The Germans believed an operation toward Mulhouse somewhat ridiculous on its face, but the feint worked because they could not discount the possibility that these American amateur soldiers might try such an attack. They began evacuating villages along the front near Belfort, reinforced their defensive line, and moved more artillery into the area.[28]

On August 30, Pershing officially took command of the forty-two miles of front that made up the Saint Mihiel sector, with his advance headquarters at Ligny-en-Barrois. That day, Foch and his chief of staff, General Maxim Weygand, arrived unexpectedly at Pershing's headquarters to request an immediate conference. The three men exchanged the usual greetings and pleasantries after which Foch dropped a political bombshell on Pershing. Foch had been endorsing the American offensive as recently as August 25, but he now told Pershing he had different plans for the Saint Mihiel Offensive and the disposition of American forces. Field Marshal Haig, commander of the British Expeditionary Force, and Marshal Foch had decided that the Allies should concentrate their forces for an offensive in the area between the Argonne Forest and the Meuse River. This action required as many as fourteen American divisions for an attack scheduled to start on September 15. The Saint Mihiel Offensive would have to be canceled or reduced in scope.[29]

Colonel George C. Marshall, chief planner for 1st Army and later U.S. Army Chief of Staff during World War II. (*National Archives*)

Foch told Pershing the French Second Army would execute the attack between the Meuse and Argonne, reinforced by four to six American divisions. This would take place as soon as possible after a limited assault on the Saint Mihiel Salient, followed a few days later by a Franco-American offensive on a front extending from the Argonne to the Souain road. Foch's plan eliminated the attack on the western flank of the Saint Mihiel

Salient and reduced the forces available for the assault on the southern flank to eight or nine divisions. There would be no strike at Metz—once American and French forces had reduced the salient, the advance would stop. Foch proposed that the scaled-down Saint Mihiel attack begin no later than September 10 with the advance between the Meuse and Argonne starting on September 15 and the offensive along the Aisne from the Argonne to the Souain road jumping off on September 20.[30]

Foch's change of heart shocked Pershing. He pointed out to the marshal that according to his new scheme the 1st Army would have little to do except hold a quiet sector once the Saint Mihiel Salient was reduced. "This virtually destroys the American army that we have been trying so long to form," Pershing said.[31] While he did not want to appear difficult, he said, speaking forcefully, "the American people and the American Government expect that the American Army shall act as such and shall not be dispersed here and there along the Western Front. Each time that we are on the point of accomplishing this organization, some proposition is presented to break it up."[32]

"Do you wish to take part in the battle (*Voulez-vous aller a la bataille*)?" an irritated Foch asked.

"Most assuredly, but as an American Army," Pershing replied.

Foch bristled. It would take a month to accomplish that, and the new offensive had to begin by September 15, he declared. Pershing was dismayed, but grasped the strategic sense of what Foch was proposing. At the same time, Pershing saw the crucial need for the American 1st Army to operate on its own.[33] Foch ended the meeting by saying that, while he was willing to listen to any new proposition, the Allies had to act in the Meuse-Argonne front on September 15.[34]

The next day, August 31, Pershing pleaded his case to Marshal Philippe Pétain, the French commander-in-chief. Meeting on Pétain's train at Nettancourt, the men found themselves in agreement for the most part. Pétain thought Foch had overstepped his authority by peremptorily abandoning the secondary attack on the western side of the Saint Mihiel Salient. The marshal said he believed this issue ought to be left to Pershing's discretion as 1st Army commander. But Pétain also urged Pershing to put off the proposed advance on Metz for the time being, instead stopping his attack along the base of the salient. Once the Americans accomplished that objective, Pétain suggested, Pershing should assume responsibility for the entire line west from Saint Mihiel to the Argonne Forest, an addition of almost fifty miles.[35]

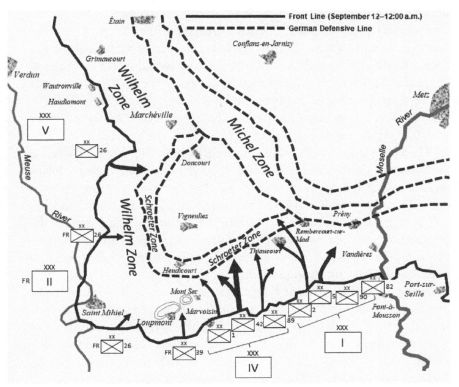

Map 4. The plan for the Saint Mihiel Offensive with German defensive lines. (*Author*)

On September 2, Pétain, Foch, and Pershing met at Foch's headquarters in Ligny. Owing to Pershing's August 31 interactions with Pétain, the atmosphere at Ligny was decidedly different. With all evidence of animosity gone, Foch agreed to Pershing's and Pétain's ideas and postponed the start of the offensive in the Meuse-Argonne sector until September 25. This delay would allow Pershing to execute his limited offensive at Saint Mihiel, then shift the 1st Army to participate in the Meuse-Argonne Offensive. Pershing's operation would begin around September 10 and attack both the southern and western faces of the Saint Mihiel Salient. Instead of driving toward Metz, however, the 1st Army would move forward in three or four days to a line from Vigneulles to Thiaucourt and Regniéville and there stop.[36]

With this agreement in place, Pershing returned to his headquarters. Jump-off was a week away, but his plan needed only adjustment, not wholesale revision. He would use four corps comprising four French divisions and eight-and-a-half divisions from the American 1st Army. The American I and IV Corps would execute the primary attack along the salient's southern boundary while the V Corps would attack in the west. The Rainbow Division would function as part of the IV Corps, entering the battle at Saint Mihiel between the 1st Division and the 89th Division. The 3rd Division, now called "The Rock of the Marne" after its tenacious mid-July stand, was in corps reserve.[37]

The key role in the offensive was the Rainbow Division's. "The 42nd Division will attack in the center and will deliver the main blow in the direction, of the heights overlooking the Madine River, exerting its main effort east of Maizerais and Essey," the 1st Army plan stated. "The division will seize its objective of the first phase, first day, without regard to the progress of neighboring divisions."[38] The 42nd's hard fighting at Champagne and in the Aisne-Marne apparently had made a strong impression at AEF and 1st Army Headquarters.

Now to get all the attacking divisions and their support in place by the jump-off date of September 10—no small undertaking. As planning continued at 1st Army Headquarters, the Rainbow Division began to move toward the lines along the salient. On August 27, orders arrived to march north, away from their rest and training areas, without explanation. Local civilians told some of the men a major American offensive was planned for the Saint Mihiel Salient in September, and many thought that was where the division was heading. Amid such loose talk, 1st Army ordered all divisions to march by night to foil daytime German aerial reconnaissance.[39]

The departure, staged over several evenings, occasioned a moving display of emotion. As whistles gave the order, men marched from their camps past masses of civilians waving goodbye. Candles in windows dimly lit the way ahead, lined by friendly faces calling out, "*Bonne chance!*"[40]

The pattern repeated nightly August 27-29. Sometime after 8:00 p.m., the units of the division would take to the roads, tramping along in time to off-color songs "as bawdy as the collective imaginations of 3,000 horny men could conceive."[41] Every forty-five minutes a bugler at the rear of the column sounded "Halt," signaling a fifteen-minute rest during which men threw themselves down at roadside until the bugler sounded "Forward March." Near dawn, the columns of exhausted men dispersed under the cover of whatever trees were available. Pitching shelter tents and lining up for chow at field kitchens, they ate and tried to sleep, hoping they were invisible to German pilots patrolling overhead. At nightfall the march resumed.[42]

On August 29, the division was ordered to camp in the Châtenois area for a few days of training that helped get "new men assimilated into the ranks of the veterans."[43] For example, the 168th Infantry spent the morning of September 2 in company and platoon drill. That afternoon the Iowans rehearsed attack formations until after dark. "Up and down the hills they charged, attacking imagined enemy positions with earnestness," John Taber wrote. "It was more than just simulating battle conditions; to every man the crest of the hill was a machine gun nest infested with Boches; to capture it he must advance cautiously and with due consideration to the possibilities of detection." Little wonder then that, as one new soldier threw himself down on his mat of straw for the night, he said, "If warfare is like that—and you call this easy—then send me back to the glorious coal mines where I can rest."[44]

This interlude was too brief. The goal had been to attack September 10, but Pershing and Foch realized all was not in readiness, so the date shifted to September 12. The Rainbow Division received orders to resume its progress toward Toul on September 4.

Heavy rain greeted this leg of the march, soaking the men and slowing supply and artillery vehicles, which often bogged down to their axles in mud. "The heavens poured themselves down in torrents all night long," Martin Hogan of the 165th recalled. "The roads churned up in gluey mud, and every few steps we splashed deep into pools of water. Our equipment was soaked; our clothes were soaked; and every yard our pack seemed to gain a ton in weight."[45]

Night marching wore on soldiers. Few got much real rest during the day. Many slept as they slogged, "depending on some sort of sixth sense to keep them on the road." When the bugler sounded a rest, most were completely asleep by the time they hit the ground. A detail behind each battalion herded stragglers, followed by a regimental detail with "hard-boiled" sergeants in charge that scooped up strays. Fresh or faltering, men marched toward a northern horizon lit by artillery fire getting ever closer with each step.[46]

On the night of September 7-8, the division got within a few miles of Toul. Raymond Cheseldine of the 166th Infantry recalled that night as a "mean one." The men were approaching exhaustion, soaked by a constant rain whose only saving grace was its late-summer warmth. The men's "tin-

Derby" helmets deflected water in sheets, soaking uniforms and packs and drenching spirits. Stopping in early morning just south of Toul, the men pitched shelter tents and fell into "dreamless sleep."[47]

Morale was wavering. Everyone now knew a major offensive was coming, but night marches in the rain had dampened any excitement and anticipation about a big, secret push. Some chattered about the division having a chance to "give 'em hell again," others openly wondered "what in Hell it was all about" and "Why do they pick on us?"[48]

On September 8, the division began a march of about nine miles north-northeast of Toul to the Forêt-de-la-Reine. Some regiments moved at night, but the 166th was told to move out in the morning of September 8, a clear signal that jump-off was near. When far from the front, the men marched in darkness. Now, with the enemy almost at hand, they marched in broad daylight. "Hell's Bells, now I know why they call us the AEF!" an Ohioan shouted. "It means 'Ass End First!'"[49]

The route from Toul took them past Bruley, Lagney, Ménil-la-Tour, and Sanzey on boggy roads crammed with trucks and wagons heading to the Saint Mihiel front. It "seemed that the entire American army was using this one artery to the front and was trying to cram all its transportation on it at the same time," John Taber wrote:

> Guns by the score, hundreds of trucks, and countless horse-drawn vehicles were moving forward in an unbroken stream. Time and again the regiment was held up by the traffic—there was scarcely a kilometer in which the column was not forced to halt for periods of five to twenty minutes. This, and the muddy, slippery roads, made the march excessively tiring.... The men were about dead—for some time there had been no sound but heavy breathing and the squush, squush of feet working up and down in the sucking mud—and they had reached the point where they were ready to lie down where they were. It was then that the order came to quicken the pace. That was piling it on a bit thick! From up near the head of the column someone burst out with the remark, loud enough for the whole company to hear: 'Oh, Hell, what's the use of hurrying—we're late anyhow.' Ordinarily this might not strike one as the most excruciatingly amusing of witticisms, but at the moment the absolute absurdity of it caught them all, and set them to laughing so that before the effect had entirely worn off they found themselves in their camp in an almost cheerful frame of mind. Such is the reaction to small things when troops are strained to the limit.[50]

American trucks struggle to make headway over the muddy roads leading to the Saint Mihiel front. (*National Archives*)

The September 9-10 overnight leg took the division farther into the Forêt-de-la-Reine toward the Étang Romé, a swampy lake, under the wettest conditions the unit had endured so far. A lieutenant in the 167th's Stokes mortar platoon wisecracked, "an attack under the existing circumstances would certainly be a failure unless the High Command used submarines for tanks, ducks for carrier-pigeons, and alligators for soldiers."[51] The forest, marshy even in dry weather, had degenerated into a "dripping swamp" thanks to constant rain.[52] Even so, the division encamped "in a state of ooziness" to await orders to move to the attack.[53] Tension rose. Smoking was banned after dark, and field kitchen crews extinguished their fires. "It was a depressing existence," wrote John Taber, "sitting around with nothing to do but listen to the endless drip of the rain, with no way of getting thoroughly dry—a poor way of conditioning troops for the rigors of battle."[54]

The war's first American-led offensive was less than forty-eight hours away.

5

INTO THE SALIENT, SEPTEMBER 12, 1918

"It was at 5 o'clock in the morning that the Rainbow Infantry left its trenches and began its "One Hundred Yard Dash" toward Metz—a speed exhibition that caught the departing Heinie just getting under way."

—Raymond Cheseldine, 166th Infantry Regiment,
in *Ohio in the Rainbow*

Early in the afternoon of September 12, I Company of the 166th Infantry was advancing. In less than eight hours, they had moved the remarkable distance of nearly five miles and were now approaching the day's objective, Pannes. As they approached the town, a machine gun opened fire. Men took cover while trying to locate the gun. Company commander Captain Henry Grave deliberately stepped into full view, hoping to draw fire that would pinpoint the nest. The German gunners pivoted their Maxim his way and fired. Grave dove for cover. His men took out the gun crew with rifle and mortar fire. In the aftermath of the brief action, Grave noticed that his .45-caliber automatic Colt sidearm only had two rounds left in its clip. So that he could have ready a full seven rounds, he emptied his gun at a can by the lip of a shell hole. Before Grave could insert a new clip, two Germans jumped from the hole, hands up, shouting "Kamerad!" Thoroughly surprised, Grave took them prisoner, covering them with an empty weapon.[1]

In the final 1st Army plans for the Saint Mihiel Offensive, American and French forces were to attack on converging axes, the French against the western flank and the main attack by the Americans from the south. If successful, these two axes would meet at the base of the salient, cutting off its nose, trapping German forces there and forcing them to surrender or die. The southern front was fifteen miles long, stretching west from the Moselle River. The American attack was to cut through German trenches along the southern boundary onto the Woëvre plain, moving northward on Vigneulles and Saint-Benoît-en-Woëvre.[2]

As the primary unit on the salient's southern face, the Rainbow Division was to attack with its four infantry regiments in line abreast across the division's front. As in the Aisne-Marne, the 83rd Brigade took the left of the line with the 84th Brigade to the immediate right. The front's terrain and expanse dictated that the infantry regiments attack in a column of battalions in which each brigade had two battalions in the assaulting wave, two battalions following in support, and a third battalion either in a third echelon or designated as brigade reserve. Each brigade was assigned a dedicated portion of the 117th Engineers, a battery of 75mm guns that would follow the infantry forward, and a platoon from A Company of the 1st Gas and Flame Regiment to mask the advance with a smokescreen.[3]

The division's first-day objective was a pair of lines. The first, south of the Rupt de Mad, a small tributary of the Moselle running northeast from the heights of the Meuse, was to be taken in the morning. The second line ran along a German barbed-wire entanglement northeast of Nonsard, south of Lamarche, and north of Thiaucourt. The Rainbow Division was to have taken that line by nightfall. On the second day, the division was to reach a line running from the middle of the Bois de Dampvitoux, then west across the Saint-Benoît-en-Woëvre to Haumont Road and north of Saint-Benoît-en-Woëvre through the Bois de Vignette to the western limits of the division's sector. After that, the division was to support the effort to reach the 1st Army objective, a line that pinched off the nose of the salient, and to advance the line of exploitation as far forward toward the Michel Zone as possible without undue struggle or losses.[4]

Within each of the division's two brigades, regiments would align as usual, the 166th, 165th, 167th, and 168th arrayed left to right. In the 83rd Brigade, the 3rd Battalion of the 166th was on the far left, and the 1st Battalion of the 165th was to their immediate right. The second support echelon consisted of the 1st Battalion of the 166th and the 2nd Battalion of the 165th, while the badly battered 3rd Battalion of the 165th was made the brigade reserve and the 2nd Battalion of the 166th was assigned as the divisional reserve.[5]

In the 84th Brigade on the division's right, the 1st Battalion of Alabama's 167th was to advance to the east of the 165th while the 1st Battalion of Iowa's 168th moved forward on the eastern boundary of the division's sector. They would move forward in line, supported by French tanks. The brigade's second echelon would consist of the 2nd Battalion of the 167th on the left and the 2nd Battalion of the 168th on the right. The reserve, or third echelon battalion, was to be the 3rd Battalion of the 167th, with the 3rd Battalion of the 168th standing in as part of the divisional reserve.[6]

The fighting along the Ourcq had taught the division not to assign each infantry battalion a company of machine guns. Instead, the division now divided the regimental machine gun companies among the infantry battalions, with each battalion having a dedicated platoon of machine gun support. The machine gun battalions assigned to the two brigades would deploy and operate by company in the rear and in direct support of the attacking infantry battalions.[7]

The Rainbow Division faced substantial obstacles in terms of terrain and enemy defenses. The German defensive lines, five miles deep behind their front line, began with two lines of trenches connected by communication trenches. These first two lines, about 200 yards apart, each were protected from frontal assault by massive tangles of barbed wire. About half a mile behind these two main trenches was a third line of trenches, also fronting barbed wire. A fourth set of support trenches and wire waited about a mile to the rear of the third line. "It looked as if the whole countryside had been sown with wire," John Taber wrote later.[8] Army planners, realizing artillery fire and tanks alone could not slice through the wire, issued each frontline squad two pair of heavy handheld wire cutters and each brigade seventy-five Bangalore torpedoes—five-foot lengths of pipe ending in explosive charges which, when connected in lengths of up to fifty feet and shoved forward into barbed wire, could be detonated to blow holes as large as ten feet in the wire.[9]

The view German observers had from atop Mont Sec. (*National Archives*)

In four years of occupation, the Germans had enhanced the salient with concrete trenches, deep dugouts, and well-protected machine gun emplacements. These defenses were manned by 23,000 troops of Composite Army C commanded by General George Fuchs and subordinate to Army Group Gallwitz. Most of these troops came from the German 10th Division, one of the salient's few first-class divisions. That division's 6th Grenadiers Regiment lay directly in the path of the 168th Infantry on the right flank of the Rainbow Division sector. The Sixth Grenadiers had tried to cross the Marne during the fighting in July but had been stopped by the U.S. 3rd Division. To the west of the 6th Grenadiers were the 47th and the 398th Regiments of the 10th Division.[10]

In terms of terrain, the initial advance would be moving slightly downhill before having to move uphill toward the first line of enemy trenches, some of which cut through the forbidding Bois de la Sonnard. These woods covered much of the right front assigned to the 84th Brigade, especially that portion given to the 168th Infantry. This area was very strongly defended; over the years the French had suffered terrible losses trying and failing to take the woods, a tangle of thickly grown trees stunted only slightly by artillery fire.[11]

As the Americans moved north, they would also have to cross two major streams. The Rupt de Mad cut diagonally across the division's path between Saint Baussant and Maizerais, while the Madine flowed from east to west. Once the division cleared a ridge north of the Rupt de Mad, it would face the Madine straight on. Both streams were relatively narrow and in dry times easily forded—a condition not necessarily present after four days of almost continuous rain.[12]

The last terrain feature of the planned action was Mont Sec, an isolated butte about four miles northwest of the Rainbow Division's line of departure. This butte jutted 451 feet above the surrounding plains and valleys, commanding the entire salient. German observers there could direct artillery fire against any force attacking from the west or the south. The unobstructed view enabled daytime spotters to see any Allied movement. Artillerists had carefully registered and surveyed the salient below and could even fire effectively at night. Rainbow Division commanders, rightly worried about Mont Sec, had to hope that darkness, weather, and tactical smoke would obscure their troops from the enemy view.[13]

Planners now chose the day for the attack, to be called "D-Day," and the exact time for the infantry assault, referred to as "H-Hour." D-Day was to be September 12 and H-Hour 5:00 a.m. Heated debate arose over artillery support. Some officers at 1st Army Headquarters argued that to achieve surprise the assault should forego preparatory fire and instead lay down a rolling barrage starting at H-Hour. Advocates of preparatory fire argued that a preliminary barrage would help silence German artillery batteries, assist in flattening barbed wire, and exert contrasting psychological effects on defenders, who would be cowed, and attackers, who would be emboldened. Pershing listened to both sides and decided that there would be no preparatory fire.[14]

Again, pre-war American military doctrine appears to have inordinately influenced strategy. Few senior officers blooded in the Philippines and Cuba had had field experience with artillery and then only with small-bore guns such as 75mm and 105mm pieces—rather than the huge tubes, ranging to 420mm and even 14-inch naval guns that the French, British, and Germans had been using for years to batter one another's trenches. As a result, against all practical evidence, American military doctrine deemphasized or altogether ignored the matter of artillery support. Colonel Conrad H. Lanza, a career artillery officer who later served in the 1st Army, noted that, in official pre-war doctrine, "the artillery was considered an auxiliary, sometimes useful, never necessary, and sometimes a nuisance."[15] Officer corps disdain for properly planned and executed artillery support had shortchanged the Rainbow Division at the Aisne-Marne, and now stood to persist for weeks.

The view German observers had from atop Mont Sec. (*National Archives*)

In four years of occupation, the Germans had enhanced the salient with concrete trenches, deep dugouts, and well-protected machine gun emplacements. These defenses were manned by 23,000 troops of Composite Army C commanded by General George Fuchs and subordinate to Army Group Gallwitz. Most of these troops came from the German 10th Division, one of the salient's few first-class divisions. That division's 6th Grenadiers Regiment lay directly in the path of the 168th Infantry on the right flank of the Rainbow Division sector. The Sixth Grenadiers had tried to cross the Marne during the fighting in July but had been stopped by the U.S. 3rd Division. To the west of the 6th Grenadiers were the 47th and the 398th Regiments of the 10th Division.[10]

In terms of terrain, the initial advance would be moving slightly downhill before having to move uphill toward the first line of enemy trenches, some of which cut through the forbidding Bois de la Sonnard. These woods covered much of the right front assigned to the 84th Brigade, especially that portion given to the 168th Infantry. This area was very strongly defended; over the years the French had suffered terrible losses trying and failing to take the woods, a tangle of thickly grown trees stunted only slightly by artillery fire.[11]

As the Americans moved north, they would also have to cross two major streams. The Rupt de Mad cut diagonally across the division's path between Saint Baussant and Maizerais, while the Madine flowed from east to west. Once the division cleared a ridge north of the Rupt de Mad, it would face the Madine straight on. Both streams were relatively narrow and in dry times easily forded—a condition not necessarily present after four days of almost continuous rain.[12]

The last terrain feature of the planned action was Mont Sec, an isolated butte about four miles northwest of the Rainbow Division's line of departure. This butte jutted 451 feet above the surrounding plains and valleys, commanding the entire salient. German observers there could direct artillery fire against any force attacking from the west or the south. The unobstructed view enabled daytime spotters to see any Allied movement. Artillerists had carefully registered and surveyed the salient below and could even fire effectively at night. Rainbow Division commanders, rightly worried about Mont Sec, had to hope that darkness, weather, and tactical smoke would obscure their troops from the enemy view.[13]

Planners now chose the day for the attack, to be called "D-Day," and the exact time for the infantry assault, referred to as "H-Hour." D-Day was to be September 12 and H-Hour 5:00 a.m. Heated debate arose over artillery support. Some officers at 1st Army Headquarters argued that to achieve surprise the assault should forego preparatory fire and instead lay down a rolling barrage starting at H-Hour. Advocates of preparatory fire argued that a preliminary barrage would help silence German artillery batteries, assist in flattening barbed wire, and exert contrasting psychological effects on defenders, who would be cowed, and attackers, who would be emboldened. Pershing listened to both sides and decided that there would be no preparatory fire.[14]

Again, pre-war American military doctrine appears to have inordinately influenced strategy. Few senior officers blooded in the Philippines and Cuba had had field experience with artillery and then only with small-bore guns such as 75mm and 105mm pieces—rather than the huge tubes, ranging to 420mm and even 14-inch naval guns that the French, British, and Germans had been using for years to batter one another's trenches. As a result, against all practical evidence, American military doctrine deemphasized or altogether ignored the matter of artillery support. Colonel Conrad H. Lanza, a career artillery officer who later served in the 1st Army, noted that, in official pre-war doctrine, "the artillery was considered an auxiliary, sometimes useful, never necessary, and sometimes a nuisance."[15] Officer corps disdain for properly planned and executed artillery support had shortchanged the Rainbow Division at the Aisne-Marne, and now stood to persist for weeks.

A 75mm gun from the 149th Field Artillery. (*National Archives*)

As Rainbow Division infantry and artillery commanders digested this news, strong opposition erupted. These men had seen the terrible results of infantry attacks undertaken without preparatory artillery fire at La Croix Rouge Farm and the Ourcq River and did not want those bloodbaths repeated. These officers went to brigade commanders, who took their deep concerns directly to 42nd Division Headquarters, asking that the division insist on preparatory fire. A reluctant Pershing ordered a four-hour barrage on the southern flank of the salient beginning at 1:00 a.m. on September 12.[16]

As artillery support, the AEF gathered nearly 3,000 guns ranging from medium wheeled 75mm pieces to 14-inch naval guns mounted on railcars and able to hurl massive shells to the fortifications around Metz, some twenty-five miles away.[17]

Artillery crews had been moving into position at night, digging in and camouflaging batteries. Battery F of the 149th Field Artillery was assigned to support the 83rd Brigade, advancing with the infantry; Battery B of the 151st Field Artillery was to do the same with the 84th Brigade. The 149th Field Artillery, two battalions of the 10th Field Artillery, and one battalion of the 150th Howitzer Field Artillery were designated as rear artillery support of the 83rd Brigade. The 151st Field Artillery, three battalions of the 228th French Field Artillery, one battalion of the 18th Howitzer Field Artillery, and the 3rd Trench Mortar Battery were to support the 84th Brigade. The remainder of the 150th Field Artillery and 18th Field Artillery, both of them howitzer regiments, and the 117th Virginia Military Police Battery were to support the entire division.[18]

On September 10, the division's battalion and company commanders were allowed to leave the Forêt-de-la-Reine to reconnoiter the German front lines; platoon commanders went forward the following day. The reconnaissance parties hiked seven miles to old French trenches now being held by the 89th Division and peered through binoculars at the German trenches, which resembled what they had seen in the Lunéville, Saint Clement, and Baccarat sectors. The reconnaissance teams looked over the ground, noting landmarks that might help troops transit no man's land in the dark. The final field order from division headquarters was awaiting them upon their return.[19]

The field order was far more detailed and complex than anything the regiment and battalion staffs had ever seen. The file, exceeding fifty pages, with ten annexes on everything from the use of artillery and engineering support to communications, supply, and air support, arrived only eighteen hours before H-Hour, too late for frontline staffs to digest all the information before troops jumped off. Regiment and battalion staffs likely flayed division planners for the tardiness, but the delay really occurred at 1st Army and IV Corps headquarters. The division G-3 staff did not receive the final plans from IV Corps until September 7, and labored nonstop for eighty-nine hours without sleep or rest to produce a field order for the division.[20]

Now infantry and artillery staffs did their best to understand these reams of information. On the positive side, the plan and field order seemed to have accounted for absolutely everything. There would be abundant artillery support and the approach to the enemy's initial defenses had been carefully planned. On the negative side, there was no time for a deep, thorough perusal of the documents. "It is almost safe to say that to this day the Colonel [Colonel Hough, 166th commander] and his adjutant, Captain Beightler, haven't read the complete file!" Raymond Cheseldine of the 166th Infantry later wrote. The regiments' battalions would begin moving forward the night of September 11-12, leaving little time to get critical information to the combat units at the company and platoon levels. The regimental supply companies and other key units had scant time to prepare. In the 166th, supply company officers and men made a "heroic effort," but could not obtain the required number of hand grenades, signal rockets, and other necessities from the division before the attack began.[21]

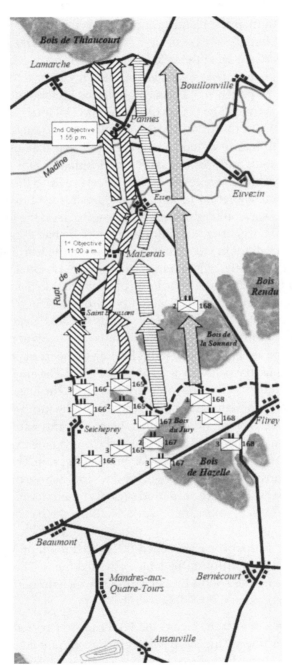

Map 5. The Rainbow Division's advance on September 12, 1918 (*Author*)

In the 165th Infantry, Lieutenant Colonel William Donovan, who was to lead the 1st Battalion "over the top," stayed up until 2:00 a.m. the night of September 10 studying the field order. In the morning, on four hours' sleep, he attended conferences on last-minute revisions to the orders that taxed everyone's patience.[22] The daylight hours of September 11 jittered with feverish activity. The details of D-Day and H-Hour had yet to reach frontline units, but the air was buzzing with anticipation.

In the 165th Infantry, chaplain Father Duffy was making plans focusing on men's souls and spiritual comfort. Hospitalized for exhaustion in the days before the move toward Toul, he returned to discover that his staff had grown. Father James Hanley, also fresh from a hospital stay for treatment of a leg wounded at the Ourcq, was back on the job along with Father George Carpentier, a Dominican priest who had taught at Aquinas College High School in Columbus, Ohio, before the war. Father Hanley was limping, so Duffy assigned him to the triage hospital. Duffy would minister to the men of the 165th. Carpentier would roam between the Ohio and Alabama regiments, seeing to Catholic soldiers.[23]

Men from the 117th Engineers were nearly finished "pegging out." This task, which had consumed two nights, required engineers to run thousands of yards of tape along roads and paths leading to the front and in trenches from which infantrymen were to go over the top.[24] The engineers marked the jump-off line as well as the routes from camp to the line, and the sector limits for each regiment along and in the rear of the jump-off line.

Early on the evening of September 11, the infantry started forward. The night turned rainy. Lieutenant Colonel Donovan described it as "impenetrably dark" and worsened by "a soul seeking rain."[25] Muddy roads became swamps crowded with trucks and wagons whose bulk forced the infantry to roadside, where deep mud sucked at their boots. To keep from wandering off track, most men kept a hand on the back of the soldier ahead.

As the 168th Infantry approached the ruined town of Mandres-aux-Quatre-Tours, a "frightful traffic jam" ensnarled them. The town was effectively "the small end of the funnel" through which thousands of vehicles and troops had to pass. John Taber wrote:

> Long lines of infantry, men of the 42nd and 3rd Divisions; machine gun carts, artillery caissons, powerful lorries, vibrant engines impatiently sputtering; back-firing motorcycles; automobiles grating their clutches; high-bodied French forage wagons, gesticulating poilus atop; great farm wagons, oxen drawn; tiny donkey carts; mounted horsemen

trotting up and down the line trying to disentangle the web—a bewildering jumble.[26]

By the time support battalions departed camp around 9:00 p.m., the weather had reached a furious intensity. Roads were "hub-deep" quagmires, and the six miles to the front felt more like twenty. "Treacherous, water-filled shell holes lined the way," remembered Taber, "and from time to time, when the column gave way to permit the passage of lorries coming from the other direction, men went floundering in up to their waists." Rain lashed down in sheets. Taber thought that all the physical elements were now in place to "presage a tragedy—blackness of night, driving rain, lightning flashes, roll of thunder."[27]

As thousands of Rainbow Division infantrymen slogged toward the jump-off line, each carried his rifle and bayonet, a small ration of hardtack and corned beef, a canteen of water, one blanket, an aid kit, and 250 rounds of ammunition. A few toted small sacks of hand grenades. Automatic rifle teams lugged Chauchats and bags of twenty-round metal ammunition clips. Officers and men had learned from hard experience to carry identical equipment so Germans could not target officers and NCOs.[28]

As the leading elements of the four infantry regiments reached the jump-off point, they relieved 89th Division men who had been holding the entire line along the salient's southern boundary. The 89th moved to their jump-off positions to the right of the Rainbow Division. Men lay down in the old French trenches, rain or no rain. Lieutenant Colonel Donovan, arriving at the 165th's trench sector, found a shelter suitable for a battalion headquarters and began to study his maps and orders yet again. Around 11:00 p.m., his company commanders reported in, telling him their men were in place—which, given conditions, was something of a miracle.[29]

Most of the infantry were positioned by around midnight. They crouched awaiting the American and French salvoes they had been told were to start at 1:00 a.m. An Alabama soldier later wrote, "Sleep, by reason of the rain and intense cold, was impossible, and one could but bear his physical discomfort in silence and wish for the break of day, with its opportunity for relieving the misery of immobility under such circumstances by a dash across the top and down and up the hill."[30]

Precisely at 1:00 a.m., the barrage began. While not as loud as at Champagne, it was still an impressive display that infantrymen at hand truly appreciated. The 75mm field pieces barked so often that the clatter was continuous and, as the noise crescendoed, a different sound joined the mix: the deep boom of long-range railroad guns. For four hours, artillerymen sent nearly a million shells at German defenses. Some rounds deliberately struck no man's land to uproot and flatten barbed wire. Others arced deeper into the salient, aiming for German troops and guns.[31]

During the barrage, Charles MacArthur and his battery of three 75mm guns from the 149th Field Artillery waited directly behind Lieutenant Colonel Donovan's 1st Battalion of the 165th Infantry. MacArthur and comrades were among the small artillery detachments that were to move forward with the infantry to provide point-blank fire. They were to go over the top with the infantrymen and try to manhandle their wheeled 3,045-lb. guns through mud and over shell holes. None had tried so dubious a task even in training. But MacArthur and cohort had signed on to the plan of their own volition. When their commanding officer received the orders for this mission, he felt compelled to send only volunteers. When he made his appeal, every soldier in the unit stepped forward. "The response was unanimous," MacArthur recalled. "That's the worst part of a call for volunteers. It takes more courage to say No than Yes."[32]

As the American and French guns fired, some men were expecting the enemy to respond based on directions from observers atop Mont Sec. But few German shells found their way to the jump-off line. Realizing there was to be no answering German barrage, Donovan turned to the men near him and said, "The Germans are pulling out."[33]

He was correct.

As early as September 3, German analysts had noted a mysterious buildup of American forces along the southern face of the salient. If there was to be an attack, they believed, that assault would only strike the salient's southern edge. German Supreme Headquarters and Army Group Gallwitz had already decided not to implement Operation Loki and its withdrawal back to the Michel Zone unless compelling intelligence indicated that the Allies intended to attack simultaneously along the salient's western and southern flanks. Until September 10, the Germans had been planning for Composite Army C to undertake a limited offensive to drive the Americans back from the southern face and were trying to gather the forces to do so.[34]

The German outlook soon began to change. On the morning of September 10, having observed the steadily increasing American buildup, German Supreme Headquarters not only canceled the Composite Army C attack, but ordered Composite Army C to prepare to withdraw from the salient to the Michel Zone. Later that afternoon, Army Group Gallwitz told General Fuchs to undertake "measures for the systematic occupation" of the Michel Zone but not to demolish ammunition and supplies unless absolutely necessary. This meant troops would begin withdrawing but abandonment of the salient was on hold. Army Group Gallwitz reminded Fuchs that commencing Operation Loki required specific orders from the army group.[35]

The Operation Loki delay arose partly from German uncertainty over the precise intentions and timing of any incipient American attack. On September 11, intelligence from the Foreign Armies Section of German Supreme Headquarters still seemed to portend an attack against only the southern flank, noting that under interrogation recently taken American prisoners indicated an attack was to come between September 15 and September 20.[36]

The September 12 Allied barrage startled the Germans. They knew something was coming and so had withdrawn certain artillery and front-line troops but believed they had several days to complete a withdrawal. As a precaution, General Fuchs had ordered the two divisions that would face any American attack on the southern flank to retreat to a secondary line. When the enemy barrage began, many of these German troops were moving to the rear, but the two divisions' commander had misinterpreted the order and left two-thirds of their infantry in position without artillery support.[37] After hours of Allied shelling and the start of the American infantry assault, Fuchs gained permission to begin Operation Loki—at noon on September 12, far too late to get much of his army away from the attacking Americans.[38]

As 5:00 a.m. approached, Rainbow Division infantrymen prepared to advance. In the 165th Infantry's trenches, Lieutenant Colonel Donovan moved up and down the line offering encouragement, especially to new men. "There's nothing to it. It will be a regular walk-over," Donovan told his troops with a smile. "It will not be as bad as some of the cross-country runs I gave you in your training period."[39] On the 168th Infantry's sector of the line, a replacement nervously asked his veteran sergeant if he thought they would be able to break through the German line. "Sure as Hell will, Buddy," the NCO growled. "You're going to see some Heinies do a quick step before long."[40]

Other veterans shared replacements' trepidation. Hugh Thompson, a lieutenant in Company L of the 168th Infantry, felt the words "five o'-clock" created a "crushing weight." Thompson, a Citadel graduate from Chattanooga, Tennessee, had been wounded and hospitalized twice, so the risk of a hat trick likely loomed in his imagination. As his wristwatch ticked, his anxiety increased. "Sulphur dials were consulted nervously amid the awe-inspiring noise," he wrote later. He knelt in the trench with his men, his .45-caliber automatic at his side. "A thousand times I felt of the chin strap of my helmet, of the gas mask on my chest, of the '45' that hung like a lead weight from my hip." He tried to whip himself into a "fury of hate," but could not summon enough rage to quell the "gnawing fear" in his heart. H-Hour arrived. "The night ahead turned inside out with a volcanic, belching roar."[41]

Twenty minutes before daylight, amid rain, mist, and fog, American artillerymen switched to a rolling barrage that stayed just ahead of the infantry, moving at 100 yards every four minutes. Shells rained on enemy trenches "kicking up red fire and black clouds where they hit." Mortar batteries began firing 105mm smoke rounds into no man's land to screen the advancing infantry.[42]

Up and down the Rainbow Division line, officers blew whistles and waved their arms, signaling men to advance. Bodies stiff and sore from laying in cold mud, doughboys began to clamber out of trenches. In a long, almost continuous wave, they moved down the hill into no man's land through the smoke and just behind the explosions of friendly artillery. Small groups of American and French tanks started out with them, but soon bogged down or tipped nose-first into craters from which tank crews could not extract their armored vehicles.

For forty minutes, the infantry slowly advanced, covering about 100 yards. Not a single German shell fell among the men, and there was no enemy machine gun fire. As the barrage rolled into the German lines, men picked up the pace.[43]

The force advanced steadily across open ground until its leading edge came to barbed wire barriers. In some places, engineering troops rushed forward, shoved Bangalore torpedoes into the entanglements, and speedily cleared lanes through the wire. Elsewhere the wire had been flattened or was so rusty and broken troops did not need shears to keep pressing forward.[44] As the Americans closed on the German trenches, enemy machine guns finally opened fire.

On the far left of the division's line, the Ohioans of the 166th advanced from trenches that ran through the village of Siecheprey. The 3rd Battalion and its machine gun company took the lead, the 1st Battalion close behind. Dawn arrived as men from these units were clearing their first belts of wire. Smoke was billowing from German rear areas where de-

Top, these were some of the barbed wire obstacles the Rainbow Division encountered in the Saint Mihiel Offensive. Bottom, artist's drawing of the assault at Saint Mihiel. (*National Archives*)

fenders were destroying ammunition dumps. A few enemy shells and rifle fire from opposing trenches constituted little more than an annoyance. Crowds of German soldiers emerged from dugouts and trenches to surrender with "the utmost docility."[45] The 3rd Battalion immediately passed prisoners to the 1st Battalion.

To the immediate right of the 166th, the New Yorkers of the 165th Infantry also moved forward quickly, initially encountering difficulties with supporting battalions. The woods of the Bois de Remieres lay on the 1st Battalion's right flank. As the battalion advanced, Lieutenant Colonel Donovan had men on the right shift left to avoid the woods. In doing so some men got lost. Amid the resulting confusion, the supporting battalion hesitated at the first belt of wire. Seeing men "picking their way rather too fastidiously" through the wire, Donovan left the 1st Battalion's front line and ran to the wire. "Get forward, there!" he shouted. "What the hell do you think this is, a wake?" This inspired one officer to bark profane encouragement at men carrying machine guns and boxes of ammunition as they struggled through craters and broken wire.[46]

Donovan's 1st Battalion swept through the first line of German trenches, taking prisoners and pressing on. At a second set of trenches, they met their first German machine gun fire. Chauchat teams and snipers rapidly crawled forward and laid down a brisk fire. As Donovan continued to move along the line giving instructions, enemy resistance evaporated, with most defenders running for the rear or surrendering en masse. As the New Yorkers swept past this second defensive line, they began to race at what Martin Hogan described as "a double-quick rollick forward in a go-as-you-please and get-there-as-fast-as-possible line of battle."[47]

On the left side of the 84th Brigade's sector, the Alabamians of the 167th advanced in what one soldier termed a "perfect formation," with the 1st Battalion in the lead and the 2nd Battalion moving up about 1,000 yards from a support position along the Beaumont to Saint Dizier highway. As they were clearing the wire belts, the Alabamians witnessed a "very fine" fireworks show as they launched star-shell rockets into the early morning sky to expose enemy positions. This display prompted the Germans to loose what seemed to be every flare and signal rocket they had, in some instances to alert artillery in rear areas to fire. But most such guns had pulled out or been destroyed. Only a few isolated German rounds were fired. When the 167th's lead battalion reached the first trenches, the men encountered only scattered rifle fire and figures in field gray surrendering. "The Germans appeared dumfounded [sic] and utterly weak."[48]

At the western edge of the dark, tangled Bois de la Sonnard the 167th experienced its first major problem. So many thousands of jagged fragments of American artillery shell littered the woods that compasses struggled to register true north. After some confusion, battalion officers decided to guide themselves based on the location of friendly flares.[49]

Events went reasonably well for the regiments from Ohio, New York, and Alabama, but the Iowans of the 168th Infantry had a rougher go. Their path of attack went directly into the teeth of the German defenses in the Bois de la Sonnard. Based on French losses incurred in previous years trying and failing to seize the Bois de la Sonnard, the Germans had expected that any attacking force would try to sweep around that forest's western edge. The Germans registered their artillery such that any force attempting to skirt the forest would run into heavy artillery fire. The boundary line between the 83rd and the 84th Brigades gave the 84th Brigade about 400 yards of leeway to the left to avoid the woods and envelop its defenders. General MacArthur decided not to take the obvious approach. He ordered the 168th to drive directly into and through the Bois de la Sonnard.[50]

The 168th's assigned front for the advance stretched eastward from the western edge of the Bois de Jury to the division's eastern boundary with the 89th Division. The men were to advance downhill into a wide valley and toward the Bois de la Sonnard. Major Guy Brewer's 3rd Battalion would lead the assault. Brewer, who had led his men up Hill 212 at the Ourcq and through the horrible days that followed, had emerged as an experienced combat leader whose men trusted him. The 2nd Battalion under Major Claude Stanley, another experienced officer who had led his men at La Croix Rouge Farm, would follow Brewer's men across no man's land, while the 1st Battalion lined up behind the 3rd Battalion of the 167th and acted as the brigade's reserve.[51]

As the Iowans stepped off, the artillery barrage reached the Germans in the Bois de la Sonnard. John Taber, leading the 3rd Platoon of K Company in Brewer's 3rd Battalion that morning, watched in awe. "The Bois de la Sonnard is a raging furnace as the hurricane of explosive sweeps through it felling trees, crushing in dugouts, battering trenches into shapelessness," he wrote later. "Through the rolling smoke shoot darts of magenta flame."[52]

L Company and M Company led the way downhill toward the wire with M Company on the left, trying to maintain contact with C Company of the 167th. L Company, on the right, was to maintain liaison with the 89th Division's 356th Infantry. These lead companies advanced in two waves, half of each platoon in each wave. I Company followed close behind M Company while K Company trailed immediately behind L Company. A platoon from the machine gun company and the 37mm gun platoon followed I and K Company. F Company from Stanley's 2nd Battalion moved up abreast of Brewer's second line to help hold the left flank of the 356th Infantry. Stanley moved up platoons from his G and H Company to help mop up stragglers and wounded.[53]

The waves broke at the wire because engineers had only been able to clear two lanes through the tangles. Men had to move through single file. But by the time they had cleared the wire, the rolling barrage had moved past the German front line. Enemy machine gunners clambered from dugouts and put their weapons into action, causing heavy casualties to the forward waves of Iowans, especially M Company. Losses were particularly severe among platoon commanders and sergeants, many of whom exposed themselves trying to keep replacements moving and in order.[54] Many replacements, panic-stricken by the Maxims, behaved more like terrified sheep than soldiers, hearing commands as meaningless noise.[55] John Taber described the scene:

> German flares, held aloft by parachutes, float over the field and silhouette the threading lines, their bayonets at the high port. They have finally worked their way through the lanes in our wire. Day is breaking, and in the half-light a magnificent picture unrolls itself as they swarm down the hill. The broad stretch of the plain is dotted with thousands of soldiers, like busy brown ants crawling over burnt sugar. Far to the left Mont Sec is boiling and foaming like an angry volcano. The Boche lines are practically obscured by the clouds of sulphurous smoke that rise high in saffron folds above it. One is awed by the immensity of it all but gives it no more than a passing glance, for the swell of the artillery from the rear and the vicious cadence of the German machine guns quickly recall one to the work in hand.[56]

In L Company, Hugh Thompson and his men traversed the wire. He had begun the attack stumbling "toward the boiling cauldron, muttering a frenzied prayer." He fell into an abandoned trench, tangling himself in an "octopus of wire." He tore loose, climbed out, and pressed on. "Groping figures followed through more grasping tentacles and through hellish furrows of clinging mud. Grotesque shadows deployed in the dazzling lights," he later wrote. Above the noise, he heard a cry: "Keep your three-yard interval!" It took him a moment to realize the voice was his own.[57]

The 168th's supporting machine guns advanced with Chauchat teams to take on German gunners. Small-bore enemy fire persisted. Defenders deployed 25cm Minenwerfers; rounds from these heavy, short-range mortars began to crash into the advancing American line. Platoon leaders chivvied men through the maze of no man's land so they could get into the enemy trenches and attack with bayonets and grenades. Advancing infantrymen could see German gunners and almost feel the heat from their Maxims' barrels as slugs whirred past their heads. One automatic rifleman was hit; another took his place. A young lieutenant seized the fallen man's Chauchat and silenced the enemy machine gun. A sniper's bullet tore through the lieutenant's head, killing him instantly. The captain commanding M Company had to leave the field streaming blood. One of his lieutenants fell nearby, killed by an enemy machine gunner.[58]

Major Brewer, hit in the leg by shrapnel, had the wind taken out of him when a German bullet hit his gas mask. He fell but quickly stood as machine gun bullets tore at his clothes. A slug struck him in the arm, breaking it. In pain and losing blood, he continued forward and remained in command of his battalion.[59]

Against fierce resistance and with extreme losses, M Company broke through on the right. By the time they forced the Germans back, every officer in the company had been killed or severely wounded. NCOs kept the men moving. The first lines of the 3rd Battalion were so strung out that their attack was on the verge of chaos. Major Brewer ordered I and K Companies to move up, carry the attack beyond the first set of trenches, and press deeper into the woods. Seeing that the enemy line had been broken, Brewer, his shattered arm bleeding profusely, relinquished command to his operations officer and started for the rear and an aid station.[60]

Hugh Thompson and his platoon from Company L had also penetrated the German trenches, where the young lieutenant from Tennessee was wounded for a third time. He felt a bullet clip his sleeve, then a "red-hot slug crushed the bones" of his leg, spinning him into a "pile of mud and rusty wire." He crawled into a crater in a "cold sweat of agony, a broken leg askew." To the chatter of machine guns and Chauchats, he fainted, not coming to until almost 8:30 a.m. Stretcher bearers got him to the regiment's aid station. Soon Thompson was on his way to Base Hospital No. 48, where he spent six months recovering.[61]

Most of the men of 3rd Battalion, having broken through, were moving into the Bois de la Sonnard. Lieutenant Taber's platoon moved forward and to the right, seeking to fill a quickly widening gap between the 168th and 356th. Apparently the 356th had met resistance; the unit was nowhere in sight. Still, orders had been to push on no matter what happened to the divisions on their flanks. The 168th continued its assault. At the second line of trenches, the men fought hand-to-hand. The Iowans quickly got the advantage and were able to move in behind the second trench line where they bayoneted dozens of the enemy. Remaining Germans, leaderless and clearly outnumbered, broke into small groups and fled north through the woods.[62]

At 6:15 a.m., as the 166th, 165th, and 167th were moving toward Saint Baussant and the day's first objective, while the 168th had subdued the Germans defending the Bois de la Sonnard. They sent a message to division remarking of the enemy, "He is kamerading." As Stanley's 2nd Battalion came up on the line, all that was left to do in the forest was to hunt down the remaining Germans, most of whom quickly surrendered with "hands held high and trembling."[63]

At the rear large groups of German prisoners collected at the 168th's headquarters, attracting curious Americans. Doughboys from the headquarters company wandered among the demoralized prisoners collecting souvenirs. Private William Greulach noticed an engraved belt buckle at a German's waist. Gesturing for the man to give it up, he examined the buckle and saw that the family name engraved on it was the same as his. Through a translator, the private learned the man whose buckle he had appropriated was a first cousin he had never met.[64]

On the left of the division, the 3rd Battalion of the 166th rapidly covered the ground north toward Saint Baussant, about a mile north of the first defensive lines. I Company, led by Captain Henry Grave, reached the village first. Grave, known to his men as "Hell Roarin' Henry," was tough but charismatic, and they revered him. As the company cautiously approached, Grave saw movement at the edge of the village. A Maxim clattered. The Americans flattened as bullets whizzed overhead. Captain Grave had a mortar crew zero in on the Maxim. Within minutes, mortar rounds from a few yards to the rear arced into the machine gun emplacement in a series of small explosions.[65]

Two Maxims opened fire on the opposite side of the village. Grave ordered more supporting fire while sending a few men to flank the guns. Part of one squad made a rapid flanking maneuver toward the gun. Carefully enveloping the crews, they opened fire and tossed grenades. As soon as the grenades exploded, the gunners cried "Kamerad!" and raised their hands.[66]

Captain Grave shouted for his men to storm the village. As the men of I Company went house to house kicking down doors, they found only hurriedly abandoned meals, supplies, and Germans anxious to surrender—except at one building. There, the men found Private George Dennis, the battalion medic. Dennis had left the rear early that morning, driving the battalion's medical cart toward the front. He lost his way and ended up heading for Saint Baussant. He saw other soldiers from the reg-

Germans captured during the Saint Mihiel Offensive march into captivity. (*National Archives*)

iment waving their arms and shouting. They were trying to tell him he was heading into German territory, but the rolling barrage drowned out their message. At Saint Baussant, seeing no one else, Dennis unloaded his cart and, thirty minutes before I Company arrived, set up a dressing station in a building.[67] History may say I Company of the 166th's 3rd Battalion captured Saint Baussant, but that town was actually taken by a single unarmed medic.

M Company was assigned to mop up in Saint Baussant while I Company moved onward to cross the Rupt de Mad and reach the first day's objective, Maizerais. The attack swept on, slowed only by token resistance and hundreds of surrendering Germans. When resistance did crop up, the men of the 3rd Battalion played it safe, calling in mortar strikes to push the enemy aside. Prisoners generally seemed to be boys or middle-aged men sapped of desire to fight and hiding in safety until surrounded and able to give themselves up.[68]

Two soldiers from the 166th's 2nd Battalion were escorting about thirty German prisoners to the rear for processing. As they passed through a small village, a German soldier left the cellar where he had been hiding and, without a word or gesture, joined the procession. Some gladly went to the rear unguarded. A wounded soldier from the regiment, head bandaged and arm in a sling, escorted five German prisoners to captivity wielding only a stick.[69] Private Dusty Boyd of the 166th wrote home, "German prisoners go back to the prison camp without any guard and seemed tickled to death to go."[70]

When I Company reached the Rupt de Mad, that stream, as expected, was badly swollen. Captain Grave found a makeshift bridge, and men began to cross the torrent. Too impatient to wait, Lieutenant Joseph Smith waded across, his platoon dutifully following him. About 300 yards ahead to the left was Maizerais, which they immediately moved to capture. By 11:00 a.m., only six hours into the offensive, the 166th had reached the first line of that day's objective.[71]

To the Ohioans' right, the New Yorkers of the 165th kept up a rapid pace and soon were at the Rupt de Mad. Donovan joined his lead platoon. The men were stumped as to how to cross the stream, at that point over eight feet wide and six feet deep, and flowing fast. Expecting any enemy troops in the town to surrender, Donovan ordered the men to swim. He jumped in and stroked to the far bank with his men right behind. They climbed ashore and swept into Mazerais, where they captured a German lieutenant and forty men, as well as a minenwerfer and four machine guns.[72]

At noon, orders arrived telling lead elements to keep advancing without pause. The 166th, 165th, and 167th soon reached the town of Essey-et-Maizerais where, greeted as liberators, they captured another large group of Germans. There was no time to celebrate with villagers; the regiments needed to press on toward Pannes and the units' objective for the day.[73]

As the 165th neared Essey-et-Maizerais, a platoon approached a hill marked on reconnaissance photos as "'Dangerous, go to the right and left." Ignoring the warning, the men climbed straight up the hill without issue. At the crest, though, they came under heavy fire from machine gun emplacements just outside the town. A French tank arrived. The lieutenant commanding the platoon jumped from the crater in which he had been taking cover. He ran to the tank, taking shelter aft, rapped on the turret, and shouted. The driver rotated the turret to the rear and opened his window as German bullets smacked the tank's front armor. A "dapper little Frenchman with the ends of his moustache waxed in points," the French tanker smiled at the American lieutenant and politely but eagerly asked how he might help. The lieutenant gave him a target at which to direct the tank's 75mm gun. The Frenchman obliged, firing several rounds that exploded among the German defenders who fled over a hill north of

Troops of the Rainbow Division advancing from Maizerais to Essey-et-Maizerais. (*National Archives*)

town. The Frenchman opened his window again and, with a broad smile, said, "How's that?" He closed the window and the tank lumbered away.[74]

As the other regiments were moving on Essey-et-Maizerais, the 168th Infantry was trying to reorganize. Lieutenant Colonel Tinley arrived on the scene west of the Maîtresse Farm, about a mile and a half southeast of Essey-et-Maizerais. The 3rd Battalion was collecting its scattered companies after the fighting at the first German defensive lines. The battalion was a tattered remnant of the unit that had jumped off that morning. In the assault's first thirty minutes, of twenty-four officers seven had been killed and six seriously wounded, including the battalion commander, Major Brewer. Four sergeants, nine corporals, and twenty-nine privates had been killed, and seventeen sergeants, twenty-three corporals, and one hundred and six privates had been wounded.[75] These losses were not as severe as what the regiment had seen in the Aisne-Marne, but the casualties among officers and NCOs were inordinately high.

Tinley ordered Major Stanley to move his 2nd Battalion into the lead position, with what was left of the 3rd Battalion to follow in support. Stanley's men moved up and continued the advance with G and H Companies deployed on the first line and F Company in support. As they approached the Rupt de Mad east of Essey-et-Maizerais, Stanley's men took numerous prisoners, also capturing the first of what would be numerous supply depots and weapons the Germans did not have time to destroy as

The town of Pannes near the final objective line for September 12, 1918. (*National Archives*)

they rushed for the rear. The Iowans took almost 300 prisoners plus ammunition and a 105mm artillery piece.[76]

It was still early afternoon when the four infantry regiments began their final advance of the day toward the second objective line north of Pannes. Upon leaving Essey-et-Maizerais, they encountered a flat plain, across which they moved quickly. As the lead battalions from the 166th, 165th, and 167th were approaching Pannes, Germans put up some resistance. Battalion commanders requested tank and artillery support. Once that materialized and firing began, the 166th's 3rd Battalion filtered up the road and into the town as the 167th was executing a flanking attack to the east of the town. In only a few minutes, the Americans had occupied the town, capturing more prisoners and supplies.[77]

The Americans took quite a haul of captured materiel. A large quartermaster's warehouse in Pannes had remained intact and now provided a bizarre assortment of souvenirs. Doughboys carted off pistols, spurs, hats, blankets, boots, underwear, and musical instruments. They even found a billiard table and a shower bath. An Ohio soldier said, "the town was a regular Woolworth Store."[78] At 1:55 p.m., the second phase line and the units' final objective for the day had been reached. What was supposed to have taken all day had been accomplished in under nine hours. All three regiments moved their headquarters into the town and Lieutenant Colonel

Soldiers from Ohio's 166th Infantry enjoy some of the food found in the numerous German supply depots captured during the offensive. (*National Archives*)

Donovan sent a request to 42nd Division Headquarters to continue the advance through the Bois de Thiaucourt. Division told Donovan to maintain his current position but scout the forest for any enemy presence. The New Yorkers sent patrols to comb the woods. They only encountered small, isolated groups of German soldiers who skedaddled when approached.[79]

The Iowans of the 168th Infantry continued to advance along the right flank of the division about a mile east of Pannes. At a German camp, Madine Lager, they found a large quantity of stores as well as twenty-three Germans hiding in a dugout who meekly surrendered. In the dugout, a table was set with a full meal, even beer, apparently on the assumption that the Americans were moving less rapidly. A few minutes later, a large wagon loaded with fish, bread, cabbage, and beer drove into camp. The astonished driver was taken prisoner. As he drove away to the south accompanied by an armed guard, he shook his head in disbelief.[80]

The four infantry regiments' speed befuddled personnel at headquarters. Given the planned objectives for the day and the expected rate of advance, headquarters staff assumed the regiments would end up in Maizerais by nightfall. Not long after the attack began, Colonel Hough and the headquarters staff of the 166th moved to Siecheprey, near the jump-off point. But as they were setting up operations at 7:45 a.m., they learned the regiment's units were already moving past Saint Baussant toward Maizerais, so they relocated headquarters to Saint Baussant, arriving at about 11:30 a.m. Before long word came that their 3rd Battalion had taken Maizerais at 11:00 a.m. Shortly after Hough sent the order back to continue the advance, he and the staff began to pack for a move to Maizerais. The biggest problem with these moves was the need to keep running new telephone lines between headquarters and advancing units. At this point, the wires had not caught up, and communication defaulted to runners. At 4:30 p.m., the 166th Regimental Headquarters arrived at Maizerais to learn that Pannes had fallen. With that news, the staff packed and moved to Pannes, arriving around 9:40 p.m.[81]

After the 165th's patrols returned near nightfall with the news that the Germans no longer occupied the Bois de Thiaucourt, the division pushed forward, establishing a line along and parallel to the southern edge of the forest. The lead companies from each regiment quickly constructed strong points four to five hundred yards apart.[82] Once that was done, the infantrymen settled in for the night.

The next day, they would continue their advance toward the Kriemhilde Stellung and the Michel Zone.

of what would be several successful American raids on Haumont-les-Lachaussee.[5]

September 13 dawned clear, very cool, and dry. The rains of recent days were gone. That morning saw the end of the Saint Mihiel Salient when troops from the 26th and 1st Divisions met near Vigneulles-lès-Attachmate, securing the line along what had been the salient's base.[6] During the advance, the Rainbow Division had taken more than 1,000 prisoners from the 10th, the 77th Reserve, the 5th Landwehr, the 8th Landwehr, the 31st, 40th, 192nd, 227th, and 35th Austro-Hungarian Divisions, from the 14th Sturm Battalion, and from fifteen miscellaneous artillery and sector troop organizations. The American division's men had liberated seven French villages and twenty-six square miles of territory. They captured huge quantities of food, clothing, medical supplies, ammunition, engineering and railroad materiél, lumber, coal, iron, and fuel. The division had seized six 77mm artillery pieces, an 88mm gun, six 105mm guns, seven 105mm howitzers, two 210mm artillery pieces, six heavy minenwerfers, a hundred each of heavy and light machine guns, two anti-tank guns, two narrow-gauge locomotives, twelve large narrow-gauge railroad cars, thirty-one small narrow-gauge railroad cars, twenty wagons, and ten artillery caissons.[7]

The Rainbow Division's advance resumed at 6:00 a.m., with the 84th Brigade swinging slightly east as the Germans retreated toward Metz and the 83rd Brigade continued moving north. The day's objective was an east-west line running through the town of Saint-Benoît-en-Woëvre, about three miles away. There had been no contact with either of the divisions on their flanks, but the division still pressed forward. Their artillery had caught up with them during the night, and division leadership was confident of being able to repel any attempt at a flanking attack.[8]

The 3rd Battalion of the 166th moved out on schedule along the division's western boundary, moving through the Bois de Thiaucourt and Bois de Beney. By 8:30 a.m., leading elements of the 3rd had reached the objective line at Saint-Benoît-en-Woëvre, and the battalion was ordered to consolidate its lines. I and K Companies had been in the lead, so they were withdrawn to support while L and M Companies dug in on the front line about 10:00 a.m. Here, the men found a garden of ripe vegetables. L Company roasted potatoes and onions for lunch, washed down with hot coffee. The 1st Battalion set up in support south of the Vigneulles to

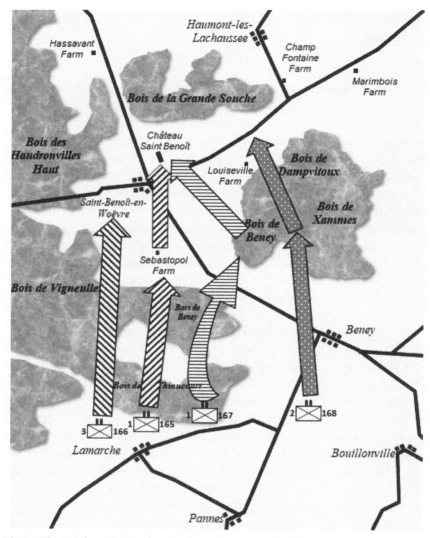

Map 6. The Rainbow Division's advance on September 13, 1918. (*Author*)

Saint-Benoît-en-Woëvre road, while the 2nd Battalion took a position in the southern edge of the Bois de Thiaucourt, northeast of the town of Lamarche-en-Woëvre.[9]

With the 166th's arrival in Saint-Benoît-en-Woëvre, the division had completed a remarkable achievement. Headquarters had expected the unit to need sixty-five hours to get to the final objective line. The Rainbow

Men from New York's 165th Infantry enter Lamarche on their way to Saint-Benoît-en-Woëvre. (*National Archives*)

Division had required only twenty-nine hours, advancing 12 miles through the center of the south face of the former Saint Mihiel Salient.[10]

As the Ohioans moved north that morning, Lieutenant Colonel Donovan had his 1st Battalion of the 165th Infantry paralleling them to the east. The battalion also advanced through the Bois de Thiaucourt and the Bois de Beney, meeting no resistance and capturing a few German soldiers hiding in the forest. At the Sebastopol Farm, about three-fourths of a mile south of Saint-Benoît-en-Woëvre, they had to pause because an American artillery barrage was falling just ahead. Waiting at the farm for the firing to stop, they saw a peasant woman and a small boy running south, away from the barrage and toward safety. She was gripping the child's hand tightly. When she arrived at the farm, Donovan asked her if there were any Germans in the village. Venting hatred of the Boche, she said a battalion of German troops had withdrawn from Saint-Benoît-en-Woëvre overnight and thanked Donovan for driving them away. He told her that his men had found a cache of food at the farm and invited her to take whatever she needed, for which she was grateful.[11]

Once the artillery fire had stopped, the New Yorkers continued their advance, arriving in Saint-Benoît-en-Woëvre around 9:15 a.m. They captured many stores from an enemy depot along the railway tracks and moved up to take the Château Saint Benoît, about 100 yards north of the village.[12] Donovan established his headquarters in the château, a magnificent building. The courtyard was filled with "valuable paintings, porcelains, and furniture" that the Germans had been unable to carry off. While Donovan and his staff were standing nearby, a German artillery shell landed, shattering every window in the château when it exploded.[13]

The 167th Infantry, which also had started out at 6:00 a.m., moved through the western edge of the Bois de Beney near the Etang de la Carpière without incident and linked up with the 165th Infantry at the Château Saint Benoît.[14]

Once again, the Iowans of the 168th Infantry had a more eventful morning than the rest of the division. Lieutenant Colonel Tinley ordered Major Stanley to lead the regiment's advance with his 2nd Battalion, and the major had his men formed up at 5:45 a.m. E Company and F Company took the lead with E on the right and F on the left, and G and H Companies moving up behind. Stanley put Lieutenant Pigeon and his scouts out ahead of the battalion by about 1,000 yards.[15]

As the battalion was moving out, men could see heavy black smoke billowing into the blue sky, indicating the Germans were trying to destroy the last of the town's ammunition dumps and storehouses. Entering the Bois de Beney, the battalion shifted to column formation to suit the narrow trails. As the scouts emerged from the lower Bois de Beney and into the Bois de Dampvitoux, a twenty-two-man enemy patrol opened fire on them from a railroad embankment north of the forest. Pigeon deployed his men in a semi-circle and had them return fire from three directions with deadly effect. In minutes, ten of the enemy were dead and the other twelve had fled north into the Bois de Dampvitoux. A small station along the railroad included a supply depot richly stocked with coal, building materials, and ammunition. After this skirmish, Pigeon sent a runner to Major Stanley saying, "Way is clear" and continued.[16]

Stanley's main body soon advanced into the Bois de Dampvitoux. Scouts and the French liaison officer, Lieutenant Kuhlmann, alerted the major to a large column of enemy troops and wagons ahead. The concentration was moving northeast along the Saint-Benoît-en-Woëvre to Dampvitoux road near the Louiseville Farm. Anxious to intercept this column, Stanley quickly formed a small force with one platoon each from both E and G Companies and sent them along a railroad track to the northwest toward the road where he hoped they would meet the enemy above the Louiseville Farm.[17]

When Stanley and his men reached the north edge of the woods, the German column had passed, leaving a rear guard of twenty-five men.

Troops from the Rainbow Division entering Saint-Benoît-en-Woëvre. (*National Archives*)

About the time the Germans saw Stanley's men, the rest of G Company arrived and opened fire on the Germans from about 500 yards northeast of the farm. The Germans, realizing they were about to be cut off, retreated into the woods on the far side. From there, they maintained rifle fire on the Americans, aided by Maxim fire from the Marimbois Farm, a bit more than a mile up the road to the northeast. The Iowans took cover and began rushing the Germans in the woods in small bounds. This assault managed to slide around the German left flank and close on the enemy. They Americans captured eighteen prisoners and killed the officer in command; survivors escaped north into Haumont-les-Lachaussee.[18]

While Stanley had been dealing with these Germans, Pigeon and his scouts encountered another German detachment at the Louiseville Farm. With H Company moving up behind the scouts, they rushed the farm and captured the defenders. The farm complex, a large collection of buildings on a three-sided square, had been a German motor vehicle repair station. Besides a large amount of materiél, the Iowans took two five-ton trucks. Major Stanley commented that the trucks would come in handy moving headquarters baggage.[19]

As the infantry regiments established a new defensive line, patrols ranged to learn the enemy's strength and location. The 165th Infantry patrols were also told to try to link with the 26th and the 1st Divisions, which were moving up on their left. The regiment's 1st Battalion had orders to establish a defensive position along the Bois de la Grande Souche by placing outposts along the road to the Hassavant Farm, a mile and a half north of Saint-Benoît-en-Woëvre. From there, additional patrols were to push forward to the Bois des Haudronvilles. Patrols for the 2nd Battalion received orders to move west along the roads to capture any small groups of Germans retreating east through the woods. That afternoon, contact was established with the 26th Division on the Saint-Benoît-en-Woëvre to Woël road, and the 1st Battalion met up with elements of the 1st Division near Bois de la Grande Souche.[20]

On the far right of the division front, Major Stanley of the 168th Infantry also received orders to send out patrols. After reforming the 2nd Battalion along the Saint-Benoît-en-Woëvre to Dampvitoux road, he began to prepare his position as a defensive line. As the men were digging in, a returning patrol reported Germans to be moving back into Haumont-les-Lachaussee. Knowing that Germans were so close, Stanley kept his men working up defensive lines. One line ran from the Etang d'Afrique to the junction of the Saint-Benoît-en-Woëvre to Dampvitoux road and the road leading northwest to Haumont-les-Lachaussee. Stanley placed E Company on the right of the line with outposts at the Farm de Champ-Fontaine and on the edge of a nearby woods. Since the 356th Infantry had still not come up on his right, the major established outposts along a line from the road intersection to the junction of the railroad with the Bois de Charey.[21] On the left of the 168th's line, that unit established liaison with the 167th Infantry's 2nd Battalion.[22]

The event of September 13 most meaningful to the doughboys of the Rainbow Division was the arrival of field kitchens. The men had been subsisting on their two-day supply of field rations since the offensive began, and many had run out of food. Combat and field trains, with kitchen crews from each company of every regiment, had been consolidated the night of September 11-12 under the Regimental Supply Officer. By noon on September 12 trains containing field kitchens were on the road trying to catch up with the infantry regiments. That task had taken herculean efforts amid massive traffic jams and roads deep with mud. But by 4:00 p.m. on September 13, all kitchens were with their respective companies and ready to serve hot meals.[23]

That night, German bombers began sortieing regularly. These flights disturbed the men's rest but did little real damage. The enemy also began an unnerving pattern of artillery bombardment. Instead of massed barrages, one long-range gun would fire at intervals, lobbing one shell left,

A patrol from the 165th Infantry dug in along a road near the Hassavant Farm. (*National Archives*)

one right, and one at a center position. The gunners jumbled targets and ranges until men went almost crazy wondering where the next round would strike. Raymond Cheseldine of the 166th Infantry wrote, "In a heavy bombardment this curiosity is not evident, but in the dead of night a lone gun can cause great anxiety."[24]

On September 14, the division issued field orders stating, "Pursuant to orders from the 4th Army Corps this Division will promptly organize its sector for defense."[25] With that order, all ideas of continuing an advance toward Metz, a pet project of General MacArthur and others ever since the division reached the final objective line, evaporated. "I could see the dust of the German trains retreating down the roads toward Metz," MacArthur said. "Prisoners captured insisted that there was only a small garrison in Metz—nothing like the large numbers needed to really garrison and hold its defenses."[26] He believed that this was not the time to stop the Allied advance. He later wrote:

> What a wonderful thing it would have been for the Division to go ahead even though the outer defenses of Metz might have held it up. What a wonderful thing it would have been for those of us who in the past had worked out so many map problems on all this famous territory never dreaming that one day we would fight on it, if on the ground of the German victories of 1870 covered with the monuments

of their regiments, the Rainbow and other divisions of the First American Army, in its first great battle could have defeated the Germans![27]

MacArthur requested permission to move the 84th Brigade forward toward Metz but, while the division, IV Corps, and 1st Army supported him, AEF Headquarters firmly rebuffed him, and for good reasons. Earlier that month, Pershing had agreed to Foch's terms regarding the Saint Mihiel Offensive, including stopping the advance at the base of the salient. Also, a drive on Metz at this time violated basic tenets of good strategy. There had been no recent, substantive planning for such an advance, nor resources allocated or organized to support one. Most importantly, the only intelligence on enemy strength and defenses had come from a few enemy prisoners, and no formal aerial reconnaissance of the area around Metz had taken place since the offensive in the salient had begun. To push forward to Metz without in-depth planning or intelligence was a waltz with disaster.

While MacArtur and other senior officers debated strategy, the soldiers of the Rainbow Division focused on comfort. Since the start of the offensive, priority on the narrow roads northward had gone to shipments of food and ammunition and movement of artillery, not individual soldiers' field packs containing their blankets. September days were warm, but nights were becoming decidedly cold. A soldier came up with an ingenious response. The commander of L Company of the 168th Infantry detailed Private Thomas Stack to travel to the rear and retrieve his men's field packs from the Forêt-de-la Reine.[28]

Stack secured a wagon and mules from the Supply Company and started south. At the forest, he located and loaded the company's packs and started back. An M.P. stopped him and told him only food, ammunition, and artillery could roll north. "This put me up a tree, for I knew the boys were sleeping in the mud and cold and wet and needed the blankets in the worst way," Stack said later. He remembered passing empty cartridge boxes a ways back. "Well," he told the M.P., "I guess I will go back and take up the ammunition first."[29]

Stack drove to the pile of empty cartridge boxes, loaded them so they covered the field packs, and rejoined the long line of northbound vehicles. When he rolled past the M.P. again, he heard him curse about "those damned guns" using so much ammunition. Stack chuckled and drove on, reaching the company's position the next morning.[30]

While Stack was helping his buddies in L Company, Major Stanley was trying to figure out how to strengthen the 2nd Battalion's defenses. He

Soldiers from Iowa's 168th Infantry man their positions near Haumont-les-Lachaussee and the Marimbois Farm. (*National Archives*)

and his men had only light entrenching shovels, insufficient for digging defensive trenches. He had the men dig foxholes, which worked to their advantage when the 42nd and the 89th Divisions accidentally began to shell his positions in the Bois de Charey. Stanley immediately asked that the gunners cease firing and correct their aiming data. If they did not, he added, he would have to withdraw his men from the line. The artillery fire stopped but an hour later resumed, killing a man from E Company. Losses from this friendly fire episode eventually totaled five killed and eight wounded.[31]

Within days, engineering support and equipment arrived, and work began on a complete defensive trench system. Forty-second Division Headquarters produced the "Plan of Defense of the Sector of Pannes." The twenty-one-page plan included detailed sketches of the communications and trench system. The 117th Engineers drew up the new defensive works and the entire division began constructing it. The first night, a large working party started digging the trenches as specified amid continuous German artillery fire. In the 168th Infantry, men from the 1st and 3rd Battalions did much of the digging. The support position was thoroughly organized, and the 3rd Battalion, besides preparing its own line, furnished wiring and carrying parties for the forward position. Working under the experienced 117th Engineers, men of the division completed a secure defensive line.[32] On September 16, the 84th Brigade took responsibility for the entire division front, and the 83rd Brigade moved back in reserve.[33]

That same day, raids on German positions began. That night a contingent from the 167th was to hit Haumont-les-Lachaussee, where the Germans seemed to have been building up their infantry forces. At the same time, the men from the 168th would attack the Marimbois Farm, just over 1,000 yards from where the Iowans' defensive line crossed the Saint-Benoît-en-Woëvre to Dampvitoux road. Both regiments planned to use a single platoon plus scouts, preceded by a preparatory barrage.[34]

The artillery commenced firing at 7:50 p.m.; the raids got underway at 8:00 p.m. The 167th was able to quickly enter Haumont-les-Lachaussee because most of the German garrison fled as soon as they saw the Alabamians. The Americans rapidly encircled a remaining machine gun emplacement, capturing eight men and killing the officer in command. Interrogations revealed that a company of the 14th Sturm Battalion had been assigned to the village with orders to stand fast except in the face of a very heavy attack.[35]

The 168th again had a tougher row to hoe. The Iowans were within 100 yards of the farm when the Germans opened fire with heavy Maxims and artillery. Major Stanley's officers rushed their men forward and a "hot fight" ensued. The Iowans employed grenades and then bayonets in hand-to-hand fighting. During the skirmish, Private Mariano Escamillo found himself surrounded by three German soldiers and "in a very tight place." Lieutenant Pigeon, Private Rudolph Mueller, and Corporal Walter Betsworth came to the rescue. Pigeon shot one German, while Betsworth and Escamillo successfully battled the remaining two. Seeing the situation resolving, Pigeon started to move on. The German he had shot raised himself to his knees and took aim at the lieutenant. Before the German could fire, Private Mueller shot him.[36] An hour later, the 168th raiders returned to their lines having killed twenty to thirty enemy and taken five prisoners against only two Americans wounded.[37]

Five days later, on September 21, the division decided to revisit Haumont-les-Lachaussee and the Marimbois Farm. Once again, the Alabamians of the 167th would attack the village while the Iowans of the 168th would assault the farm complex. Commanders figured that the Germans would be better prepared and offer more substantial resistance, probably from recently arrived artillery. This was confirmed late that afternoon by a heavy German barrage from guns near Haumont-les-Lachaussee that continued into the night.[38]

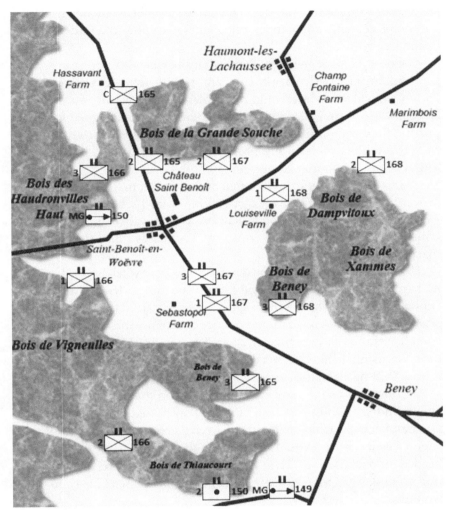

Map 7. The Rainbow Division's final positions in the Saint Benoît Sector. (*Author*)

In response, the division added two batteries of 120mm guns. Those eight tubes brought the raid's artillery element to eighty pieces, including forty-eight 75mm guns and twenty-four 155mm guns. Division artillery chief Colonel Henry Reilly planned to use the guns to their maximum capacity. Reilly had three objectives. His gunners would try to smash German defensive positions and reduce or eliminate resistance. Crews would shift their fire beyond both targets to box them in and keep the Germans from counterattacking. And Reilly meant to smother all enemy machine gun emplacements and supporting artillery, keeping the raiders from coming under fire.[39]

At 4:00 a.m. on September 22, the attack began with a barrage of village and farm by twelve heavy guns and twenty-four light pieces. Two 75mm guns blasted the farm at point-blank range, tearing down walls and blowing off roofs. Thirty American machine guns assigned for supporting fire began rattling away at the farm. The Germans sent signal rockets into the pre-dawn sky, prompting German artillery into action. Thirty minutes into that hammering of both target areas, men from the 167th Infantry's M Company, covered by forty-eight machine guns, crept forward to a point 300 yards east of Haumont-les-Lachaussee. Corporal Fleckenstein, revisiting ground he had stalked the night of September 16, remembered, "The noise was terrific, and it actually seemed to be raining machine gun bullets."[40]

The barrage that had been striking the village now fell beyond it. The Alabamians leapt up and sprinted toward the village. Each of the company's four platoons had been assigned a specific part of the town to clear, after which they were to report to the company commander at the church.[41] At the village perimeter, a wire fence stopped Fleckenstein's platoon. German machine gunners facing them seemed to be out of ammunition. Shifting right, the Americans end-ran the fence into the village.[42]

Fleckenstein's platoon swept left onto the main street, hurling grenades and incendiary bombs into each building they passed. The street led to a German barracks which had already been seized, with fourteen of the enemy taken captive. With mop-up soon accomplished, the Alabamians headed for friendly lines. They and their prisoners reached that destination around 5:30 a.m. A casualty count revealed two men killed and four wounded.[43]

Slightly in advance of the barrage, the Iowans of the 168th Infantry had sneaked forward about 200 yards, lying flat and waiting for the guns to start. They were to attack as three detachments of fifty men each. One group was to rush left to destroy dugouts on the farm's northern edge. Another was to hit the center and clear out the main buildings, while the third detachment was to neutralize German pillboxes at the farm's southern corner.[44]

Waiting out the barrage, the Iowans realized they were coming under friendly fire at their rear, so they fast-crawled forward, anxiously poised to attack once the gunners knocked off.[45] When an officer shouted, "All

Men from Alabama's 167th Infantry in positions along the road toward Haumont-les-Lachaussee. Five minutes after a Signal Corps photographer took this photo, this position was hit by a German artillery shell that killed two of these men. (*National Archives*)

together, let's go!" the men ran toward the farm as fast as they could, tearing through rusty, broken barbed wire. They surrounded the ten farm buildings, penetrated each, and tossed grenades into the dugouts, shooting anyone who resisted. Within minutes, the farm secured, the Iowans headed home with nine prisoners.[46]

Germans taken during the dual raids wound up at the Château Saint Benoît, headquarters for the 84th Brigade and 167th Infantry. Prisoners told interrogators the Germans were bringing up a big gun to destroy the building. Two days later, on September 24, a 280mm gun boomed in the distance; its 600-lb. round barely overshot the château. Fifteen minutes later, another huge shell screamed in; as headquarters personnel were fleeing the château that behemoth smashed a stable. Explosive rounds struck the headquarters at its midsection and one wing, followed by two incendiary shells that exploded inside the château, setting the entire building afire.[47] Of the structure, established as part of an abbey in 1128 and of late decorated with pink and blue draperies and vintage tapestries, only blackened exterior walls remained. The ruins still stand.

On September 27, the 166th Infantry received orders to relieve the 167th Infantry along the front of the Saint Benoît Sector. The change took place without incident. The 1st Battalion took the forward positions along

The charred remains of the Château Saint Benoît after being destroyed by German artillery shells on September 24, 1918. (*National Archives*)

with a machine gun company at hand, the 2nd Battalion for support, and the 3rd Battalion in reserve. As yet, this stretch of defensive line featured no dugouts or trench complexes, only foxholes that offered scant cover for what became regular enemy shelling with high explosive rounds, shrapnel, and mustard gas. The 166th's Supply Company carried in food every night, but the men lived in misery.[48]

The division continued to order raids as well as nightly scouting patrols into no man's land. September 28 saw a rare daylight raid, with Haumont-les-Lachaussee again the objective. Twenty men from the 166th's A Company and another twenty from B Company were to assess whether the Germans had withdrawn by the fraught method of aggressively engaging the enemy.[49]

Preceded by a three-hour barrage, the Ohioans set off at 5:30 a.m. The A Company men approached the village from the left; the B Company party split in two to attempt to enter the town. One B Company group was nearing the town's north edge when a large number of Germans opened fire on the interlopers. The corporal leading the second B Company party heard a telegraph clacking inside the church—apparently calling for artillery support, as a German barrage was soon slamming the Ohioans. Germans opened fire on the A Company men with machine guns.[50]

Red German flares announced the Americans' presence as enemy rounds crashed into Haumont-les-Lachaussee and to the right of B Company. Two three-star white rockets flew up from the American lines behind the raiders, signaling American artillery to get working. Within seconds, American shells were falling about 150 yards northeast of the village, striking enemy machine gun emplacements. A raider was hit and killed, lying where he fell. When another man was wounded, Sergeant David Russell went forward under heavy machine gun fire to carry him to the American lines.[51] Having proved at high cost that Haumont-les-Lachaussee still harbored Germans, the raiders withdrew.

Before returning to the front line, the 166th Infantry had bivouacked for weeks on the southern edge of the Bois de Nonsard, a fabulous place to do so. In four years occupying the locale, the Germans had established permanent and, by Ohio standards, luxurious facilities, including cinder roadways lined with "rustic cottages completely furnished and equipped with electric lights." The Germans, of course, knew the site's coordinates and shelled the locale nightly.[52]

Another problem at the complex arose from the army's class system. The 166th's Supply Company was first to occupy the place. The quartermasters had made themselves quite comfortable when General Lenihan, commander of the 83rd Brigade, decided he wanted to billet there. The General and his staff moved into the most luxurious of the cottages. There was more than enough room to accommodate him, his people, and the supply company, but Lenihan, fearing that the bustle around ration dumps would attract shelling or an aerial attack, bounced the quartermasters.[53]

The quartermasters quickly colonized a site back from the main road as nice as their previous quarters. But no sooner had the company moved in then General MacArthur, unhoused by the destruction of the Château Saint Benoît, arrived with his staff. MacArthur evicted the supply company.[54]

This time, deep in the forest, the resourceful quartermasters found a "model village" of bungalows set in a lovely clearing around a wonderful single-story log building with four bedrooms and a big living room that had a large stone fireplace. Adjoining the lodge were smaller houses, along with stables fit for mules and horses. The setting was perfect, but the supply company's stewardship of it was fleeting.[55]

With his staff, Major General Menoher, the Rainbow Division commander, had quartered nearby in the Forest of the Lovely Willow, where another bungalow camp beckoned. Menoher was perfectly happy there, but his chief artillery officer, General Gately, insisted on obtaining his own cottages for use as a Division Artillery P.C. He ordered the quartermasters to hit the bricks.[56]

The supply company commander chose veteran Stable Sergeant Red Waggoman to step in as the unit's real estate agent. Waggoman, a keen student of staff officer thinking, knew to seek a campsite desirable except for being "too damned close to the front for any generals!" He did exactly that, and the wandering company set up housekeeping, able to tout themselves as "the best billeting party the Division Generals ever had,"[57] undisturbed until the regiment again moved to the front.

On September 30, a secret field order relieved the Rainbow Division of its duties and assigned the 89th Division to take over the front in the Saint Benoît Sector. That night, as the 42nd Division men were withdrawing, another order directed the division to be ready to march on October 1. Optimists pictured a stroll to a rear area for extended rest and recuperation. Realists knew better. A 165th Infantry man snorted, "Hell, we're going to something worse!"[58] He was right—they were headed for the new offensive raging in the Meuse-Argonne.

In his September 30 diary entry, John Taber wrote that, while the war seemed to be going the Allies' way, the fighting needed to end "before the rest of us are shot up."[59]

7

TO THE MEUSE-ARGONNE, SEPTEMBER 30– OCTOBER 12, 1918

"It was a cloudless night and clear, so that the sheets of gun-lightning that illuminated the northern sky seemed doubly brilliant and alarming. At a crossroad someone read aloud the road direction, Vers Verdun. We weren't in for any picnic this time."
—John H. Taber from *The Story of the 168th Infantry*

On the night of October 10-11, 1918, the Rainbow Division's four infantry regiments slowly began to make their way north to relieve the 1st Division, which had fought desperately to take the ground on which the Rainbow men were marching. Dawn was still to come when the Rainbow men all had collected at their intended position aft of the 1st Division and the front. Foxholes and craters had to suffice as bunks beneath the roar of American and German guns.

Morning dawned wet, cold, and foggy in as horrific a setting as any they had seen during the war—"one that can never be forgotten,"[1] wrote Alison Reppy of the 166th Infantry. All around sprawled dozens upon dozens of dead doughboys from the 1st and the 35th Divisions. German machine gunners "lay dead in their gun emplacements, where they had fired until the last minute,"[2] killing many of the Americans lying in the Meuse-Argonne mud. Sergeant Dana Daniels of the 166th wrote in his diary, "I took a walk over to look over the scene of the battle and there lay on the ground 34 dead Boche & 35 dead American Boys." Before the day was done, Daniels would count fifty more decomposing corpses overdue for collection, processing, and burial.[3]

Besides dead men, rotting animal remains layered the ridges with "horses and mules, killed by artillery fire, or, perhaps, having fallen in the harness, dead from sheer strain and exhaustion." The stench defied description. John Hayes of Alabama's 167th Infantry remembered, "The cold rains to which the battlefields were then exposed had turned the flesh of the corpses to a livid blue or an ashy gray."[4] On the far right of the division's line where the 168th had moved into position, men found 288 dead from the 1st and the 32nd Divisions.[5] The regiment's chaplains, Major Winfred Robb, Lieutenant Roscoe Hatch, and Lieutenant Henry Strickland, led details that undertook the somber task of burying dead doughboys.

A soldier from the 150th Machine Gun Battalion came upon a dead man seated against a tree trunk, a rifle beside him leaning on the trunk. Another dead American had a gaping hole in his head. "I needed tobacco bad, and there lay a sack of Bull Durham," the passerby wrote. "It was wet from the rain, but I used it as I knew he never would again." Now he found a dead German in a foxhole, a bullet hole at the center of his forehead, hand grasping a potato masher. "He lay there on his back stretched out, with eyes wide open," the soldier wrote. "I can still see him there as he lay. I'll never forget that."[6]

"There was no doubt about it," John Taber wrote of the silent message conveyed by the 1st Division dead. "The regiment was in for a desperate struggle."[7] Captain Leon Miesse of the 166th wrote in his diary, "The sights which met our eyes are too sad to relate, but somebody blundered."[8]

Someone had blundered: Lieutenant General John J. Pershing and the staff at AEF and 1st Army Headquarters. Errors, rash decisions, and poor planning at the Meuse-Argonne cost the American 1st Army 121,000 casualties, including more than 26,000 dead.[9]

By the time the Rainbow Division received orders to start moving west, the Meuse-Argonne Offensive had been raging for four days. Its auteur, Marshal Foch, insisted on shifting American divisions from Saint Mihiel to the Meuse as soon as the earlier action concluded. That was Foch's con-

A dead American doughboy lies next to his foxhole in the Meuse-Argonne. (*Library of Congress*)

dition for creating the U.S. 1st Army and allowing Pershing his scaled-down assault on Saint Mihiel. Foch was basing his choice of the Meuse-Argonne as a battlefield on Allied successes during the summer of 1918. Prior to the Second Battle of the Marne, Allied leaders believed that, although steadily increasing American strength was shifting the balance of power on the Western Front, victory was not to come until 1919. Events at the Marne and Saint Mihiel had convinced Foch that a major offensive might finish off the weakened Germans before 1918 was out.

To accomplish that, Foch developed an offensive in the form of a massive set of pincers. One Allied blade would slash in the Somme, the other in the Champagne-Argonne. The rest of the Allied armies were to attack across the entire Western Front. So sustained and concerted an assault, Foch believed, would bleed Germany dry, crippling the entire imperial army. The French Fourth Army and the American 1st Army would form the right wing of an attack designed to envelop German forces deployed along the central part of the Western Front in northern France. Together, these two groups would thrust toward key rail lines at Sedan and Mézières, moving between the Meuse River on their right and the Suippe River on the left.[10] Besides being a key rail center, Sedan held massive symbolic meaning for the French. There, in 1871, France had ended the Franco-Prussian War in a state of profound humiliation when Napoleon III surrendered to Wilhelm I, King of Prussia and the current Kaiser's sire.[11]

Foch had insisted that Pershing have the 1st Army ready by September 26 to attack an area bounded by the Forêt d'Argonne and the Meuse River. Pershing was to have independent command of a unified American sector that comprised a sizable portion of the eastern flank of the Western Front. Foch meant for the Franco-American attack on the right to pry the Germans from their bastions in northern France and make them use strategic reserves that Allied forces would destroy. This, the marshal hoped, would push the enemy to the breaking point as the Allies forced the Boche out of France and Belgium.[12]

Once Foch's plan was set, AEF Headquarters and 1st Army went about creating one of their own—up to that point the biggest military operation in American history, to be spun up in twenty-three days and fraught with risks that came to be made real. "Pershing's men would soon be paying a price for the concessions he had yielded to Foch as the price of keeping the American Army intact," historian John Eisenhower wrote. "He had agreed to launch a major campaign in formidable defensive terrain with inadequate time to prepare, a combination that would inevitably bring hardships on his men."[13]

The 1st Army G-3 plans team, led again by Colonel George Marshall, had to figure out how to move an army more than sixty miles and provide all the artillery, food, forage, and ammunition for a sustained campaign. Marshall and cohort convinced Pershing that while it would be impossible to move the divisions positioned around Saint Mihiel by September 26, the artillery transport effort could shift the full complement of some 2,000 guns and 600,000 tons of supplies and ammunition in time—even though one division's supporting artillery consisted of seventy-two guns, a road train stretching more than ten miles.[14]

The scale of the requisite artillery force demanded 300 highway miles of a road network inadequate for repositioning major armies. Late-summer rains had made nearly impassable slogs of the three roads leading into the American sector of the front. These same roads, long overdue for repair, also were needed by French forces moving across the rear of the 1st Army to join French Army units on the western flank. And most of the supplies and ammunition for 1st Army waited along what had been the southern face of the Saint Mihiel Salient.[15]

With a plan for moving guns, crews, and matériel in hand, Marshall and staff weighed how to deliver more than 600,000 men to the front to

Traffic jams like this one in the roads leading to the Meuse-Argonne front would limit logistical support throughout the offensive. (*National Archives*)

relieve 200,000 French troops there. This even bigger set of headaches fell to the AEF logistics organization, the Services of Supply, or SOS. By the late summer of 1918, troops working in the SOS numbered over 500,000, more than the combined armies that Ulysses Grant and Robert E. Lee led. Chronically short of critical personnel and equipment, the SOS bore down and established nineteen railheads, thirty-four evacuation hospitals, and fifty-six ordnance, quartermaster, ammunition, petroleum, gas warfare, and engineer depots for the coming attack. In the seventeen days preceding the Meuse-Argonne jump-off, the SOS staged 40,000 tons of shells, enough to support five days of artillery fire.[16] But the task of providing continuous logistics support to a massive army on the attack severely challenged the unit.

Pershing ordered that his extremely ambitious attack occur in four phases. The first, on September 26, had the 1st Army on day one driving ten miles into the German lines across an eighteen-mile front between the Forêt d'Argonne and the Meuse River. On September 27, the day after achieving that breakthrough, the 1st Army would join with the French Fourth Army on their left north of the Forêt d'Argonne at Grandpré. The second phase required the Americans to advance another ten miles and push the Germans back beyond the line of Stenay to Le Chesne. In the third phase, French forces under American command were to attack east of the Meuse River to eliminate any German forces on the Heights of the Meuse, protecting the 1st Army's right flank. In the fourth phase, the 1st Army and the French Fourth Army were to attack and seize Sedan and Mézières.[17] Pershing figured the entire sector to fall in mere days.

Pershing's extremely ambitious scheme and its objectives rested on a solid foundation. The enemy divisions involved were under strength, but the 1st Army's G-2 Intelligence staff believed the Germans capable of reinforcing them with four divisions on day one, two more the second day, and on the third day providing as many as nine additional divisions. To achieve its initial objectives before reinforcements could help underpin a strong, cohesive defense, the 1st Army had to attain, maintain, and sustain fierce momentum.[18]

In daily mileage covered, the Saint Mihiel Offensive had advanced only about half of what Pershing wanted troops to achieve in the Meuse-Argonne, and at Saint Mihiel the terrain and defenses had been far less challenging. The area of the planned American attack gave the Germans every physical advantage. Brigadier General Hugh Drum, 1st Army Chief of Staff, later remarked, "This was the most ideal defensive terrain I have ever seen or read about."[19] Major General Hunter Liggett, who commanded the I Corps at the start of the offensive before being made commander of the 1st Army, said, "The region was a natural fortress beside which the Virginia Wilderness in which Grant and Lee fought was a park."[20]

The 1st Army area of operations was a north-south corridor in a shallow valley about twenty miles wide. The corridor's western boundary encompassed most of the Forêt d'Argonne, which sat atop a plateau between the Aisne and Aire Rivers. The forest was a tangle of dense undergrowth and trees crisscrossed by hills, draws, and deep ravines deleterious to mobility, communications, and artillery support. East of the forest, the valley formed by the Aire River offered a natural corridor suitable for moving troops, but that valley spread below the hills of the Forêt d'Argonne to the west. In addition, the large buttes of Montfaucon and Vauquois to the east dominated the valley, ideal locations for artillery observers and guns poised to pound any advancing forces. In the center of the American sector jutted the Barrois Plateau, a series of hills rising from south of the town of Montfaucon northeast to Romagne-sous-Montfaucon and Cunel and ending at the Barricourt Heights. East of the Barrois Plateau on the right flank of the American sector was the Meuse River valley, another natural movement corridor. But, as at the Aire River valley, high ground flanked the pathway. On the Heights of the Meuse east of the river, the Germans had massed artillery.[21]

The Germans had made the most of the terrain. Having occupied the area for four years, the foe had built a formidable defensive system. Heavy losses at Verdun and the Somme in 1916 had forced the German high command to update its defensive thinking and develop the Siegfried Stellung, a series of fortifications the Allies called the Hindenburg Line. The new German doctrine emphasized defense in depth to conserve manpower and counter improving Allied firepower and offensive tactics. The Germans skillfully sited field fortifications and interlocked fields of fire to blunt Allied attacks.[22]

Fortifications and artillery shelters peppered the sector; a light rail line supported logistics. Four major defensive belts strapped the area to a depth of nine to fifteen miles, with the third and fourth belts, the Brunhild Stellung and the Kriemhilde Stellung, being the most formidable. In the sector assigned to the 1st Army, these lines ran from Grandpré on the western boundary of the sector across the heights of Côte Dame Marie, Romagne, and Cunel, to Brieulles on the Meuse. Defenders were to man mazes of concrete-reinforced shelters and machine gun nests, earthen strong points, and support and communications trenches. These defenses exploited the terrain, as did barbed wire entanglements meant to funnel attackers into narrow corridors overlain by a web of interlocking machine gun axes and pre-planned artillery targets.[23]

The soldiers defending the 1st Army's area of operations came from the German Third and Fifth Armies. The Third Army held the Forêt d'Argonne and the area west of the forest where the French Fourth Army would attack. The Fifth Army defended the area east of the forest through the Aire River valley to east of Saint Mihiel. The Third Army assigned the 76th Reserve Division from its Group Aisne while the Fifth Army deployed the 2nd Landwehr Division and the 1st Guards Division from its Group Argonne along the line east of the forest. The Landwehr had been stripped of most of its younger soldiers to support those spring 1918 offensives, costing the division the intimate familiarity with the Meuse-Argonne and its defensive positions that troops had gained serving there since 1915. The elite 1st Guards Division had endured four draining years of combat. The Fifth Army's Group Meuse West placed the 117th Division and the 7th Reserve Division in the Forêt d'Argonne; the AEF considered both second-class divisions.[24]

The German divisions aligned across the 1st Army's front may have been under strength and tired, but their core consisted of hardened veterans steeped in defense-in-depth strategy and thoroughly prepared to hold their ground. What they had lost in numbers of men they made up in weaponry and firepower. One division could field almost 200 heavy and light machine guns, a Maxim for every nine soldiers. Also, as seemed to be the case everywhere on the Western Front, these units could call on thousands of artillery pieces, carefully placed to obstruct any attacking force. A doughboy said, "every goddamn German there who didn't have a machine gun had a cannon."[25]

Arguably, the 1st Army's greatest challenge was the position and the condition of its own divisions. Given the terrain, the defenses, and Pershing's ambitious objectives, the divisions available for the opening phases of the offensive were completely inadequate. Needing the Saint Mihiel Offensive to prove the AEF could operate independently, Pershing had chosen his most experienced, veteran divisions to attack the salient. But now those divisions were tied down securing that prize, unable to shift to the Meuse-Argonne and leaving the 1st Army with few good choices with which to stage its initial assault there. A total of nine divisions made up the attack forces of the 1st Army's I, III, and V Corps. Of those nine divisions, four were National Guard, four were National Army, and one was Regular Army. The Regular Army's 1st Division plus the 77th, 4th, and 28th Divisions had combat experience, but the 79th, 35th, 91st, 37th, 80th, and 33rd Divisions were unbloodied. The 80th and 33rd Divisions, new to France, had received almost no supplemental training.[26] "They had never been under shell-fire before," *Baltimore Sun* reporter Raymond Tompkins wrote. "They had never heard the sound of a German gun or the whine of a German shell."[27] It would take a miracle for these men to overcome what awaited in the Meuse-Argonne; asking them to achieve objectives likely unattainable by even veteran divisions was a major blunder. As these green troops failed to meet Pershing's objectives, he and the AEF barked draconian edicts and fired command personnel, making matters worse.

Assigning inexperienced divisions to the 1st Army helped conceal the nature of the coming offensive and preserve the element of surprise. To avoid triggering reinforcements by the Germans, 1st Army planners moved men and matériel at night. This partly succeeded, but the Germans did identify arriving American divisions, pegging them as "new and only partly trained." German Supreme Headquarters labeled the likelihood of an immediate attack in the area "improbable."[28] As late as September 27, a day into the Allied offensive, German intelligence officers were stating that they believed any new American offensive would be aimed at Metz and the Saar coal basin.[29] Once the offensive was underway, the degree of inexperience in many American units surprised even the Germans. Three days in, the German Supreme Headquarters in the Field referred to the use of these untrained divisions as a "reckless commitment of all available means."[30]

Pershing was undaunted. On the afternoon of September 25, the day before jump-off, he visited every division and corps headquarters to buck up his men and to gauge his officers' sentiments about their prospects. Pershing later wrote, "They were all alert and confident and I returned feeling that all would go as planned."[31]

"No judgement was ever more wrong,"[32] a biographer wrote. The exuberance of the Headquarters staff discouraged dissent further down the command ladder. Major General James Harbord, who had been Pershing's chief of staff and was commanding the SOS at the time, said, "To doubt audibly was to be a traitor."[33]

The Meuse-Argonne Offensive opened as planned at 2:30 a.m. on September 26, 1918, when 1st Army gunners opened fire all along the line between the Forêt d'Argonne and the Meuse River. The three-hour barrage sought to flatten barbed wire, suppress German artillery, destroy enemy field fortifications, and kill or wound defenders. The gunfire was some of the most impressive of the war. "I was as deaf as a post from the noise," Captain Harry Truman of the 35th Division's Battery D, 129th Field Artillery, said. "It looked as though every gun in France was turned loose."[34]

H-Hour arrived at 5:30 a.m., and the 1st Army's infantry began its assault with what was supposed to be that day's ten-mile drive into the German defenses—they would not come close to taking that much ground. At best the American attack in Pershing's first phase was a mixed bag. On the far right in the III Corps area along the Meuse, the infantry of the veteran 4th Division, aided by fog that prevented effective German artillery fire, advanced through the marshes of the Meuse River amid heavy machine gun fire to seize their first day's objective line; their westernmost brigade advanced nearly a mile past the strategic town of Montfaucon.[35] Little good could be said about the performance of I Corps and V Corps.

The key objective for V Corps was the high terrain and crossroads at Montfaucon. The corps attacked using the 91st, 37th, and 79th Divisions, none of which had any combat experience. Even though V Corps had enveloped the Germans defending Montfaucon, the inexperienced 79th Division could not push through the thick undergrowth, fallen trees, and shell holes complicating the approach to the town. This division had only been in France a few weeks, had received less than a month of training, and had seen less than ten days of service in the quiet trenches of the Avocourt sector. While the 37th Division was able to clear the Bois de Montfaucon and advance to the western slope of the Butte de Montfaucon, by early afternoon the men were exhausted and completely disorganized. The 91st Division advanced almost ten miles, but a fierce German counterattack pushed it back.[36]

The worst performance was that of I Corps, assigned the grim task of taking the Forêt d'Argonne on the western flank of the 1st Army's sector. One I Corps division, the 35th, was able to push forward to take Cheppy and Vauquois, but that advance stalled. The division took heavy casualties, but their biggest problem was leadership. Only five days before the offensive, the division commander had relieved all his brigade and regiment commanders. His choices of replacements were virtually unknown to the units' soldiers and officers, crippling the new men's capacity to coordinate attacks and communicate with subordinates. By the end of the day, the 35th was almost incapable of sustained battle.[37]

On the far left of I Corps, the green troops of the 77th Division struggled through dense undergrowth deep in the Forêt d'Argonne. Further frustrated by a labyrinth of German trenches and machine gun emplacements, they became disoriented, ending the day having advanced only a mile and lost contact with the French Fourth Army on their left. The 77th Division's infantry "was poorly handled, without any sense of the need to hurry before the enemy brought up reinforcements" and merely "sauntered" into the forest, a senior officer said.[38] The one experienced division in I Corps, the 28th, was able to overrun Varennes but came to a complete stop north and west of the town amid heavy German artillery fire.[39]

That night, Pershing realized the fast advance he had envisioned had been a mirage. And the Germans may have realized the attack was not a feint designed to distract from a thrust toward Metz and were beginning to rush three fresh divisions and part of a fourth to the Meuse-Argonne front. The 1st Army staff was struggling to maintain a semblance of command and control over a large force in an operation far more difficult and complex than the offensive at Saint Mihiel. Pershing responded to lack of progress with threats. In what was the start of a downward lead-

Soldiers from the 77th Division struggle through the dense undergrowth of the Forêt d'Argonne. (*National Archives*)

ership spiral, he not only exhorted subordinate commanders to try harder, but he also threatened to relieve them if they did not achieve his objectives or slacked off.[40]

Over the next three days, the Germans poured in more reinforcements, getting six more divisions into place by September 30. The combined German defensive forces brought the offensive to a standstill and even forced some American units to retreat. "Morale brilliant," the 52nd Jaeger Division reported. "The troops rejoice to have the Americans in front of them and want to attack for the booty."[41]

As the last day of September arrived, the 1st Army slowly clawed its way forward. Four days of bitter fighting had not delivered most of their first-day objectives. As more experienced divisions began to arrive from Saint Mihiel, Pershing ordered the relief of divisions that had lost effectiveness. The 3rd and the 32nd Divisions replaced all three divisions in V Corps, and the veteran 1st Division replaced the 35th Division in I Corps. With those changes in place, Pershing and the 1st Army began to plan for an October 4 resumption of the general attack.

On September 30, while the 1st Army was trying to get the offensive back on track, the Rainbow Division got orders to depart Saint Mihiel for the Meuse-Argonne. Units from the 89th Division moved in as Rainbow infantry regiments moved out. The 166th Infantry, on the front lines in the Saint Benoît Sector, began to pull back that night to lessen chances of the Germans spotting the changeover. Darkness complicated the shift. Roy Bailey, a platoon sergeant in D Company of the 166th, wrote in his diary that he "had a time getting [the] platoon together," but he had them off the line by 10:00 p.m. "Don't know where am taking platoon," he noted in closing for that entry, "but on my way."[42]

Except for the 3rd Battalion, the 166th was off the line by midnight, moving about six miles in an hour to a bivouac on the western edge of the Bois de Pannes. The next morning, the 3rd Battalion was in camp, but only briefly. Orders soon came for the regiment to march to Saint Mihiel that afternoon. Before departing the regiment enjoyed a mail call, the men's first since before the start of the Saint Mihiel assault.[43]

Preceded by "feverish preparations," at 12:30 p.m. on October 1, the 166th started for Saint Mihiel. Arriving around 6:00 p.m., the men found trucks waiting to haul them west of Verdun to join the new offensive.[44] The sight of the convoy rattled many men. The trucks were the same make as they had ridden into the Aisne-Marne Offensive and, as at the Marne, had Vietnamese drivers—a disturbing flashback to horrors they had been trying to forget. Some referred to the drivers as "undertakers," and many "seemed to shy a bit at trucks," a man with the 167th said later.[45]

Once loaded, the trucks rumbled all night. Around 7:00 a.m. on October 2, after a drive of about thirteen miles,[46] the column stopped near Neuville-en-Verdunoi, the men unloaded, and the 166th went into a two-day bivouac. At 9:00 a.m. on October 4, they began a fourteen-mile march northeast to Jubécourt, followed the next day by a twelve-mile foray on foot deep into the Bois de Montfaucon over ground recently captured by the 37th Division. As they marched through the forest, driving rains typical of the French autumn began. At nightfall the wind rose and the temperature fell. Red flashes from artillery lit the northern sky, and a "deep, reverberating murmur at intervals kept alive the fact that the war was no myth, no dream, but terribly real."[47]

The New Yorkers of the 165th Infantry had been in a reserve position on September 30 when the withdrawal order arrived. They moved to the Bois de la Belle Ozière and spent a night, in the morning marching to meet their trucks and make for the Meuse-Argonne. Leaving at 4:00 p.m., the regiment rolled overnight in the cold along a highway that French troops in 1916 had dubbed the *Voie Sacrée* ("Sacred Way") for its vital role in sustaining them at Verdun. On October 2, at about 5:00 a.m., the 165th disembarked to get a "primitive rest" in a wet wood.[48]

At 6:00 p.m., the New Yorkers were marching to Mondrecourt, remaining there, sodden and sleep-deprived, several days. Of that interlude, Martin Hogan later said, "Camping out in a wet wood with one's clothes wet through and a feeling of sogginess even in one's dreams is an adventure that soon stales." The 3rd Battalion's chronically late hours prompted a wag to suggest renaming the unit the "night owl battalion." Another jokester cracked that their marches "would make even Old Broadway jealous." Hitting the road again October 4, men speculated, as ever, about their destination. Hope for a rest camp stay dimmed when the booming from artillery suggested they were traveling parallel to the front, and at an intersection they saw a battered road sign reading "Verdun." Everyone grasped what this meant. "We were heading straight for trouble," Hogan recalled, "and by the shortest route." On October 5, they moved north again toward the Bois de Montfaucon on a road clogged by all the division's infantry.[49]

The 167th Infantry had moved into the Forêt d'Apremont on the night of September 30, departing October 1 by truck. Passing through Lérouville and crossing the Meuse River, the Alabamians passed Ligny-en-Barrois and Bar-le-Duc, reaching Bulainville around midnight. The regiment remained there until October 4, marching north to Parois, a village about twelve miles west of Verdun. At Parois, the regiment camped for a frosty night on a hillside, making an early start toward the Bois de Montfaucon. Fortified by field kitchen coffee and a hot breakfast, they marched through Avocourt amid heavy traffic and the ruins of many small villages.[50]

The 168th Infantry was camped in the Bois de Pannes when ordered west. Like the 167th, they moved to the Forêt d'Apremont on the night of September 30, camping in a field near old German trenches. The very cold night had even more chilling accompaniment: encounters with French skeletons. The Iowans found two found in a shack, rotting equipment at their sides, a legacy of earlier attempts to reduce the Saint Mihiel Salient.[51]

On October 1, with a Meuse-Argonne-bound truck convoy due, Major Robb, the 168th's chaplain from the Church of Christ, held a memorial service. At a crude flag-draped altar, he choked up as he prayed for the war's end and in remembrance of the many men of the regiment who had fallen. As the chaplain concluded his sermon, the band struck up "Onward Christian Soldiers" and men resumed breaking camp.[52]

Late that afternoon, Vietnamese drivers arrived in a mile-long procession and within two hours pulled out for Bar-le-Duc, an eight-hour drive after which the doughboys marched toward Deuxnouds-devant-Beauzée. The night was cloudless and clear, the northern sky illuminated by "sheets of gun-lightning" that seemed "doubly brilliant and alarming." At a sign for Verdun, a man portentously said the name aloud. The men all knew they "weren't in for any picnic this time," John Taber wrote.[53]

In Deuxnouds-devant-Beauzée, their billet was the hard, cold ground in an orchard. While they waited there two days for orders, grisly rumors abounded, such as one that had the Germans flanking and annihilating an entire American corps.

On October 5, the entire 42nd Division, including its artillery, which had been supporting 1st Army's initial advances, crawled amid heavy traffic to the Bois de Montfaucon. The route, through Récicourt, swarmed with pioneers struggling to make the roadway usable for artillery and supply trucks and wagons. Dead stops accounted for over half the time some regiments spent getting to the Bois de Montfaucon. Every village and town through which the division passed was in ruins, a "desolate and hopeless country" made up of "tragic silhouettes against a leaden sky."[54]

At 4:30 a.m. on October 6, the division turned off the muddy artery onto a narrow German-built plank road, and there was the Bois de Montfaucon, the very picture of what happened when industrial war and nature collided. In the last ten days fighting had shattered and splintered the forest's old-growth trees. What remained lay coated green with mustard gas. Craters as deep as fifteen feet so closely pocked the ground that it was impossible to pitch camp in what a man called a "shell-torn graveyard of timber."[55] Charles MacArthur wrote:

> There wasn't a live leaf in twenty miles. Thousands of dead men sprawled in the ulcerated fields. Horses, their legs awkwardly pointing up, general litter and junk. Wagons, rifles, socks, rations, love letters. ... One of the kids [of the 79th Division] lay on the ground dying with a bullet in his guts. He had been yanked from a stenographer's job in New York, trained (as they say) and exposed to his first fire—all in thirty-seven days. He was slightly bewildered by it all.[56]

The Bois de Montfaucon was a horrible place to bivouac—damp, cold, crowded, and filthy—but it was also the only bivouac available, and the division stayed five miserable days awaiting orders to the front. Pershing had resumed the assault on October 4 convinced that his men, slightly rested and reinforced by the veteran 1st and 3rd Divisions, would make that breakthrough he so desperately needed. Instead, the Germans, also

The view looking south toward the grim and uninviting remains of the Bois de Montfaucon. (*National Archives*)

reinforced, held their positions and when they did lose ground, retook it with fierce counterattacks. This resulted in the bloodiest two weeks in American history—that first week of October the 1st Army lost over 6,000 men killed in action; by the end of the second week, more than 12,000 Americans had died in frontal attacks. These losses gained less than a mile of ground.[57]

On October 4, German Prince Max von Baden sent President Wilson a message asking for negotiations that might lead to an armistice. Washington and Berlin had been interacting through neutral countries since August 14. No matter the cost in troops and civilian misery, the Germans intended to keep up the pressure in the Meuse-Argonne, hoping to strengthen their negotiating position.[58]

By the time the Rainbow Division had made camp in the Bois de Montfaucon, cheering rumors of an imminent armistice were rippling through the AEF rank and file. Rainbow Division leaders were doubtful. In the 165th Infantry, Colonel Mitchell and Lieutenant Colonel Donovan feared morale might plummet if talks failed. They asked Father Duffy to query the men on peace talks, and "set them right if necessary." He found some men emphatic about the need to keep pressing the Germans; others just wanted the war to end.[59]

German intelligence had noted the Rainbow Division's arrival. On October 9, a report by the Headquarters of the German Group of Armies characterized American divisions along the Meuse-Argonne front. "The engagement of the 42nd Division is to be expected soon," the report stated of the National Guardsmen Pershing had wanted to relegate to replacement status. "It is in splendid fighting condition and is counted among the best American divisions."[60]

On October 10, orders came for the Rainbow Division to begin replacing the 1st Division along the front line on October 11 and accomplish that task fully by the night of October 11-12. At heinous cost, the 1st Division had done its best to prepare the battlefield so the Rainbow Division could break the Kriemhilde Stellung. On the left of the division's sector, the 1st had taken the ground on the outskirts of the town of Sommerance and captured the heights of the Côte de Maldah about a mile southeast of the town. On the right, the 1st Division had advanced into the Bois de Romagne and driven out German defenders. From these positions, the Rainbow Division was to advance and break the German lines, a brutal job.[61] "The resistance of the enemy was very obstinate," 1st Army G-3 reported. "A strong line of resistance ran from Grandpré to Landres-et-St. Georges."[62]

The 168th Infantry began to move north toward the eastern edge of the division's sector just before midnight on October 10. Clouds deepened the icy gloom as the men stumbled forward. An Iowa soldier said, "It was in many ways the worst march that the regiment ever made."[63]

By the time the Iowans reached the main road, the men were chilled to the bone; many men's nerves were already worn thin. They marched north and around Montfaucon, turning west onto a highway jammed with trucks and French troops. Forced to march roadside, the men endured constant splattering as trucks bounced through mudholes. A few enemy shells went overhead before landing well to the south until the division reached a crossroads at Éclisfontaine. A section of motorized artillery pieces was blocking the way, stopping forward progress. German shells came in, producing "sharp tearing of air" followed by a "deafening burst," as shrapnel sprayed A and B Companies, scything men "like ripe grain before a hail storm."[64]

Private Charles Southwick of B Company recalled that hot metal shards "seemed to come right up under" his helmet. He only realized enemy rounds were incoming when he saw a bright flash and a strong concussion wave struck him "full in the face, neck, and chest." Bent forward as he was under the weight of his pack, the wave hit under his chin like a punch, lifting him into the air. "It seemed that I whirled upward for several seconds," he said, "and I remember dreading the fall." Ears ringing, he briefly lost consciousness. When he awoke, the ringing had stopped. He found himself in the roadway, wounded, and quickly crawled under a truck.[65]

Trapped on the road, men began to run in bewildered confusion as the wounded sobbed and cried out. Officers and sergeants remained cool amid the onslaught, calmly uttering words of caution and encouragement and regaining control. As the wounded were being moved off the road, medical teams arrived and began to treat them. The shelling cost the regiment fifty-four men killed or mortally wounded. Somewhat disheartened, the regiment reformed and continued somberly and silently toward the front.[66]

Covering only nine miles in ten hours, the column paused to rest. A few hours later, after dusk, they were up and moving again. Passing through Exermont they turned north onto muddy, treacherous trails winding up and down steep hills. In one of many ravines, mustard gas from German shells hung in the air like mist, prompting officers to keep the march route on higher ground as much as possible. At the ravine-stitched d'Ariétal Farm, the men had to don gas masks.[67]

It was almost midnight when C and D Companies from the 168th's 1st Battalion reached those units' assigned positions on the north edge of the Bois de Romagne, relieving the 1st Division's 26th Infantry Regiment. The 26th had lost so many men that the entire regiment had fewer soldiers than the 1st Battalion of the 168th. The new arrivals quietly filed into the rough line of foxholes comprising the American front line and settled in. German trenches and fortifications were only about 75 to 100 yards away across the exposed ground of no man's land. The rest of the 168th deployed about three-fourths of a mile to the rear on Hill 263, where the 2nd Battalion soon joined them.[68]

To the Iowans' immediate left was the 167th Infantry. They had also arrived after dark on October 11 and en route been shelled but suffered no casualties. They replaced the men of the 1st Division's 18th Infantry on the western edge of the Bois de Romagne. The 3rd Battalion and the Machine Gun Company move into place along the front line, while the 2nd Battalion was placed in support and the 1st Battalion assumed the reserve position.[69] Like all the other regiments, the Alabamians found themselves surrounded by corpses. At a location that had changed hands two or three times, John Hayes of I Company recalled seeing "scores of unburied soldiers." Every dead man was barefoot; before being driven back, Germans apparently had stripped dead men, friend and foe, of their boots, a "ghoulish expedient." Hayes attributed the morbid scrounging to a desperate equipment shortage. "The spectacle of these dead men despoiled of their shoes," he remembered, "was a gruesome sight, sad and terrible to behold."[70]

The 165th Infantry arrived just to the west of the 167th around 11:00 p.m. on October 11. As 3rd Battalion, assigned the lead position in the line, neared the front, the men passed American and German dead in great numbers among shell holes, along with abandoned equipment. At the front waited not the shelter of trenches but miscellaneous foxholes and craters, as was so all along the front line. The men formed up below the crest of a hill with I and M Companies in the lead and K and L Companies behind in support.[71]

The 166th marched about four miles through rain to positions near Exermont on the night of October 10-11. The regiment halted short so officers and NCOs could reconnoiter the unit's destination along a line near Sommerance designated as Hill 240, Hill 263, and Hill 269. That night, the men quietly advanced to relieve exhausted soldiers of the 1st Division and by dawn were in place. The 2nd Battalion under Major Geran took forward positions southeast of Sommerance, with the 3rd Battalion in support on the southwestern side of Hill 240 and the 1st Battalion in reserve in the Bois de Montrebeau.[72]

The Americans could see why the Germans had been able to hold out so long, and how the same ground would make it hard to resupply the entire Rainbow Division. The rugged landscape was marked by four large conical hills, two in perfect alignment front to rear in each of the division's brigade sectors. The only access to these hills was via deep valleys and ravines over muddy passageways barely qualifying for the term "road." Mud in them ran a foot deep, and runoff made them more canals than paths. Pack animals were useless here, as were ambulances. To get to and from the front everything from food to ammunition to wounded men had to be carried by soldiers.[73]

AEF and 1st Army headquarters had grown profoundly unsettled. Pershing ordered a reorganization in which he relinquished command of 1st Army and divided that force into the 1st Army and 2nd Army. He gave command of the 1st Army to General Liggett and placed the 2nd Army under Major General Robert Bullard. Both men were trusted friends of Pershing's, and he felt confident they could get the offensive on track. He also conducted a draconian housecleaning of senior officers, firing men who had been with the AEF since its arrival in France in 1917. The dismissals raised apprehension in the senior ranks such that some commanders pushed faltering attacks long past any hope of success, costing many lives.[74]

An AEF document, *Notes on Recent Operations No. 3*, dated October 12, 1918, presented useful tactical insights to commanders from the battalion to the division level. But the publication's instructions indicated that AEF leaders had reverted to the disastrous Allied doctrine of 1914-15. The authors criticized some commanders for being overly concerned with reducing casualties and, in a throwback to pre-war American doctrine, said many were relying too heavily on artillery fire to destroy enemy machine guns. Commanders should simply rely on the power of the infantry and their rifles to overcome Maxims, the booklet said. Its contents reflected Pershing's belief that troops needed to be more aggressive. "It is seldom wrong to go forward. It is seldom wrong to attack," the authors wrote. "In the attack it is much better to lose many men than to fail to gain ground."[75]

Multiple 1st and 2nd Army commanders embraced these faulty precepts, at the cost of thousands of American lives, many lost by men of the Rainbow Division.

8

THE ASSAULT ON THE KRIEMHILDE STELLUNG BEGINS, OCTOBER 14, 1918

"The struggle was foot by foot and of the grimmest type."
—Major Walter Wolf, Adjutant, 84th Brigade,
in *A Brief Story of the Rainbow Division*

The night of October 14, 1918, Martin Hogan was in the 165th Regiment's dressing station, a particularly horrible setting.

A corporal in the New York regiment's 3rd Battalion, Hogan had joined up in the summer of 1917. He was as old as the century, which was to say a year short of minimum enlistment age. His older brother was a sergeant in one of the city's other National Guard units, his parents were long dead, and he was single. He saw nothing to keep him from going to France to fight except his age. He decided that was merely an obstacle to overcome. "I felt that I looked old enough to pass a recruiting sergeant, and that the call for men was urgent enough to justify me in camouflaging my age by one year," he wrote later. "Anyhow, I thought, I can go to France and grow up with the war."[1]

Now here he sat among other damaged men. Some, terribly wounded, cried out in agony, wanting only for their pain to end and their bleeding to stop. Others suffered from extreme exhaustion or exposure to cold and rain. Men with "shell shock" sat staring into the distance or shaking uncontrollably, minds damaged by all they had seen and endured. Martin felt perhaps he had no right to be among them because of a bullet wound to his left hand.[2]

He had been hit during a duel with a German sniper at the end of a day of terrible fighting. His 3rd Battalion had gone over the top at 9:00 a.m., seeking to do what the 1st Division and others had been unable to do—break the Germans' vaunted defensive line, the Kriemhilde Stellung. He and his comrades had barely risen from their shell holes when they encountered a blazing gauntlet of machine gun and artillery fire. Men began to fall like kingpins. "This was not to be the walk-away of St. Mihiel," he thought.[3]

After about two hours of fighting through boulders, gullies, brambles, and dark ravines, all lined with deep belts of barbed wire placed with "devilish ingenuity," the assault ground to a halt. There was just no way to advance. "Time and again I had turned corners, crossed stretches, and passed beneath fruit-bearing trees, and, beyond, had paused a moment in surprise at finding myself still alive," Hogan wrote later, "until I had become convinced that I was bullet-proof."[4]

About 12:30 p.m., Hogan was leading his squad into a clearing. He was ten to fifteen paces ahead, approaching a shell hole, when he spied the glint of gunmetal in a tree about twenty yards uphill. He signaled his men to take cover, then dove into the crater. Peering over the lip, Hogan could make out a rifle muzzle occasionally poking out among the dark green leaves of a sharpshooter's hide.[5]

Hogan fired his Springfield several times at where he thought the sharpshooter to be. The shell hole was not much protection given the sniper's elevated position. Hogan's shots seemed only to increase the sniper's "earnestness." The two had exchanged about a dozen shots, with several hitting the ground around the young New Yorker, when the sniper stopped firing. Hogan thought that perhaps his shots were zeroing in, prompting the sniper to bear down in his attempt do away with his foe, what Hogan later called "a very natural and worthy determination."[6]

Hogan reloaded and, as he was taking aim, the man in the tree fired. Hogan felt "a sharp stab" in his left hand. The sniper's slug had hit the back of his hand, "tearing this knuckle away and ripping up the bones and flesh." Hogan ducked as the sniper fired several more shots.[7]

Realizing he was vulnerable to capture, Hogan looked for an angle to play. Another doughboy was crouching nearby in a shell hole to his left. Hogan crawled over to him as the sniper fired again and missed. Hogan wrestled himself into the other crater and had the other man bandage his hand. Looking back, he saw his men setting up a machine gun. He decided to make a run for their position.[8]

He crawled from the hole, ran a few feet, then dropped and crawled, again under fire by the sniper. Reaching safety, he pointed out the sniper. The gunners fired. Hogan's opponent dropped from the tree, likely dead before he hit the ground.[9]

Soon it was dark. Hogan and his men stayed put, awaiting reinforcements or a message telling them to pull back. By 6:00 p.m., neither had arrived. Badly weakened by loss of blood and restless from intense pain, Hogan nonetheless meant to stay with his squad—until an officer arrived and ordered him to head to the rear, no easy task.[10]

Hogan later wrote, "It was still more dangerous to go back than it was to go forward." As he joined a pack of wounded, exhausted men, German barrages found the route to the aid station. Hogan "saw men being carried with legs shattered, with blood-drenched clothes from the flow of ghastly body wounds," and passed by a doughboy "sitting against a tree with half of his head torn away." Hogan figured the dead soldier had been trying to make his way to the dressing station. He must have seated himself by the tree after the first shock to rest and died.[11]

By the time he arrived at the dressing station, Hogan was "half fainting" from blood loss. Medical orderlies cleaned his wound with iodine and put a fresh bandage on his hand. As Hogan looked about, horror overcame him. He wrote later, "So badly wounded were some of the men brought in that the place called to mind nothing so strongly as an abattoir, with human beings as victims." An ambulance crew shuttled him to Evacuation Hospital 110, where doctors amputated his finger.[12]

Martin Hogan's war had ended. For the rest of the Rainbow Division, more death and suffering awaited.

The next phase in the offensive had its genesis the night of October 12 when General Liggett, who Pershing had just reassigned to the post of 1st Army commander, drove south from his V Corps headquarters to 1st Army Headquarters at Souilly. Pershing had invited Liggett to dine with him aboard the AEF commander's private railcar on a siding at Souilly.

Evacuation Hospital 110 where Martin Hogan was treated. (*National Archives*)

When Liggett entered the car, he found Pershing deep in thought while several other officers sat nearby. After a few minutes, Pershing began to talk with Liggett about the lack of progress on the Meuse-Argonne front. He told Liggett the French were pressing him to move faster. Marshal Foch had asked Pershing why the Americans were not advancing as speedily as the British and French elsewhere on the Western Front.[13]

This enraged Liggett and the others at the table. There was no question why the American advance had been so slow, and those at Pershing's dinner believed Foch knew the reason. They reminded Pershing that when the offensive had begun on September 26, only five German divisions had been defending the lines in the Meuse-Argonne. Now the foe had as many as forty divisions in place. Still, Pershing knew he had to do something to get things moving forward.[14]

The AEF commander's plan was to renew the offensive starting October 14. After dinner, General Drum, Pershing's chief of staff, and the 1st Army operations staff at Souilly scrutinized maps. They decided a pincer movement might break the German line. The main effort of the attack would fall on General Pelot Summerall's V Corps, while I Corps protected the V Corps left flank. A stretch of high ground about eight miles wide between the town of Romagne-sous-Montfaucon, on Andon Creek, and Fléville, on the Aire River, controlled a road network that bottlenecked through Landres-et-Saint Georges. That area was also favorable for the assault because, unlike lanes of attack on the far right, it was far from German guns on the Heights of the Meuse. Enemy artillery that had posed so great a threat in the Forêt d'Argonne had been eliminated, disposing of enfilading artillery fire on the assault's left flank. The Rainbow Division and the 32nd Division would take up the V Corps front and push to take two key pieces of terrain: the Côte de Châtillon, southeast of Landres-et-Saint Georges, and the Côte Dame Marie, which overlooked the town of Romagne-sous-Montfaucon.[15]

Pershing and Drum believed these hills to be the keys to breaking the Kriemhilde Stellung. If the hills were taken, the 1st Army could exploit that success by pushing on to seize the Bois de Bantheville, making the remainder of the Kriemhilde Stellung untenable for the Germans. The Rainbow Division was to advance from the Bois de Romagne to take the heights that ran from Saint Georges through Landres-et-Saint Georges to the Côte de Châtillon. Once this line was secure, the 42nd was to swing east into the Bois de Bantheville. On the right wing of this double envelopment, the 3rd and the 5th Divisions of III Corps were to clear Germans from the heights above Cunel and the hills east of Romagne-sous-Montfaucon. Then the 3rd and 5th were to move northwest to assist V Corps in securing the Bois de Bantheville. The 32nd Division, at the center of the envelopment, was to attack the Côte Dame Marie to prevent the Germans from shifting forces to block the wings of the envelopment. To draw attention from the main attacks on the right and left wings, the 32nd Division was to launch its attack three hours prior to the assaults by the 5th and 42nd Divisions.[16]

The Rainbow Division's four infantry regiments would face daunting terrain and defenses, and the terrain the 83rd Brigade would confront on the left differed drastically from that encountered by the 84th Brigade on the right of the division's front. The ground over which the 83rd Brigade was to advance was probably the most level of any along the Meuse-Argonne front. The ground between the lines of the 166th and the 165th Infantry and the German trenches was, for the most part, open save for scattered patches of woods. From the Côte de Maldah, the terrain sloped slightly downhill toward a small stream that ran generally east to west, bordered in places by swampy ground. From there, the terrain rose gradually to the plateau on which the Germans had dug trenches.[17]

Right of the 165th's position, the terrain changed markedly. The plateau rose and was characterized by densely wooded hills. At the center of the plateau was the Côte de Châtillon, a steep, conical hill covered in

Looking east over the interlocking bands of barbed wire towards the Côte de Châtillon from where German machine guns could sweep the right flank pf the 83rd Brigade. (*National Archives*)

dense woods. South of the Côte de Châtillon was the steepest rise, Hill 288, which would have to be taken before moving against the Côte de Châtillon. The slopes of Hill 288 were almost vertical in places, and the ravines around it were heavily wooded with no trails or paths on which to advance. However, between the Côte de Châtillon and Hill 288 was Hill 242, and on the north fringe of the opening between the Bois de Romagne and the woods of the Côte de Châtillon were La Musarde Farm on the west and Le Tuilerie Farm, less than half a mile to the northeast.[18]

The Germans had fully exploited the terrain along this front. The Kriemhilde Stellung was slightly under two miles from the lines of the 83rd Brigade and only about a mile from the 84th Brigade. German defenses there consisted of three lines of barbed wire and trenches. The first bands of wire were breast-high and as much as twenty feet across. Unlike at Saint Mihiel, this barbed wire was well-maintained. The wire bands were tethered to iron supports that formed small squares. This reinforcement would thwart efforts by artillery or Bangalore torpedo to flatten or penetrate the wire. Behind the wire well-constructed trenches about four feet deep sported numerous machine gun emplacements. Further back were two more lines of wire and trenches about thirty yards apart, although these wire bands were lower and the trenches shallower.[19]

Starting from the left of the division's front, these trenches ran west to east just south of Saint Georges and Landres-et-Saint Georges. At Landres-et-Saint Georges, the wire turned southeast toward the American lines to follow the lowest slope of the Côte de Châtillon and embrace La Musarde Farm before swinging east again to Le Tuilerie Farm.[20] This array let the Germans sweep the entire front with devastating Maxim fire, while from the dominating heights of the Côte de Châtillon they could blast the right flank of the advancing 83rd Brigade with enfilading fire. Unless the Americans took the Côte de Châtillon before the 166th and the 165th Infantry advanced, they might not make any gains at all.

All four of the division's infantry regiments had completed relief of the 1st and the 35th Divisions by October 12, as scheduled. At 5:00 p.m. on October 13, 42nd Division Headquarters issued Field Order No. 36, detailing the attack plan for the morning of October 14. The opening paragraph stated, "The enemy is withdrawing on the entire western front." This assertion reflected a fantasy that headquarters staff at AEF and 1st Army seemed determined to perpetuate. German forces had withdrawn voluntarily in places along the front, but not in the Meuse-Argonne Sector. The Germans had never withdrawn from an American front voluntarily and in fact had fought furiously and stubbornly for every inch of ground.[21]

Field Order No. 36 directed the Rainbow Division to advance and seize a line running from about the Bois l'Epasse on the east to Côte 253 and on to the ridge approximately half a mile northwest of Saint Georges. Headquarters expected troops to advance across more than two miles of rough, heavily defended terrain and through three lines of German wire and trenches. The orders also stated that, while the four infantry regiments would attack in parallel areas, they were not assigned the standard single jump-off line that ran through all lanes of attack as at Saint Mihiel. Instead, the jump-off line was echeloned in three different steps with a fourth step for the 32nd Division on its right. The 166th and the 165th Infantry, on the far left of the division front, were the farthest forward, aligned with the jump-off line for the 82nd Division on their left. The jump-off line for the 167th Infantry was slightly forward of that unit's line, while the 168th Infantry jump-off line was to the right rear of the Alabama regiment, creating a gap between the regiments.[22]

To accommodate these echeloned jump-off lines, the orders specified different times for the brigades and their regiments to move forward. The 32nd Division was to advance at 5:30 a.m. The Iowans of the 168th Infantry were to attack as soon as the 32nd Division had moved abreast of its jump-off line. By 8:30 a.m., the orders said, the 168th should have advanced to a point opposite the 167th's jump-off line, at which time the Alabamians would also attack. Once the 167th had reached a point opposite the 166th and 165th's jump-off line, approximately two hours later, the last two regiments would attack.[23]

In addition to the infantry regiments, two companies of the 117th Engineers were assigned one each to the 83rd and the 84th Brigades to assist the infantry in cutting through the bands of barbed wire and to maintain lines of communication to the rear. An artillery platoon of two guns would accompany each of the infantry assault battalions and provide fire support.[24]

Major General Pelot Summerall, commander of V Corps. (*National Archives*)

At 9:30 p.m. on the night of October 13, a revised field order modified the original order; two of those revisions had major impact. One ordered the 83rd Brigade to provide any fire support that it could on enemy positions that might threaten the left flank of the 84th Brigade as the 167th and the 168th advanced. This demonstrated that headquarters recognized that the 83rd Brigade could not successfully advance until the 84th Brigade was abreast.[25]

A second modification, regarding artillery support, had more dire consequences. The original field order reflected the artillery strategy used successfully by the 67th Field Artillery Brigade to support the advance of the 1st Division. This strategy, a major departure from historical American artillery planning, called for all division guns to focus on key target areas, shifting fire according to advancing infantry units' demands. In this case, this meant that, as the attack began, all guns were to pound the area confronting the 167th and the 168th Infantry on the right of the advance. The original order specified, "Especial attention will be devoted by the divisional artillery to: Côte de Châtillon—Hill 262—Northern part of Bois de Romagne—Hill 288 and Enemy Trenches." Annex 1 to *The Plan for the Employment of Artillery* provided further detail regarding concentration of artillery fire.[26]

Almost as soon as the original field order reached the affected artillery units, the 67th Field Artillery Brigade Headquarters countermanded the planned approach in a memorandum dictating a return to traditional strategy in which all division guns provided a uniform barrage across the entire division front. This change remains a mystery, as everyone from the V Corps commander, General Summerall, to 67th Field Artillery Brigade commander General George Gatley were strong advocates of using specific concentrations of artillery fire to support infantry. Most historians seem to believe the change reflected a critical shortage of artillery ammunition. As 1st Army advanced away from SOS railheads and traffic jammed highways, ammunition deliveries lagged.[27]

This and challenges presented by the terrain and German defenses caused great concern among tactical commanders at the brigade and regimental levels. On the night of October 13, after the field order had arrived, been amended, and been digested by staffs, General Lenihan, the 83rd Brigade commander, called a meeting at his P.C. with Colonel Hough of the 166th, Colonel Mitchell of the 165th, and Colonel Reilly from the artillery brigade. Lenihan began the meeting by asking Hough and Mitchell for their thoughts on the attack plan. Each said he thought the attack would be very difficult because men would be advancing into a salient whose front and right face were held by German forces deployed in a well-fortified, naturally strong position. Pointing to the map, they indicated that the Côte de Châtillon dominated the terrain and provided the Germans a clear view of the land over which the Ohioans and New Yorkers had to advance. From that high ground, Germans could pour severe flanking fire onto the right of the assault force—unless the Americans secured that hill before their men attacked. Hough and Mitchell said they did not believe the 167th and 168th could push through the considerable obstacles impeding them and take the Côte de Châtillon in the three hours dictated by the field order.[28]

Reilly agreed with Hough and Mitchell, calling the artillery change a mistake. He said he believed that the Alabamians and the Iowans would need concentrated fire support if they were to move over Hills 288 and 242 to take the Côte de Châtillon in the time allocated. The three colonels suggested Lenihan communicate these grave concerns to General Menoher, the Rainbow Division commander, and request not only the artillery ammunition needed for concentrated fire support but more time for the 167th and 168th to take the Côte de Châtillon before their regiments began advancing. Lenihan listened intently but ended the conference

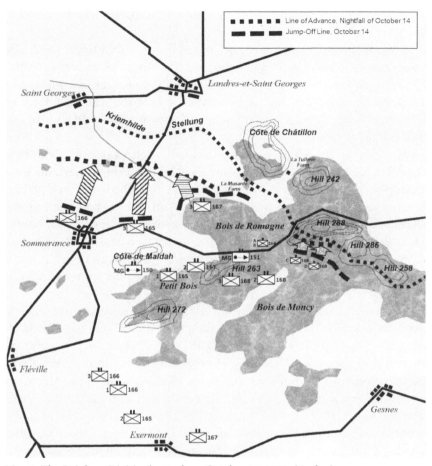

Map 8. The Rainbow Division's attack on October 14, 1918. (*Author*)

without deciding about the suggested changes to the plan of attack.[29] The flawed plan stood.

The infantry regiments prepared for their attack through the night and into the early hours of October 14. On the right, where the challenges posed by the foe and the terrain were most severe, Major Lloyd Ross of the 168th Infantry's 1st Battalion reported to regimental headquarters by telephone that his battalion and its machine gun company were in position. Colonel Mathew Tinley told Ross about the early morning timing of the attack and the great responsibility being placed on him and his men. Tinley said General MacArthur had declared, "Ross is the absolute key to the whole situation."[30]

Ross, from Red Oak, Iowa, had joined the state militia in 1893. His company was mobilized into federal service in 1898 and sent to the Philippines. He saw combat in the insurrection and returned home in 1899. By October 1918, he had become an officer some characterized as a "natural soldier," and a "man of great judgement who could control sizable bodies of troops."[31]

Hanging up the telephone, Ross decided to send a patrol to pinpoint the enemy in his front. He knew planners at higher headquarters, working from plots on a map, were struggling to determine the front lines' precise locations. His concern was that the jump-off line he had been given, slightly forward of his current position, actually might be in enemy hands. He ordered Lieutenant Raymond Turner to lead a patrol of fifteen scouts from A Company as well as five men from D Company to reconnoiter the proposed jump-off position along the line of hills from Hill 286 to Hill 288.[32]

Turner selected his men, who included his second-in-command, Sergeant William Fleming. In darkness the patrol moved out, paralleling an old grass road up the slopes of Hill 288 with Sergeant Fleming and six men taking the point. They were approaching a fork in the road about 500 yards west of the hill's summit when Fleming spotted two Germans about 200 yards up the road. He alerted Turner, who halted the patrol and checked his bearings on the map. The Germans were well within the sector incorporating the 1st Battalion's jump-off line. Turner was discussing the situation with another officer when Fleming suggested he take a small detail up the road to see if there were any more Germans there and to try to capture the two he had seen.[33]

Turner agreed. The sergeant chose six privates. Fleming would take the lead with three men close behind him and the others about twenty yards back. Turner and the rest of the patrol remained about fifty yards in the rear to support them. As Fleming and his men crept forward, machine gun fire erupted from the crest of the hill where a German trench crossed the road. Two of Fleming's men were killed. The survivors scattered. Turner advanced his group until enemy fire drove them to take cover. Some thirty Germans who had been lying in wait to ambush the patrol moved between Turner's position and Fleming's men. Fleming returned fire. Another of his men was badly wounded. The sergeant ran out of ammunition. Germans pounced, knocking Fleming unconscious with a rifle butt. They dragged him and the wounded soldier to their rear. The wounded man died four days later. Fleming remained in enemy hands until war's end.[34]

Turner returned and reported to Major Ross. At no small cost he had confirmed that the Germans held the position assigned the battalion as its jump-off line. Ross immediately chose a position to the south of the hill as his new jump-off line.[35]

Ross moved C Company and D Company into the new positions south of Hill 288 in the north edge of the Bois de Romagne facing La Musarde Farm. Their assignment would be to take Hill 288, then seize Hill 242, about half a mile north. They then were to take a strong point centered around La Tuilerie Farm at the base of the Côte de Châtillon. All this was to occur within 90 minutes, even without opposition an imposing undertaking given the rough, heavily wooded terrain. A Company and B Company were in support at the bend of the road northeast of Côte 263, and the 2nd Battalion moved into position on the south slope of Hill 263.[36]

About 8:00 p.m. that evening, Ross learned that the 127th Infantry of the 32nd Division, which was to advance on his right, had not received any orders for the attack and was making no preparations to advance. While attempting to sort out this miscommunication, Ross heard a rumor that the attack had been called off because the Germans had accepted President Wilson's peace terms. Absent substantiation, Ross continued his preparations to attack.[37]

To the Iowans' left, Alabama's 167th Infantry also spent the night staging. Colonel Screws, the regiment's commander, had been hospitalized with influenza; the very capable Lieutenant Colonel Walter Bare was in command. Because the 3rd Battalion had not participated in the attack at Saint Mihiel and was in better shape than the other two battalions, Bare assigned them as the assault battalion. He moved the 2nd Battalion into the support position on the forward slope of Hill 263 about half a mile to the rear and placed the 1st Battalion in reserve on the rear slope of the hill. The only problems the regiment had that night were from friendly artillery that kept dropping rounds short and onto the 167th and 168th, causing casualties neither regiment could afford.[38]

The other unit preparing on the right was Georgia's 151st Machine Gun Battalion, which moved into position along with the 3rd Battalion of the 167th on the forward slope of Hill 263. The 151st commander, Major Cooper Winn, felt he had proven the value of mass overhead machine gun fire at Saint Mihiel and in the dual raids on Haumont-les-Lachaussee and the Marimbois Farm. Winn was very confident that, properly organized and employed, his guns could provide the dedicated fire support the infantry would need. He and his battalion were placed under the direct command of General MacArthur and were assigned to provide fire support against the Germans on the Côte de Châtillon.[39]

As soon as the 167th's lead battalion was in place on October 12, Winn began to deploy men and guns. At first, he had trouble positioning his battalion because the unit he was relieving had their machine guns deployed with the departing infantry battalions. Winn took matters into his own hands. He moved his B Company and D Company into position on Hill 263 with his two other companies in the rear near Exermont. Ordered to provide mass overhead fire support for the October 14 assault, he personally placed all sixty-four of his Hotchkiss guns high on the forward slope of Hill 263, from which gunners could shoot down into all of the Côte de Châtillon. Winn sighted target areas himself and provided written instructions for each of the sixty-four guns, including their respective targets and times for engagement. He himself saw to the ammunition supply; by the time the assault was to begin, he had brought up more than a million rounds.[40]

In New York's 165th Infantry, Colonel Mitchell had decided to place command of all the men at the front under the redoubtable Lieutenant Colonel Donovan. Mitchell would remain at the regiment's P.C. in Exermont with Captain Merle-Smith, the operations officer, while the intelligence officer, Lieutenant Lawrence Living, relayed information from an observation post to the rear of the front. Donovan assigned I Company and M Company of the 3rd Battalion as the lead elements for the assault, with K Company and L Company in immediate support to their rear.[41]

"The sun never shone," wrote Father Duffy, "and a large part of the time it rained steadily." Low clouds foreshortened the views aloft from observation balloons. Donovan labored to get ammunition and food over flooded trails. Rampant moisture in the air and on the ground hampered communications. Field telephones often failed and neither horses nor men could traverse what had become "seas of mud."[42]

That night, Donovan sent a patrol to scout the sunken road chosen as the regiment's jump-off line. The patrol reported that, as best they could tell, the Germans had no men between the regiment's front and the jump-off line. Donovan made his way along the line to remind his battalion and company commanders not to use the attack formation standard in a

Machine gunners of the 151st Machine Gun Battalion, seen here with their French comrades. (*Major William Carraway, Historian, Georgia Army National Guard*)

simultaneous advance, instead adapting to the echeloned jump-off lessons learned at Saint Mihiel and the Ourcq, with men advancing in small groups, running and crawling until they could infiltrate enemy trenches.[43]

Surveying the terrain to the 165th's front, Donovan saw a gap of mostly open ground to the right between them and the Bois de Romagne. The Sommerance to Romagne-sous-Montfaucon road ran in front of the Côte de Maldah before turning up through the same gap between the 165th and 167th, and then through the Bois de Romagne and over the crest of Hill 288. The terrain to the immediate front of the Côte de Maldah was "entirely open and devoid of any cover except a few small groups of trees and holes in the ground." But the ground just beyond the Sommerance to Romagne-sous-Montfaucon road dipped where a small stream ran. This depression offered at least some cover and was to the immediate left of the northern edge of the Bois de Romagne from which the 167th was to be attacking. Donovan chose the low spot for a jump-off line. Like everyone else, he could see the Côte de Châtillon to his right, and he realized that unless the 167th and 168th secured the hill, the Germans would be able to hit his men hard with fire on their right flank.[44]

Donovan had never agreed with the attack plan. Like almost everyone else, he could see the importance of taking the Côte de Châtillon, whose capture was key to any successful assault. He had proposed to advance his men until they were abreast of the wire to their right and hold that line with just enough men to ward off counterattacks while the rest of the regiment swung into position to the immediate left of the 167th and the 168th. The 165th could attack the Côte de Châtillon from the west while the Alabamians and Iowans assaulted the hill from the south. Once the hill was secured, the 165th could turn west and attack the German flank to take Landres-et-Saint Georges. No one at division headquarters had been interested in his plan and they insisted on a direct frontal attack across the division's front.[45]

To Donovan's left, the Ohioans of the 166th moved their 2nd Battalion under Major Geran into line as the assault battalion. Geran's plan was for G Company and H Company to lead the attack with E Company and F Company right behind. On Geran's left was the 325th Infantry of the 82nd Division, and his own H Company was placed about a half-mile south of the town of Sommerance. G Company, which had driven the Germans out of the town on the night of October 12, would step off from protected positions in Sommerance.[46]

The division's artillery opened fire as scheduled, spreading limited ammunition across the entire division front. October 14 dawned "dark, misty, and forbidding," which did little to assuage the fears of men waiting to advance. They had slept, if what they had done could be called sleep, in muddy foxholes, wearing summer underclothes with one blanket per man and no overcoats. They arose stiffly, steeling themselves. The Germans sensed something was coming and added their heavy artillery to the friendly guns' roar.[47]

Enemy machine gunners also went to work. A pair of Maxims was ravaging Company D of the 168th's 1st Battalion. Lieutenant Roger Spaulding called Sergeant Bernard Nelson over. "There's a couple of Boche machine guns out there," he said, "think we'll have to get them."

Nelson looked calmly toward the German emplacement. "Think we will, lieutenant," he replied. "How many men shall I take?"

Before Spaulding could answer, Nelson chose two squads and, using the dense morning mist as cover, led the men through brush, cutting barbed wire and crawling up the slope and behind the German gunners' trench. One enemy soldier was sitting quietly on the trench lip, smoking a cigarette. At Nelson's signal, the Iowans rushed into the trench with a wild yell, killing all twelve Germans and destroying the Maxims. Thirty minutes later, Nelson and his men were back inside the 168th's lines. Reporting to Lieutenant Spaulding, the sergeant simply said, "We got the

Soldiers from New York's 165th Infantry prepare to advance towards Landres-et-Saint Georges. (*National Archives*)

guns, lieutenant," and walked back to his platoon as if he had been strolling in a park.[48]

When H-Hour arrived at 5:30 a.m., Major Ross waited on the far right of the division front for word from the 127th Infantry of the 32nd Division that the 127th had advanced abreast of the 168th's lines and was ready to protect his right flank. Without that protection, Ross's battalion would face severe enfilading fire from Maxims atop Hill 286 able to sweep the entire valley between their jump-off line and the slopes of Hill 288. By 7:30 a.m., there was still no sign of the 127th, and Ross received orders to advance immediately with or without flank support. The orders also told him to take Hill 288 no matter the cost.[49]

Ross sent word to prepare to advance down the line to his companies. Friendly artillery support had never really touched Hill 288 and the German trenches that ran across it, so Colonel Tinsley had the headquarters company's Stokes mortar platoon shell the enemy positions for fifteen minutes before Ross's men went over the top. At 8:00 a.m., C Company and D Company climbed out of their foxholes and advanced, followed by A Company, B Company, and the 2nd Platoon of the machine gun company.[50]

As soon as they appeared, they met a "hail of steel." Part of the advancing line took advantage of limited cover in dense woods, but Germans on Hill

288 could see them coming and poured artillery and machine gun fire into the valley below. The Iowans hit the ground and crawled steadily forward, using every bit of cover they could find. Watching from Hill 263, General MacArthur reminded Colonel Tinley that Hill 288 had to be taken or the rest of the division could not advance. Tinley turned to Major Stanley and told him he should throw the entire regiment into the effort if necessary.[51]

At 8:30 a.m., while the 168th was fighting across the valley toward Hill 288, the 167th began to advance to their left. The Alabamians' 3rd Battalion led the attack with K Company and L Company in the van and M Company and I Company supporting. K Company was supposed to maintain contact with the 168th on the right but fierce resistance against the Iowans prevented effective cooperation, creating a large gap between the two regiments. As soon as the 3rd Battalion began to advance from the Bois de Romagne, German observers on the Côte de Châtillon directed a very heavy and accurate barrage their way.[52]

Amid artillery and machine gun fire, the Alabamians in K Company had managed to advance about 200 yards when they encountered the first of the enemy's heavy barbed wire belts, well-engineered and without a trace of rust or breakage. American artillery shells had had virtually no impact on the wire, and the men from the 117th Engineers could make a pathway through the tangles only with wire cutters or Bangalore torpedoes. All K Company could do was occupy a narrow strip of the Côte de Châtillon inside the enemy wire and use rifle grenades to drive Maxim gunners from the cover of La Musarde Farm.[53]

L Company was able to advance about 300 yards on the right because wire entanglements there ran diagonally across the regiment's front, so L Company did not reach the wire as soon as K Company. About 9:40 a.m., K Company stopped in a narrow woods west of La Musarde Farm because of heavy flanking machine gun fire from the Côte de Châtillon. On Lieutenant Colonel Bare's orders, the two lead companies dug in where they were because Bare saw the futility of attempting a frontal assault on the Côte de Châtillon under these conditions. He also moved I Company in between K Company and L Company and assigned H Company to move forward to the left and make contact with the right wing of the 165th Infantry.[54]

The New Yorkers of the 165th jumped off at 8:30 a.m., as did the 167th to their right and the 166th to their left. Despite Donovan's concerns, those units advanced even though the Côte de Châtillon remained in German hands.

The view south from the ridges above Saint Georges and Landres-et-Saint Georges toward the ground over which the 165th and 166th Infantry would try to advance. (*National Archives*)

As soon as I Company and M Company reached a line abreast of the northern edge of the Bois de Romagne, they began to take fire from Maxim guns on the Côte de Châtillon and directly to their front in trenches south of Landres-et-Saint Georges. German artillery fire joined the deadly mix, as did strafing German aircraft. M Company tried to stay in contact with L Company of the 167th but the Alabama advance stalled, exposing the New Yorkers' right flank. As they moved through the ravine where the small stream ran across their front, the New Yorkers found a little cover in a patch of woods, but not enough to lessen the toll being inflicted on the regiment's right flank by Germans firing from the Côte de Châtillon.[55]

Seeing men on the right falling, Donovan turned to the battalion commander, Major Thomas Reilley. "'Where the hell is that coming from?" Donovan asked. Reilley told him the fire was coming from the Côte de Châtillon. "We're worse off here than we would be if we moved forward," Donovan said. Urging men on, Donovan, Reilley, and the rest of the battalion crossed the stream into the small woods on the far slope. A few reached the first belt of wire, but withering machine gun fire swept them as they tried in vain to cut their way through. Donovan recalled, "Those who got into the wire were killed or wounded." Everyone else halted on the slope above the stream and took whatever cover they could.[56]

Martin Hogan was in the 3rd Battalion support line as the 3rd advanced. Passing through the woods along the stream, men in his company found Germans hiding among the trees, leading to what he called "many a beautiful individual fight." "Every bad tangle was a machine gun nest," Hogan recalled, "and every tree was a turret." He watched men suddenly disappear off the path into a thicket to emerge a few minutes later, "their bayonets clotted with red."[57]

The companies in the lead, I Company and M Company, were receiving "stinging fire" from seemingly every angle. Hogan recalled that the "whole front was a series of individual actions and short-ranged duels." Soon, L Company and K Company caught up with the two lead companies. Germans, apparently thinking the New Yorkers were going to withdraw, began shelling the rear of the American position, their snipers firing on anyone still trying to cross the stream.[58]

Around 11:00 a.m., the 165th's advance slowed but sustained its intensity. "Each man was putting into the fight all of his strength, all of his skill as a marksman, all of his acuteness of vision, and all that he had learned about fighting against men in cover," Hogan wrote. The forward line of German machine guns was well-placed and almost impossible to approach. Despite this, Hogan's comrades would rush the gunners "in a headlong charge, by encircling, by being stumbled upon accidentally, fallen into, and captured after silent arguments with blood-dripping bayonets." Doughboys fell everywhere. Men "would break out before a thicket, and far ahead the rat-a-tat would sing, and a man would lie clawing frenziedly at stones and tangled roots." Men would rise and run toward a patch of woods when snipers or hidden machine guns opened fire, "leaving some of their number in death convulsions on the ground and others sorely wounded."[59]

The Ohioans of the 166th went over the top at the same time as the 165th on their right and units from the 82nd Division on their left. The 2nd Battalion jumped off about 200 yards north of Sommerance with G Company on the right and H Company on the left. E Company and F Company in order from right to left followed close behind in support. Facing relentless machine gun fire from the enemy trenches south of Saint Georges, the leading elements of both G Company and H Company took Hill 230 about a mile south of the German lines around 9:30 a.m. and dug in amid heavy artillery and machine gun fire.[60]

On the left, H Company was being fired on by German machine guns emplaced in several patches of woods west of Hill 230. Maxim by Maxim,

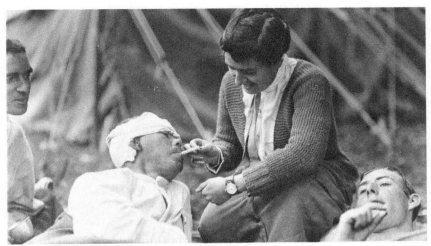

Private Ernest Stambach of the 165th Infantry's K Company at an Evacuation Hospital after being wounded on October 14, 1918. (*National Archives*)

the Americans cleared these woods using rifles, grenades, and bayonets, taking some eighty prisoners. Orders came to push on and break the German lines south of Saint Georges, which was impossible against such heavy resistance and with little to no friendly artillery support.[61]

By day's end, Major Geran's 2nd Battalion had suffered more than 300 casualties. As in the Aisne-Marne and at Saint Mihiel, most were recent arrivals. While the regiment was still bivouacked in the Bois de Montfaucon before the attack, Geran's battalion had received 300 replacements. None had had more than four weeks of training before being sent to France, and Geran's veterans had no time to school them. Geran tried to distribute new men among veterans. Only hours before the attack, he learned that many of these replacements had never been taught how to load or fire a rifle. Veterans were trying to give a crash course on weapons. "Of the 300 men we lost that day, 240 of them were these new men, and the majority of the balance were non-commissioned officers who lost their lives in attempting, during the fighting, to keep these untrained men from bunching up," Geran said later.[62] Once again, the AEF's process for training and assigning replacements had amounted to little more than murder.

Back on the division's right flank, the 168th struggled slowly forward. Clearly they were not going to meet the deadlines set for them to take Hill

288 and the Côte de Châtillon. The left of C Company, advancing on the regiment's right, had been firmly anchored, but the right wing was taking heavy fire and could not advance an inch. The situation was in doubt until a small group of men from the company's headquarters company began to move stealthily through the wire belt and dense brush toward the German guns on the crest of Hill 288. Once in position with good cover, they brought their rifles to bear on the machine gunners, achieving complete surprise. The enemy quickly fled, and the Iowans seized the first part of the Kriemhilde Stellung.[63]

By this time, Major Winn had his machine guns on Hill 263 pouring fire into the German trenches. With this supporting fire, C Company came up on a new line, while D Company was able to fill out the line on the left. The Iowa infantrymen began to crawl across the valley. When they were within a few yards of the enemy, Winn had his guns lift their fire. This was the signal for the infantry to leap into the German trenches, whose startled occupants they quickly subdued.[64] With this action, the crest of Hill 288, which some considered the "keystone of the Kriemhilde Stellung,"[65] was in American hands. But the vital forward slope, site of the main German defenses, remained in enemy control.

Fire from the Germans on Hill 286 harassed the Iowans until the 127th Infantry took the hill. As late afternoon approached, Major Ross organized his men to seize German trenches lining the forward slope of Hill 288. He had A Company and B Company move forward to relieve C Company and D Company and form the lead wave.

The Germans were ready, secure behind a barbed wire belt that "ran from tree to tree like the matted undergrowth of a jungle." The attacking Iowans could not surmount "murderous fire" and get close enough to rush the trenches. B Company, which attacked on the left, managed to push through into the woods they faced, unaware that C Company was not able to cover B's right flank. Suddenly wire was blocking their path and, as machine gun fire raked them, the company fell back and dug in. B Company remained in its own small salient until dark, when the men withdrew to the battalion's line.[66]

While that fight was occurring, the 167th remained in position to the 168th's left, unable to advance. The 165th and 166th, also stalemated, were fending off counterattacks. The division had advanced about a mile on the left toward Saint Georges and Landres-et-Saint Georges and on the right had taken the crest of Hill 288, but their objectives remained remote. The trenches running east to west below Saint Georges and Landres-et-

Saint Georges and most of the Côte de Châtillon, the key to breaking the Kriemhilde Stellung, were still in enemy hands.

9

TAKING HILL 288 AND HILL 242, OCTOBER 15, 1918

"The enemy's resistance on the front of our army is breaking."
—Field Order No.37, Headquarters, 42nd Division,
October 14, 1918, 11:30 p.m.

Captain Mike Walsh, an expert marksman Father Duffy described as a "rugged, whole-souled soldier and leader of men,"[1] stood out among the 165th Infantry's officers in that he had once served in the Regular Army. Between his time in the Regular Army and the National Guard, he had accumulated twenty-seven years of service.[2] To Walsh's great frustration, the knowledge he had gained in all those years made him indispensable to the regiment's rear echelon, chaining him to a succession of desk jobs. He continually pressed to serve in combat. On the night of October 13-14, 1918, he was told to report to Major Tom Reilley's 3rd Battalion where he was to command I Company. He immediately made his way to Reilley at the front facing Landres-et-Saint Georges. Barely able to contain his enthusiasm, Walsh told Reilley, "After twenty-seven years I am finally in the war."[3] Reilley later recalled, "Walsh seemed like a kid out of school."[4]

The next morning, as the regiment was advancing against intense resistance, Walsh's men received fire. Reilley had come to I Company's position. He and Walsh were conferring when bullets hit nearby, making a "plopping" sound.

"That's a sniper," Walsh said. "That means a chance for us."

Enlisting a young private, Walsh set off with him. After a prolonged search, they spotted a rifleman hiding in bushes on a hillside at a turn in the road about 600 yards away.[5]

Walsh unstrapped his Springfield and aimed. His shot went wide. The sniper replied in kind. The two exchanged several shots, whereupon the German jumped from cover and began sprinting uphill toward the main line of enemy trenches. Walsh took aim and hit the German, who threw up his arms, dropped his rifle, and fell dead. Walsh returned to his company.

"I'm in the army now," he told Reilley. "I'm out of the boy scouts at last."[6]

That night, Major Reilley heard Walsh had been wounded. He headed for a sunken road where I Company had dug in. He found Walsh in a shell hole with his men.

"What is the matter, Mike?" Reilley asked. "Are you hit?"

"Yes, I am hit in the arm," Walsh said, revealing "a long tearing wound" made by a sniper's bullet.[7]

"That's all right, Mike," Reilley replied. "You have it coming to you. You will now get a nice rest between white sheets with plenty to eat and be warm and comfortable and come back to us when you are well again. You go back now and get your arm fixed."

Walsh protested that he did not want to leave his men, but Reilley was adamant. He said the regiment had to stay put for the moment, so Walsh was to head to the rear for treatment and hospital rest, then rejoin the battalion.[8]

A disappointed Walsh asked if that was an order.

"You're damn right it is."

Walsh smiled, turned over command to one of his lieutenants, and began the long hike to the regiment's dressing station.[9]

Just before dawn, Reilley was crouched in his shell hole with men from the battalion staff when Private Edward Healy of Walsh's company slid in beside him.

"Major, as we were coming up just at dusk tonight, we saw the body of Captain Walsh on the right of the road about 150 or 175 yards in the rear of the sunken road," Healy said. "The whole back of his head is caved in." Apparently, the concussion from an artillery round had killed Walsh. For his one day in combat, Walsh had paid the ultimate price, one that many more men would pay in the days ahead. Letting the news sink in, Healy said to Reilley, "We would like to go out and bring his body in."[10]

"I will give you no such order," Reilley said. "He is dead, and I am not sending live men after dead men. But I am not stopping you."

Healy got another soldier to help him, and the two carried the captain's body to the rear. Healy was careful not to tell anyone else in the company that their commander was dead. Father Duffy later said, "It was well for his Company that they did not know the misfortune they had sustained because no loss in our whole campaign was more deeply felt."[11]

Walsh, posthumously awarded the Distinguished Service Cross, lies in the Meuse-Argonne American Cemetery, Plot F, Row 1, Grave 9, one of more than 14,000 American soldiers buried there.[12]

The night of October 14, the men along the Rainbow Division's front got what rest they could a few thousand yards from the enemy. Their commanding officers took stock, reorganized, and tried to make sure all was in readiness for the morning attack. At higher echelons, staff officers pondered how to improve that attack's prospects by having a force move down the far side of Hill 288, up and over Hill 242, and seize the Côte de Châtillon.

A first plan, from General Menoher and General MacArthur, was distributed to the 167th and 168th just after dark on October 15. This approach called for three companies from the 167th to join the 1st Battalion of the 168th in a night bayonet assault—no gunfire—on the Côte de Châtillon.

The field officers, knowing the ground involved, instantly recognized the idea's complete insanity.[13] Men would be trying to find their way through dense woods and underbrush in the dark to try to penetrate barbed wire engineers could not cut through in broad daylight. The orders called for the 167th Infantry to attack from a woods southwest of La Musarde Farm, while the 168th Infantry advanced north toward La Tuilerie Farm and on to the Côte de Châtillon. As the Iowans had learned, it was impossible to move in that direction because of the wire and machine gun fire on the 168th's front and right flank. To clear the wire and evade the Maxims the 168th would have to make a flanking movement to the left. This would cause the regiments to collide and intermingle in the dark.[14] Major Ross, whose battalion had been tagged to make the assault, recommended in the strongest possible terms these orders be rescinded. Colonel Tinley called 84th Brigade Headquarters to relay Ross's concerns. The 168th's orders were soon withdrawn; those for the 167th's attack remained in place.

Major Ravee Norris of the 167th viewed those orders with "surprise and consternation." Norris, whose three companies were supposed to make the attack, telephoned the 167th P.C. to lodge a vehement protest, telling Lieutenant Colonel Bare, "It is nothing short of murder to send men in on such an assault when everything which has happened during the past two days and two nights has shown that such an attack simply cannot succeed." Step by step, Norris enumerated his deep concerns.

"I am sorry, Norris, but this is a direct order and must be obeyed," Bare replied.[15]

Norris decided he could not agree to the orders until he had at least spoken to Bare in person. As he was leaving his P.C., two of his company commanders approached him. "What in hell does this order mean? Such an attack will never succeed," the two officers said practically in unison. "You know that, Norris, as well as we do!" Norris told them that until and unless the order was rescinded, they would have to attack as ordered and that they should start preparations immediately.[16]

Talking with Bare at the regimental P.C., Norris could see that the lieutenant colonel felt the same. But Bare continued to maintain that unless General MacArthur cancelled the orders the attack was on. Norris returned to his battalion P.C. "decidedly down cast." He said later that he knew this sort of attack "could not succeed and that the more courageously it was pushed the greater the number of men who would be killed and wounded trying to do the impossible."[17]

No final order to execute the plan came the next day. Apparently, Colonel Tinley's protest had made a difference with MacArthur. At 6:00 p.m. Norris received a summons to be at the regimental P.C. in the morning. Expecting to be relieved, he packed his musette bag, shook hands with all the battalion officers, and said his goodbyes. He turned over command of the battalion to his senior captain, I Company's Thomas Fallow, and headed through the woods to see Lieutenant Colonel Bare.[18]

At Bare's P.C., the regiment's commander told Norris the bayonet attack had been cancelled. "We have other plans," Bare said. "And we want you here so that there can be no mistakes." Norris said his "spirits went about as far up as they had been down," a glee not from being cashiered but being spared, he said later: "Rather, it was the thought that the lives and limbs of the men for whom I was responsible and many of whom I not only knew but also knew their parents were not to be needlessly sacrificed."[19]

1st Army Headquarters decided that, despite casualties and lack of success, the Rainbow Division must resume its attack and continue until the division achieved its original objectives. At 11:30 p.m. on October 14, 42nd Division Headquarters issued Field Order No. 37, directing a resumption of the assault on the morning of October 15. The first paragraph read, "The enemy's resistance on the front of our army is breaking." Division historian Henry Reilly later wrote, "The first paragraph was cheering, but not convincing, particularly in so far as the 83rd Infantry Brigade and the Alabama Regiment on its right flank, which faced both north and east, were concerned."[20]

The order stipulated the same zones of action as the previous day's order. Artillery would fire on the Germans from 7:15 a.m. to 7:30 a.m. before lifting so the barrage could shift 300 yards while the infantry transited enemy wire belts. At 7:40 a.m., beneath a rolling barrage, the 166th and the 165th were to advance. The 167th and the 168th were to "exploit" the Côte de Châtillon and the woods near La Tuilerie Farm.[21]

At 1:00 a.m., 83rd Brigade Headquarters issued a field order directing the 166th Infantry to resume its assault on Saint Georges at 7:30 a.m. L and M Companies from the 3rd Battalion were to make up the first wave, with I and K Companies in the second.[22]

The 83rd's plan included a potentially important element. Throughout the offensive, the 1st Army had used armor, mostly French-built Renault PT light tanks, but breakdowns sapped the machines' effectiveness. At one point, over half of the 1st Army's tanks were inoperable. For the day's attack, the 1st Army planned to provide sixteen tanks from the U.S. 3rd Tank Brigade, commanded by Lieutenant Colonel George Patton.[23]

At sunrise, the men from the 3rd Battalion were waiting for their tanks to show. At 6:20 a.m., the Germans began to send high explosive and gas shells into the regiment's positions around Sommerance. German infantry counterattacked an hour later. At H-Hour, 7:30 a.m., the regiment, still tankless, moved forward as scheduled.[24]

Not long after the 3rd Battalion got under way, the regiment received messages that the tanks would arrive soon. The regiment's men crept across no man's land, and M Company sent patrols into woods to deal with German infantry whose numbers turned out to be considerable. In

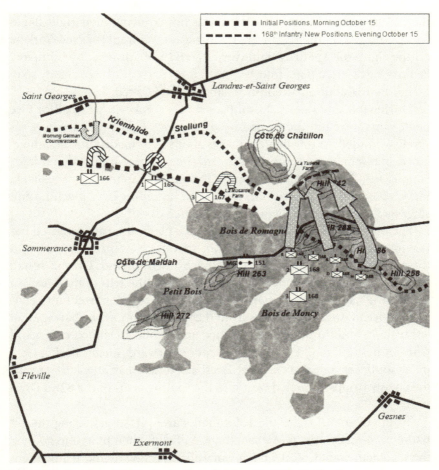

Map 9. The Rainbow Division's attack on October 15, 1918. (Author)

a brief firefight, the Americans inflicted heavy casualties on the enemy, who quickly withdrew. M Company lost twenty men.[25]

The rest of the assault was getting nowhere, and, at 8:55 a.m., word came that there would be no tanks after all. So many of the sixteen tanks allocated for the attack had broken down that Patton had had to withdraw and reorganize.[26]

At 9:35 a.m., a call went out for a barrage to sweep all enemy trenches in the zone. The gunners went to work at 10:15 a.m., firing until noon. The infantry from the regiment again tried to advance but discovered that the 165th, unable to move forward, was not covering their right flank, which Maxims on the right were raking again. Without the New Yorkers on the right, the 166th's assault waves could not advance. M Company kept trying. By 1:30 p.m., four failed attempts had cost the company sixty men.[27] By nightfall, all attempts to advance had halted.

During that day's attack, I Company officers took heavy casualties. Five lieutenants were hit; the company commander, Captain Grave, was severely wounded. As one lieutenant was about to be loaded into an ambulance, he sent a message to the 3rd Battalion commander, Major Haubrich: "Please send tanks at once. Excuse holes in this message blank, but it's the only one I have." On the way to wounding him, machine gun slugs had perforated the lieutenant's dispatch case.[28]

H Company, part of the first wave, sent a platoon on an advanced patrol toward the regiment's left. Wounds sent the platoon's two leaders to the rear, leaving Sergeant Irvin Dresbach in command. Dresbach had joined the old 4th Ohio in June 1916. He made the trip to the Mexican border and had risen to corporal by the time the regiment went into Federal service in August 1917. Gas from the Germans' morning barrage had left his eyes and throat severely burned and swollen. He took command without hesitation and pushed the platoon forward. Encountering Germans southwest of Saint Georges, Dresbach ordered an attack that broke the enemy troops, who fled west into the waiting arms of the 82nd Division.[29]

To the Ohioans' right, the 165th had started its attack using the 1st Battalion under Captain Michael Kelly. As Kelly's men poised to go over the top, Lieutenant Colonel Donovan walked among them, "telling them that we had to go through and that they were the fellows to do it." Kelly blew his whistle and the soldiers emerged, Donovan with them. He had only gone a few steps when a machine gun bullet hit him below the knee, going through the bone. He crawled into a crater as Germans were counterattacking from trenches south of Landres-et-Saint Georges against the New Yorkers' right[30] The night before, Donovan had had Stokes mortars and additional machine guns brought up, and those crews went into action. Within minutes, the mortarmen and machine gunners, firing from the woods along the stream, broke the assault.[31]

This enemy counterattack convinced Donovan that another German assault could cut off Kelly's advance with the 1st Battalion, so he sent word to Kelly to fall back. Kelly refused unless he had written orders. Donovan rummaged in his dispatch case for a message form and, lying in mud, wrote an order that he sent to Kelly via runner. As the message was going to Kelly, Major Alex Anderson and Captain Henry Fecheimer from the supporting 2nd Battalion, who had heard about Donovan's leg, materialized to check on him.[32]

Donovan's shell hole shelter was on the reverse slope of the hill in front of the German wire, a position both isolated and dangerous. Fecheimer later remembered thinking, "'How in hell is anybody going to get him out of here?" Donovan calmly said hello and advised the pair to take cover in an adjoining hole but two men already were in it. Seeing another hole, Fecheimer quick-crawled into it as a German round vaporized the other two.[33]

Colonel Henry Reilly, right, the Rainbow Division's artillery chief and later 83rd Brigade commander. (*National Archives*)

Donovan refused to be evacuated until the attack had ended. Not that he could easily have made his getaway—German gunners had bracketed his position with fearsome precision. Being boxed in, Father Duffy wrote later, was "one of the creepiest feelings in war."

"A shell lands to the right of a group of men; no harm in that—all safe," Duffy said. "Then one lands to the left, to front, or rear, and the next is closer in between them. Then everybody knows what is happening. That square is in for a shelling until nothing living inside it will escape except by miracle."[34] Anderson and Fecheimer fetched stretcher bearers who extracted Donovan to the rear before the artillery box closed in on him.

Kelly and the 1st Battalion fell back to the line along the streambed. They had met intense fire from their left brought to bear by Germans who had infiltrated a draw that ran from Saint Georges to a patch of trees called Woods 199, north of the 165th's forward line. In the early afternoon, the 2nd Battalion relieved the 1st Battalion as the regiment established an east-west line about 400 yards north of Woods 199—the farthest the 165th was to advance during three days of fighting.[35]

To the right of the two 83rd Brigade regiments, the 167th made little progress. During the night of October 14-15, L Company and I Company crossed no man's land to a position near the wire belts where a deep gully provided some protection from enemy flanking fire. L Company advanced the farthest; I Company filtered in behind. H Company moved into the regiment's main line to fill a gap between the 167th and 165th on their left. Shortly thereafter, K Company was pulled back to the edge of the Bois de Romagne so the artillery could try again to flatten wire to the company's front.[36] That effort failed.

During the early hours of October 15, a patrol consisting of one platoon each from F Company and K Company, with a platoon from M Company in support, was ordered to advance toward the Côte de Châtillon. Intelligence suggested the Germans may have fallen back from their trenches there; the patrol was to confirm or contradict that suspicion. The patrol crept toward the wire without incident until a hail of German machine gun fire dropped many men dead or wounded. Germans got close enough to hurl grenades into the Alabamians' midst, forcing survivors to shelter in craters before falling back to the Bois de Romagne.[37] A few daylight patrols went out to check the status of the German wire, but otherwise the 167th remained where it had gotten to on October 14.[38]

The 168th spent the latter hours of October 14-15 organizing their positions and preparing for an assault after dawn. Stokes mortars and 37mm guns were brought forward. Engineers, carrying as many pairs of wire cutters as they could find, moved up to help address that stubborn wire. Major Ross's 1st Battalion held its place in the line on the slope of Hill 288 overnight while H Company of the 2nd Battalion protected the right flank and maintained liaison with the 32nd Division. The remainder of the 2nd Battalion advanced to support the 1st Battalion, and the 3rd Battalion came forward to Hill 269.[39]

Misery reigned that night. Major Ross had lost over 100 men on October 14 and sent that many again to be treated for the prolonged effects of exposure to rain and cold. Trails and roads to the rear were impassable; the only way to get badly wounded men to care was to carry them on litters for miles. This strained the regiment's Sanitary Detachment; thirty-five F Company men had to be detailed to evacuate wounded in a bloody procession through the valley amid bursting German gas rounds.[40]

The infantry regiments struggled to keep men nourished. The 168th's field kitchens were more than two miles to the rear, and ration carts could only roll about halfway from there to the front. To reach some units, porters had to lug heavy containers the entire distance over boggy trails amid constant shelling. The 168th's Supply Company, operating in a

Hill 288 as seen from approximately three-fourths of a mile to the south. (*National Archives*)

ravine near Exermont, worked minor miracles. John Taber wrote that "in spite of the roads, the gas, and the constant punishment from enemy artillery, somehow or other rations, ammunition, and supplies were delivered."[41]

Mist and drizzle degenerated into downpour. By midnight, shell holes and foxholes were brimming with cold water. Their occupants had as "a lullaby" the "crackle of machine gun fire and the slamming of artillery" from over the ridge of Hill 288.[42]

After an all-night artillery preparation, Major Ross ordered his 1st Battalion forward just after dawn. Now better informed about the enemy's positions, he ordered A Company under Lieutenant Robert Bly to swing right and make an encircling movement to clear the forward slope of Hill 288 and the east and west slopes of Hill 242. Ross was hoping this would allow the rest of the battalion to advance to the base of the Côte de Châtillon. With B Company to A company's left, the battalion went over the top and down the wooded slope on the heels of a brief mortar bombardment. A Company's maneuver right only partially succeeded but did secure a foothold Ross thought he could exploit.[43]

As A Company was trying to clear the slopes of Hill 288 to the right, the 1st Platoon of B Company advanced half a mile, reaching La Tuilerie Farm where two enemy machine guns were in the woods. In a fast, furious fight, the platoon, enduring heavy losses, destroyed one gun and captured four Germans; only twelve Americans came out whole. Lieutenant Howard Smith's platoon took on a four-Maxim emplacement. In great pain from a shoulder wound, Smith led the attack. He and his small detachment put the guns out of action and captured thirty-six Germans. Weak from blood loss, Smith guided sixty Germans to the rear. At the 168th's lines, an observer seeing Smith noted that "his blouse had been torn off, his shirt was streaming with blood that exaggerated the pallor of his face, and it was evident that he was about all in." Smith declined treatment until he had delivered his prisoners. He approached Major Ross.

"Where do you want 'em, Major?" he asked.

"Why, you have been wounded," Ross said. "How do you feel?"

Smith grinned and replied, "Like the devil, sir."[44]

For ninety minutes, the entire battalion took cover as enemy artillery and minenwerfer crews rained ordnance that inflicted numerous casualties. By noon, Ross had moved forces forward and now had a front line composed of B, C, A, and H Companies, with D Company in support. He assigned H Company to circle Hill 242 from the right and capture La Tuilerie Farm while the other three companies assaulted the left of the hill. After a forty-five-minute American barrage on Hill 242, Ross sent his men at the enemy in a driving rainstorm at 3:00 p.m., their fourth attack in two days.[45]

The battalion made its way quietly through woods into a meadow on the final ridge south of the Côte de Châtillon. Just beyond was a hedge, and beyond that the ground dipped and rose to the edge of a woods at the foot of the hill. The woods covered the Côte de Châtillon's southern slope, extending right to within about 100 yards of La Tuilerie Farm. As the men were deploying into combat groups, the Germans opened fire "with a blast and roar that could not have been more startling if it had been launched automatically by the touch of an electric button." Machine gun rounds poured down from the hill and 88mm guns fired into the battalion at close range.[46]

Startled, the Iowans quickly maneuvered into skirmish formation and continued to advance. B Company and C Company rushed the hedge with bayonets fixed. Defenders fired about twenty shots before abandoning their guns and running for the woods as the doughboys fired, killing many as they fled.[47]

While that attack was happening, H Company was breaking through on the right of Hill 242, reaching La Tuilerie Farm at the edge of a clearing. The men dashed across the open ground, drove the defenders back, and seized every one of the stone buildings except the barn. They held the farm until a heavy enemy barrage that evening drove them back to the edge of the Bois de Romagne. Ross consolidated his line at the base of the hill, summoned reinforcements, and dug in for the night as the "relentless heavens continued to drench the unprotected men on the line," who had no blankets or shelter. Men shivered in foxholes, waiting for dawn and another assault on the Côte de Châtillon.[48]

10

THE CÔTE DE CHÂTILLON, OCTOBER 16, 1918

"The two battalions, like the arms of a relentless pincer, closed in from both sides. Officers fell and sergeants leaped in to take command. Companies dwindled to platoons and corporals took over. At the end, Major Ross had only 300 men and six officers left out of 1,450 men and 25 officers. That is the way those gallant citizen-soldiers, so far from home, won the approach to final victory."
—General of the Army Douglas MacArthur in *Reminiscences*

Overnight on October 15, Captain Thomas Fallow and 100 of his men crept to the right of the 167th Infantry's main line west of the Côte de Châtillon. Their objective was an existing opening in the barbed wire that everywhere else had blocked attempts to gain this steep hill, key to breaking the German line. The enemy had built this "chicane," French for "trickery," in order to move supplies from the Côte de Châtillon to German positions on Hill 288. The Americans now held the hill but, as revealed by aerial reconnaissance, the Germans had neglected to close the chicane, a narrow passageway through the wire.

Fallow was a "mustang," Army slang for an NCO raised to officer's rank. A sergeant during the 4th Alabama's 1916 deployment to the Mexican border in 1916, he became an officer at Camp Mills. He had become one of Major Norris's most capable and reliable combat officers, hence his selection to take the chicane and attack up the slope of the Côte de Châtillon to flank the German defenses.

The chicane was as described. Fallow motioned his men forward through it toward a hedge at the foot of the hill. A little after 6:00 a.m., Fallow deployed a skirmish line behind the hedge. Once men were in position, the captain convened his officers and NCOs to discuss their plan of attack. All agreed the best and simplest approach was to charge en masse up the hill to their front, on which no German wire spread.[1] The signal for the attack would be three tweets from Fallow's whistle.

Fallow's small detachment waited in silence for Major Winn's machine guns to start in at 10:00 a.m. As Winn's guns battered German positions, enemy gunners and infantrymen took cover in dugouts. The American machine guns fired for 30 minutes above the 167th, a fusillade "like a million bees overhead."[2] Now Winn held his fire so the infantry massed along the hill's base could attack. Fallow could see that the Iowans to his right were in position and ready to attack on the eastern side of the hill. He lifted his whistle and blew three times, loud and shrill.

In AEF and 1st Army planning rooms and across the front, the afternoon and evening of October 15 had been consumed with meetings and debates about how to attack on October 16.[3] Everyone in the Rainbow Division saw the need to seize the Côte de Châtillon. Colonel William Hughes, the 42nd Division Chief of Staff, later said, "A careful study of the situation showed that the Côte de Châtillon was the key to the whole situation, not only because of its physical characteristics and the position which it occupied, but also because it was very strongly held by the Germans, who apparently after our first attacks had increased its garrison." On October 15, MacArthur visited Hughes to ask permission to concentrate his brigade's attacks on the Côte de Châtillon with direct support from the 151st Field Artillery, which MacArthur wanted placed under his direct command.[4]

Intrigued by MacArthur's idea, Hughes took MacArthur to meet with Menoher, after which all three paid a visit on General Summerall at the V Corps P.C. After a discussion, Summerall took them to see General Drum, the 1st Army Chief of Staff. Drum listened intently but neither he nor Summerall thought MacArthur could take the Côte de Châtillon using only his brigade and some dedicated artillery support. They believed that the way to take the hill was to continue the general advance across the front.[5]

This assumption guided the division's Field Order No. 38, issued October 15. That order stated that the 83rd Brigade was to attack German trenches south of Saint Georges and Landres-et-Saint Georges with tank support, occupy and mop up both towns, then advance upon and seize the ridges to the north. At the same time, the 84th Brigade was to use its positions to exploit the Côte de Châtillon and the woods around La Tuilerie Farm, but not attempt to advance further. Yet again, artillery support would be distributed across the front, though this approach had yet to support the infantry as needed.[6]

Intelligence from a German prisoner changed American plans. The captive told interrogators the Germans were to stage a major counterattack against V Corps on October 16. At 11:45 p.m. on October 15, V Corps Headquarters told the Rainbow Division to cancel Field Order No. 38 and prepare to defend the right flank of the I Corps as it advanced and stand ready to repulse a counterattack.[7]

As V Corps and 42nd Division Headquarters were sorting out these matters, discussions about taking the Côte de Châtillon went on at regimental levels, particularly the 167th Infantry. Earlier in the day, MacArthur had shown the Alabama commander, Lieutenant Colonel Bare, an aerial photo indicating a passage through the wire to the right of La Musarde Farm. Called a "chicane," the opening likely had been built to supply men stationed in woods that American forces now controlled.[8]

Bare briefed his battalion commanders, showing around the photo and telling them that the division's plans still called for another frontal attack, to be led by Major Norris and his 3rd Battalion, with the 2nd Battalion in support and the 1st Battalion in reserve. Once Bare finished, Norris spoke.

"I have been up there forty-eight hours!" Norris said. "I am to make the attack. Am I to have nothing to say about it?"

"'Well, what have you got to say about it?'"[9]

Norris declared that the hill would never fall to frontal assault. He urged concentrated artillery and overhead machine gun fire to keep the Germans' heads down while exploiting the chicane. He suggested about 100 men infiltrate along a hedge that ran from the woods to the gap in the wire. Once through the chicane, these men could reach another hedge parallel to the southwestern face of the Côte de Châtillon. He pointed out that the western side of the hill, facing open ground where three of his

This Army Signal Corps photo provides a 1918 view of the Côte de Châtillon. (*National Archives*)

companies were deployed, was actually the Côte de Châtillon's front. The southwestern slope that faced the woods and La Musarde Farm was the German left flank.[10]

Norris predicted the Germans would read artillery and machine gun fire as the start of another frontal attack on the Côte de Châtillon's western face. While the enemy prepared to repulse this supposed attack, the infiltrators would hit the Germans' exposed left flank. If the 168th made a cooperating attack on the eastern face, the entire German position on the Côte de Châtillon might collapse.[11]

Bare approved the plan and headed to a meeting called by MacArthur at the 84th Brigade P.C. Bare was met there by Colonel Tinley from the 168th and Major Winn of the 151st Machine Gun Battalion. Inside, MacArthur and Summerall were on a phone call loud enough for Bare, Tinley, and Winn to hear the V Corps commander tell MacArthur 1st Army leadership was demanding the Côte de Châtillon be taken by 6:00 p.m. October 16.

"We will take the Côte de Châtillon by tomorrow afternoon by 6 o'clock or report a casualty list of 6,000 dead," the ever-theatrical MacArthur replied. "That will include me."[12]

MacArthur hung up and asked for the best approach to taking the hill. Bare summarized the plan Norris had proposed. He pointed out that this approach would mean some of his men would encroach on the 168th's sector, perhaps causing friction since Colonel Tinley outranked Bare.

Tinley interrupted. "I will be delighted to not only cooperate in every way I can but will take orders, if necessary, from [Lieutenant] Col. Bare," he said.

Talk turned to how the 168th could advance to the east rear face of the hill and make an attack from yet another flank of the enemy position. A pleased MacArthur immediately approved the undertaking and Bare, Tinley, and Winn returned to work.[13]

Just before dawn, Major Ross called the officers of the 168th Infantry's 1st Battalion and those from F Company and H Company to his P.C. John Taber wrote, "They knew that their men were at the breaking point, that they were exhausted from long exposure, lack of sleep and proper nourishment." In preceding days half their officers and many of their best men had been killed and wounded. They numbly made preparations "as if working out a dream in which there was no such thing as life and death— a dream in which one sets about methodically to achieve the impossible."[14]

When Captain William Kelley, commander of B Company, told his men, many of whom were expecting to be relieved, about the attack, the news staggered them.[15] Going over the plan with his sergeants at the company P.C., Kelley tried with little success to seem cool and reassuring.

"We will attack at eleven o'clock this morning," he told the NCOs. "There will be a barrage. I know it's tough that we've got to hit it again, but the brigade has been ordered to take the hill, even if it is wiped out in doing it." Looking his NCOs in their faces, Kelley was blunt but professional.

"Now men, it's serious," he added. "We're going to have losses. We've only eighty-five [men] left. We must keep casualties as low as possible. We'll advance one man from each squad at a time. I think that way we can hold losses to the minimum."

He urged them to keep the men busy until jump-off. That would keep their minds occupied and their bodies warm.[16]

Ross began to adjust his lines. He reorganized his front and shifted it a little to the right with B, C, H, and F Companies in line left to right. He placed D Company in reserve on the left flank and A Company on the right, while E Company and G Company advanced to a point behind Hill 242, putting them in position to be thrown in as circumstance demanded. As the 1st Battalion commander ordered the men out of their muddy fox-

THE CÔTE DE CHÂTILLON

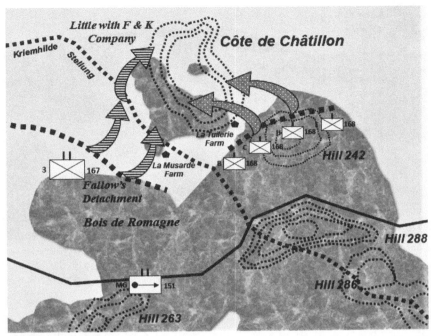

Map 10. The Rainbow Division's attack against the Côte de Châtillon on October 16, 1918. (*Author*)

holes, many were shivering and "their hands, crinkly from continued soaking, could scarcely grasp their rifles." Some, John Taber wrote, "wondered if they were equal to the task set before them—if they could make the grade."[17]

At 10:00 a.m., the division's artillery began barraging the German lines atop the Côte de Châtillon; Major Winn's machine guns began blasting their trenches. The artillery was to fire for thirty minutes. Winn's guns would continue another fifteen minutes, during which they would fire only at the hill's crest. Winn designated a stand of fir trees near the top of the hill as a reference point for his gunners. Every Hotchkiss gun was assigned a space about fifty yards wide to blanket with lead. Winn had carefully calculated firing data for each of his sixty guns, and his three-man crews were to fire as rapidly as possible without overheating their weapons.[18]

Ross had the four guns from the 1st Battalion's Machine Gun Company and his Stokes mortars fire during the final fifteen minutes of the

This recent photo of the Côte de Châtillon with La Musarde Farm in the foreground shows the view men from the left-wing units of 168th Infantry would have seen on the morning of October 16, 1918. (*Major William Carraway, Historian, Georgia Army National Guard*)

artillery barrage. At 10:30 a.m., F, H, C, and B Companies attacked from right to left. As the wave of infantrymen stepped off, they met a "tornado of bullets" from Maxims in the woods on the slopes of the Côte de Châtillon. German bullets swept the open ground from La Musarde Farm to La Tuilerie Farm. B Company tried to cross that space, but any man who left the cover of a hedge was cut down.[19]

German fire on the right was less severe, and the Iowans there began to make progress which steadily spread to the left. Two platoons from F Company attacked the lower eastern slope of the hill and were about to reach their first objective when a well-manned Maxim to their left began firing. At the same time, all of H Company made a run for La Tuilerie Farm. Despite heavy losses, the men entered the farm complex, shooting Germans as they went. Moving beyond the farm, they advanced up the hill until they encountered a circular trench defended by four heavy machine guns and more than twenty Germans. These gunners were swinging right to fire on F Company when the men of H Company put their Springfields to work. As the Germans tried to take cover, H Company overran the trench, killing or capturing all defenders. Seeing this strongpoint taken, German gunners up the slope abandoned their positions as H and F Companies double-timed to the hilltop.[20]

This photo shows the view the Germans near La Musarde Farm had of the ground over which the left-wing units of the 168th Infantry attacked. (*Major William Carraway, Historian, Georgia Army National Guard*)

To the immediate left of H Company, C Company began advancing through about fifty yards of woods and undergrowth. At the edge of the woods, bursts from Maxims caused "an involuntary recoil, as one would attempt to escape a draught-forced flame at a suddenly opened furnace door." Maxims in the wood opposite were sweeping the "naked swale with a merciless completeness." The first men from C Company who tried to cross fell in heaps. On the right an enemy gun was put out of action, spurring the two lieutenants leading C Company's attack to lead their men across the boggy open ground as fast as they could run while "yelling at the top of their lungs like wild Comanches." They quickly reached the base of the hill, in the process losing eight men.[21] While the artillery barrage continued and the 168th prepared to advance, Major Norris's 100-man detachment under Captain Thomas Fallow poised to attack.

The night before, Fallow had led his detachment along the hedge toward the chicane, finding it to match its description. Hastening through the gap, they continued along the hedge that ran parallel to the southwest face of the Côte de Châtillon. Major Norris left the rest of the attacking force under Captain Robert Joerg and followed close behind Fallow's force.[22]

When the barrage lifted at 10:30 a.m. and the Iowans of the 168th began their advance to the right at La Tuilerie Farm, Fallow's men scattered along the hedge, which was on a slight rise in the terrain. Once the barrage stopped, the Germans rose and saw Fallow's contingent. They opened fire with machine guns while Fallow's men waited for the captain to signal the attack. A round hit Major Norris's heel, toppling him.

"As I lay there," he recalled, "I heard Fallow's three blasts on the whistle and then the yell of our men as they jumped forward to charge."[23]

The men swept uphill, clearing out enemy machine guns on the side of the hill before breaking through the left rear of the German lines facing west. Obviously flanked, Germans not dead or badly wounded fell back to the north. As enemy reserves came up, the Germans formed a new line across the northern slope of the Cote de Chatillon. Fallow's men did the same, taking cover wherever they could.[24]

As Fallow's men were moving uphill, the 168th's C Company, having traversed the open ground to the left of La Tuilerie Farm, reached a place where a wood narrowed to a blunt salient of open ground stretching to the hilltop. Panting and sweating, they rapidly skirted the woods to a point at which two enemy machine guns were firing on H Company and F Company. Lieutenant William Witherell shot at them with his pistol with no effect, then dropped back into the woods and prepared his men to rush the enemy guns. Before the company could advance again, Corporal Joseph Pruette took matters into his own hands.[25]

During the advance, Pruette had collected an armful of German grenades. Crawling forward on the right, he got close enough to the enemy trench to lob in a potato masher. The gunners dove into a dugout. The grenade exploded. Pruette leaped atop the dugout as the rest of C Company arrived. Hopping delightedly, face "streaked with mud and perspiration," the corporal grinned broadly, a grenade in either hand.

"I've got 'em!" he shouted. "I've got 'em!"[26]

From inside the dugout, Pruette and his comrades heard pitiful cries of "Kamerad," followed by Germans emerging, hands held high.

"Come out!" Pruette, thinking he had captured a few men, shouted. "Come out!"

The parade went on until seventy-two Germans had surrendered, prompting some Iowans to think they might have taken on more than they could handle. A German officer noticed Pruette's two chevrons and remarked in broken English that he would prefer to surrender his arms to an officer. "To Hell with that noise," Pruette replied, waving a grenade.

"Give me those guns, or up you go in smoke." The officer did as ordered, "gracefully and with alacrity."[27]

Lieutenant Witherell realized only about fifteen men from C Company were with him. The rest of the company had been held up along with B Company by enemy machine gun fire on the left. The woods had to be cleared to the right, and quickly. F Company had moved to the top of the ridge, safe from enemy fire for now, while H Company was advancing into the woods above La Tuilerie Farm. But the entire slope of the hill was under heavy fire from the right flank as well as from the summit of the hill to the left. The Germans were now dropping minenwerfer rounds onto the hillside. If Witherell waited for reinforcements, they might lose all they had gained.[28]

The young lieutenant sent five men led by Sergeant Merl Clark into the woods to figure out the strength of the machine guns punishing the Iowans' left flank and, if possible, take them out. Clark sent one man circling left to make sure none of the 168th would fire on the patrol while the others spread out in a semicircle. They moved cautiously but quickly through the trees until they found the German guns. Coming up on the enemy's rear, Clark realized the Germans had no support behind, leaving their rear and flank exposed. He signaled his men to rush the guns. The crewmen at the first Maxim were dead or wounded before they could react. The second crew surrendered. The rest of the German gunners realized they had been flanked and fled up the hill. With these guns silenced, B Company and C Company advanced uphill and into the woods.[29]

While the 168th's men were struggling past La Tuilerie Farm and into the woods, a provisional battalion made up of the 167th's E Company and M Company, along with portions of I Company and K Company, began shifting to the right toward the chicane. The move took time, and until the Alabamians could reach the southwestern slope of the hill, the 168th could advance no farther.[30] The Germans wisely increased their fire on the Iowans and launched counterattacks. F Company warded off one such attack. C Company pressed toward the top of the ridge under very severe artillery and machine gun fire. The men made it and came up on the left of H Company. But German guns on the top of the Côte de Châtillon rendered this line untenable, especially for H Company. The H Company commander, Captain Oscar Nelson, was hit. He dragged himself to a shell hole for cover. Litter bearers tried to reach him. "I'm done for, boys!" he yelled. "You can't help me. Don't risk it." He died within minutes.[31]

Command of H Company fell to Second Lieutenant Charles Seeley, who ordered his men to fall back down the hill to La Tuilerie Farm. That exposed both of C Company's flanks, forcing that unit to withdraw to the edge of the woods below. By the time C Company and H Company reached the farm, H Company had lost all its officers killed or wounded and was down to twenty-five men, a tenth of full strength. C Company had one officer and fifty men. A Company had lost all its officers, and D Company had but two officers and only about forty-eight men.[32]

By 2:00 p.m., the 167th's provisional battalion had traversed the chicane and formed a line with the 168th across the southern slope of the Côte de Châtillon. At 3:30 p.m., Germans there seemed to be on the verge of counterattacking to drive the Americans off the hill. The 168th sent E Company and G Company to bolster the line. Before these units could take their positions, the 167th's men began to move up the hill along with the Iowans of B Company. They stormed the summit with the 168th's E Company and C Company joining them in the attack. The Germans did counterattack but were quickly repelled with assistance from a well-timed and well-placed artillery barrage and the determined effort of one American with a Chauchat.

Private Thomas Neibaur, an automatic rifleman in M Company of the 167th Infantry, lay in a shell hole with his loader and observer awaiting that counterattack. Major Ravee Norris, his battalion commander, later described him as "a little fellow and quite young."[33] Neibaur was a rarity in the Alabama regiment, being from Idaho, where his family had settled in the 1880s.[34]

Only weeks before the U.S. entered the war, Neibaur had enlisted in the Idaho National Guard. At Camp Mills, his unit became part of the new 41st Division, which in France was designated as a replacement unit for the AEF. Neibaur was transferred to the 167th Infantry prior to its deployment to the trenches at Lunéville.[35] Surviving the trenches and the fighting at Champagne, La Croix Rouge Farm, the Ourcq, and Saint Mihiel, Neibaur and his Alabama comrades had come to the Meuse-Argonne.

Since falling back from their trenches earlier in the day, the Germans had begun to shell the positions occupied by the 167th and to fire at M Company from isolated machine gun positions about 100 yards away. Neibaur volunteered to try to flank the Maxims and moved forward with his two-man support team. They crawled up a draw where they ran into barbed wire. Neibaur decided to set up there. As he was getting into position, German fire killed his observer and loader. Neibaur caught three bullets in a thigh.³⁶

The Germans, again counterattacking, had just about gained the top of the ridge to his front. He propped his Chauchat on a small dirt berm and began firing. It did not take long for the enemy to make out Neibaur's position; about fifty soldiers rushed him. He killed or wounded most of the attackers, firing more than fifty rounds and going through two and a half clips.³⁷

Neibaur decided to try to make it back to his own lines. He abandoned his Chauchat and was crawling down the hill when he was hit again, this time in the hip. He rolled into a shell hole and lost consciousness. When he awoke, he had company—fifteen Germans had dis-

Private Thomas Neibaur who served in M Company of the 167th Infantry. (*U.S. Army History Center*)

armed him, tossing his Colt M1911 pistol beyond his reach. When the Germans' attention drifted, Neibaur clambered to the weapon and snatched it. Four Germans came at him with bayonets. Neibaur killed all four and leveled his pistol at the others, who dropped their rifles and surrendered to the diminutive soldier from Idaho.³⁸

Neibaur waved his pistol, indicating that they should leave the crater and, limping badly, took his prisoners to the 167th's lines. Neibaur received the Medal of Honor; his citation for valor read in part, "The counterattack in full force was arrested to a large extent by the single efforts of this soldier."³⁹

About that time, the remainder of the 167th's K Company and F Company under the command of Captain Royal Little shifted left and moved through a hole in the wire on the hill's northwest side. Once those units connected with the rest of the American line, the remaining Germans withdrew from the hill. With their retreat, the Alabamians and Iowans had secured the critical ground atop the Côte de Châtillon.⁴⁰

Major Norris, lying wounded on the ground at the bottom of the hill, had been listening to the battle, trying to figure out what was happening to his men. When their yells grew fainter, he was almost sure they had not been turned back. "I was terribly anxious," he said, "as after all in war you never can be sure a fight is all over." A sergeant appeared. He yelled, "Captain, we've got the hill and a lot of these —d d— mned Heinies as well!" Norris laughed with relief while weeping for joy.[41]

As the two regiments of the 84th Brigade were fighting to take the Côte de Châtillon, the 165th Infantry remained where dug in from the day before; the 166th was ordered to remain in position as the 82nd Division tried to advance to the Ohioans' left. If the 82nd succeeded, K Company was to send out strong patrols to link up with the 82nd, then try to enter Saint Georges from the west. If K Company was able to enter the town, M Company would attack on the flank of the enemy trenches east of Saint Georges.[42]

At noon, Captain Hutchcraft, commander of K Company, left the regiment's positions near Sommerance and took a patrol to the western edge of Saint Georges. He thought the 82nd was making its advance as planned. Soon after the patrol had left, the 3rd Battalion P.C. in Sommerance received word that the 82nd was not advancing but, instead, had been ordered to keep pace with the 78th Division on its left. Captain Hutchcraft soon discovered this error when he advanced and found that the 82nd was a considerable distance down the road south of Saint Georges. Before he could contact the 82nd, a German observation plane spotted his patrol and directed heavy machine gun fire at his men. Realizing he had no way into Saint Georges, he withdrew his patrol, losing two men killed and four wounded.[43] The 166th's efforts to break the Kriemhilde Stellung were over.

In the eyes of AEF, 1st Army, and V Corps Headquarters, Rainbow Division attacks of October 14-16 had not met expectations. Pressure for results was increasing. Given the 83rd Brigade's slow advance toward Saint Georges and Landres-et-Saint Georges, that locale was where upper command was going to apply most of that pressure.

On the night of October 16, General Summerall, the V Corps commander, visited the 83rd Brigade and the 165th Infantry. At the 165th P.C. in Exermont, he met with Colonel Mitchell, the regiment's commander, and demanded to know why the New Yorkers had been unable to take the low ridge beyond Landres-et-Saint Georges.

Summerall "was not well handled," Father Duffy said.[44] According to Duffy, while Mitchell was a good soldier, he was a modest officer, not the sort "to say a strong word in his own defense." He made a "poor figure on the witness stand."

Mitchell and his operations officer, Captain Merle-Smith, attempted to explain the situation.[45] They highlighted the unending enfilading fire from the Côte de Châtillon on the right flank. From the beginning, taking that hill had been seen as critical to the 83rd Brigade's ability to advance, but the 84th Brigade had been unable to take the hill and silence those guns. Then there were the enemy's wire belts, which had resisted all attempts at cutting by hand or flattening with artillery. And the overall artillery plan was severely flawed. Not only was broad uniform fire across the entire division front a failure, but too many rounds were falling short, killing the regiment's own soldiers. These factors, combined with lack of tank support, had led to heavy losses that made reaching the regiment's objective all but impossible.[46]

The V Corps commander was in no mood for an argument. He told Mitchell and Merle-Smith that he "wanted results, no matter how many men were killed."[47] Summerall left the P.C. to see General Menoher at 42nd Division Headquarters. After discussing the situation in the 83rd Brigade, Menoher and Summerall decided, per Pershing's edict to clean house of ineffective officers, to assign blame and make changes—coincidentally exempting Summerall, Menoher, and their staffs from any finding of fault.

On October 17, Summerall issued orders immediately relieving the 83rd Brigade commander, General Lenihan, as well as Colonel Mitchell, Captain Merle-Smith, and the 165th's adjutant, Lieutenant Harold Betty. Summerall also indicated he thought Colonel Hough of the 166th Infantry should be relieved but left that to Menoher. Menoher called Hough to division headquarters and conveyed Summerall's opinion. Menoher also commented on what he saw as low morale in the 166th, apparently blaming attitude for the regiment's inability to take Saint Georges.[48]

Hough gave as good as he got. "No one man can take [the] fatigue out of men who have been living in water-filled holes in the ground with no overcoats and but one blanket seeing their comrades killed by shell fire or dying from pneumonia," he roared at Menoher. "The men want action. If you hold me responsible for the condition which you allege to be true, then remove me now."[49] Menoher immediately truckled.

Colonel Reilly, who had been commanding the division's 67th Field Artillery Brigade, was assigned to replace Lenihan while Lieutenant Colonel Charles Dravo, who had been division machine gun officer, was assigned to lead the 165th Infantry. Many New York regiment officers knew Dravo, who became very popular when his first action upon assuming command was to issue a report on conditions in the regiment aimed at restoring Colonel Mitchell to command.[50]

Summerall had not been entirely wrong to flag low morale. By October 15, peace talk rumors were rampant, and with some justification. Berlin had been exchanging messages with President Wilson since October 14 regarding his proposed "Fourteen Points" as a basis for peace. Dana Daniels of the 166th wrote in his diary on October 15 that the men were "very anxious about peace talk."[51] At least some men had little appetite for facing enemy machine gun fire in a meaningless gesture.

With the Côte de Châtillon captured and the Kriemhilde Stellung pierced at last, the question for the Rainbow Division and 1st Army was when to exploit the break and who would make that attack.

Those decisions were not long in coming.

11

EXPLOITING THE BREAKTHROUGH, OCTOBER 17–NOVEMBER 1, 1918

"A mighty unbroken rumble and roar of thousands of batteries that caused the earth to tremble as if in fear of its very existence—this was the final death knell of the Hohenzollerns."
—John Taber in *The Story of the 168th Infantry*

The morning of November 1, 1918, soldiers and Marines of the 2nd Division watched clock hands tick toward 5:30 a.m., when they were to go over the top to assault remnants of the Kriemhilde Stellung. The combined artillery of the 42nd, 2nd, and 89th Divisions had been firing all night at the German trenches near Saint Georges and Landres-et-Saint Georges. At 3:30 a.m., that barrage intensified.

General Summerall, the V Corps commander, had gathered enough artillery pieces to provide the fire support men like Colonel Henry Reilly had been advocating for weeks. Reilly, who had been the Rainbow Division's chief of artillery before becoming the 83rd Brigade commander on October 17, believed in mass firepower concentrated in a focused front as opposed to an evenly distributed blanket of fire across a broad front using fewer guns. For the November 1 attack, Summerall had collected thousands of artillery pieces of all calibers to provide a deep, fierce barrage of high explosives and shrapnel to support two divisions across a four-mile front of operations.[1]

The barrage, from 3:30 a.m. to 5:30 a.m., would be followed by a rain of shells more than 1,200 yards deep across the entire front behind which the infantry was to advance. This latter barrage was to be accompanied by massed overhead machine gun fire, as at the Côte de Châtillon. If successful, this support would allow the 2nd and the 89th Divisions to break through the Kriemhilde Stellung and begin rapidly pushing the Germans toward the Meuse River and the strategic city of Sedan.[2]

At 3:30 a.m. "all the guns in France seemed to unite in one tremendous whoop." John Taber called it a "mighty unbroken rumble and roar of thousands of batteries that caused the earth to tremble as if in fear of its very existence."[3] Men from the Rainbow Division's 83rd Brigade were still manning positions along the front as the artillery fire began, and the 2nd Division moved through the 83rd's lines toward the German positions. "As the light came and the mist cleared," recalled Major Thomas Reilley of the 165th Infantry, "it looked as if a volcano was riding, right up the hill to the front."[4] Even before the final barrage, numerous Germans came across no man's land to surrender. Major Geran of the 166th Infantry's 2nd Battalion reported that several hundred had come through his lines north of Sommerance before sunrise. He and his men shepherded them into groups as large as 150 they sent unguarded to the rear with just a guide.[5]

The 2nd Division made quick work of the German forces, and after the first few battalions had advanced, some 83rd Brigade officers moved forward to see what the barrage had accomplished. What they saw left them dumbstruck. They noted the remarkable density and regularity of the shell craters but most importantly they saw only a few dead and wounded Americans. Enemy casualties littered the ground in and around trenches, so many that it was apparent that any German "manning a weapon would be promptly hit." American machine gun fire had been so dense "there was not a tree lining the road between Landres-et-St. George and St. George which did not have several machine gun bullet holes in it."[6]

Among officers moving up behind the 2nd Division advance was Father Duffy. Accompanied by a sergeant, he went looking for American dead in the wire belts that for so many days had blocked the 83rd Brigade.

Two German artillery pieces lie damaged and abandoned on the ridges north of Saint Georges and Landres-et-Saint Georges after the American bombardment of November 1, 1918. (National Archives)

As he and the NCO passed through Sommerance, they saw five German prisoners approaching, guarded by four Americans. A German round exploded among the nine, blowing them in all directions. Duffy ran forward while the sergeant dashed for an ambulance. Three men were dead. The blast had torn away one American's legs. He told Duffy his name was Conover and that he was a Catholic. Duffy began to give him absolution while the soldier said the prayers. "He had no idea his legs were gone until a soldier lifted him on a stretcher, when I could see in his eyes that he was aware that his body was lifting light," remembered Duffy. "He started to look but I placed my hand on his chest and kept him from seeing." Duffy next went to the aid of a badly wounded German officer. The man "cursed his fate that brought him to this death by the fire of his own guns after lasting through four years of war."[7]

The 2nd Division and the 89th Division continued to chase Germans retreating toward the Meuse. Soon, the Rainbow Division was to follow them and take the lead, then begin its own race to Sedan.

The capture of the Côte de Châtillon began a period of relative inactivity for the Rainbow Division. Patrols went out and some front-line units were relieved, but little else of note occurred. The patrols sought to see if the

Germans had decided to withdraw now that the Côte de Châtillon was in American hands, threatening the German lines west of the hill and south of Landres-et-Saint Georges and Saint Georges. On the afternoon of October 17, reports indicated that the Germans had fallen back. The 166th Infantry was told to send a confirmatory patrol that night.

Lieutenant Alison Reppy, the 1st Battalion Intelligence Officer, organized a patrol that departed the extreme left of the division's front line around 3:00 a.m. on October 18. The men headed northwest to a small woodland southeast of Hill 230, 300 yards south of German trenches. In the woods, Reppy sent one scout and one observer to the crest of the hill. From the top, the pair could not see well enough to determine if the enemy was present. They moved down the counter-slope until they were about 150 yards south of the road that entered Saint Georges from the west-southwest. It was getting light, and German heavy machine gunners there fired on them. Reppy's scouts quick-timed up the hill, where they remained to observe the enemy.[8]

Now six machine guns on both flanks of the observation position were firing, soon joined by artillery and more machine guns. White alarm flares rose all along the German lines, "denoting suspicion and great nervousness." A heavy fog formed, limiting visibility. Reppy decided to pull the patrol back to friendly lines around 5:30 a.m. Clearly the Germans were still afoot.[9]

On the far right of the Rainbow Division's line, the 3rd Battalion of the 168th Infantry was moving forward to relieve the 1st and 2nd Battalions, which had borne the brunt of the fighting for the Côte de Châtillon. While the 3rd Battalion had been held in reserve, the task of relieving the other two battalions "was not a pleasant prospect." Those units had spent three days under continuous shelling with high explosive and gas rounds and now had to advance "through the glutinous mud and chilling rain" to a newly established front line that lacked any shelter or protection. But the men knew what their comrades in the 1st and 2nd Battalions had gone through in seizing the hill, and "their philosophical attitude" overcame any reluctance to advance. Once the 3rd Battalion arrived, the men of the other battalions slowly pulled themselves from foxholes and began to move listlessly toward the reverse slope of Hill 288 and Hill 242. Once there, they fell immediately to sleep despite the cold and rain.[10]

When I Company of the 3rd Battalion reached the front to relieve E Company and C Company, it was dark and raining steadily. As E Company began to pull out, several men voiced concern that one of the forward outposts had not been relieved. Hearing this, Corporal Arthur Brandt of I Company volunteered to lead a group to relieve the outpost. Before the war, Brandt, a twenty-six-year-old from Pottsville, Iowa, had been a carpenter. He had a reputation in his unit for habitually taking on the most difficult and dangerous assignments. As the corporal led his team forward, German artillery began to hammer the American lines. The group was about 100 yards forward of the main line when a shell burst wounded four men, including Brandt, whose face was shot away. In addition, he had a serious hip wound and too many pieces of shrapnel in his body to count.[11]

Only Brandt knew the way to the regiment's lines. Using hand signals, he told the other men that he would take the lead and get them to safety. Despite intense pain, he led the men to the 168th's positions through "impenetrable blackness." Brandt then headed for Hill 242 to have his wounds dressed. There he found many more wounded, all needing to get to the regiment's dressing station. Again, only Brandt knew the way. He led a column of wounded men and litter bearers on a torturous march to the rear over Hill 288. At the dressing station, he collapsed. He died the next day.[12]

As Brandt had been making his way to the rear, the rest of the 3rd Battalion had been trying to consolidate new forward positions while awaiting orders to continue the advance. The first challenge was to dig in. But excavating foxholes was almost impossible in soil "the consistency of thick soup" and finished holes quickly filled with water. Someone suggested digging each hole more deeply at one end, then installing a "nest" of branches; occupants perching on these platforms could bail out the sump using a helmet or a mess kit. The 168th remained in these positions for six days. John Taber wrote:[13]

> It took courage merely to stay at the front without the urgency of attack to relieve the strain or to distract from incessant shelling. The water was bad, the food cold and insufficient, clothing inadequate, and the rain—the sun did not shine from the day the regiment first entered the line until it left—and wind seemed allied to wear men down.[14]

All along the division's front, men suffered from exposure, and sickness became the main threat. It was typical for a hundred sick men or more to leave each regiment daily. Colonel Tinley of the 168th reported to the 84th Brigade, "The morale is still up to the old Rainbow standard, and the men will go up against anything to which they are assigned, but they are so worn out, physically and mentally, from exposure, lack of nutrition, nervous strain, and depleted numbers, that they could not hold out against more than three hours of severe fighting."[15]

Reports like Tinley's began to strike home. On October 18, the division's Supply Companies started distributing new uniforms, underwear, blankets, and overcoats to men who had been living in wet clothes for almost three weeks. This boosted morale, but food was still a problem. So long as the regiments remained in the line, canned meat, dehydrated potatoes and onions, and hard bread remained staples.[16]

Little happened for five days. An attack planned for October 20 was canceled when a staff officer from 42nd Division Headquarters got lost while carrying all the orders and maps for the assault and got captured.[17] Men sat in foxholes and tried to take cover from enemy artillery. Every entry in the diary kept by the 166th Infantry's Sergeant Roy Bailey from October 16 through October 23 said the same thing: "Still on hill, shelled."[18]

Private Enoch Williams of the 166th was able to secure a scrap of YMCA paper on which to write home. "Am in the lines now but expect to be relieved soon as we have been in about 14 days," he told his mother. "Say, you ought to see my home. It's a hole in the ground [with] a few boards and dirt on top. The entrance is just big enough to crawl in and runs enough inside for two to lay squeezed up close together. But that don't matter as long as we are dry and warm. Gee, but I would like to sleep in a real bed once."[19]

This extended pause arose from deliberation and cogitation at AEF and 1st Army Headquarters over how to exploit the break made in the Kriemhilde Stellung at the Côte de Châtillon. Prisoners taken during this time indicated that the German high command believed American possession of the strategic hill had made the remainder of the defensive line west of Landres-et-Saint Georges into a mere outpost position for the main German line of defense. Deciding how to exploit the gains made by the 84th Brigade and who should make the next attack got intense study by the AEF.[20]

General Pershing believed that, with the positions on the Romagne heights, including the Côte de Châtillon, in American hands, German defeat "was merely a question of time." He thought his forces could advance without special preparation and drive the Germans from the field. But, acknowledging his men's condition, he concluded that it would be better to pause, plan, and organize a single powerful offensive, then to drive the Germans back over the Meuse River. As supplies were gathered and lines of communication improved, planners at 1st Army tentatively set October

28 as the starting date for that offensive. The French Fourth Army, which would be needed to support the American left flank during the attack, would not be ready by then, so jump-off was changed to November 1.[21]

During the relative quiet enforced by AEF and 1st Army planning, divisions along the front were ordered to hew to custom and have a single brigade hold each division's front while the other brigade rested. The Rainbow Division directed that the 84th Brigade pull back while the 83rd Brigade took over the division front line. On October 20, the division issued Field Order No. 41, requiring the 83rd Brigade to assume all coverage of the front while also changing the division's sector boundaries. The new boundaries equalized the areas covered by the 42nd Division and the 89th Division, which had just replaced the 32nd Division on the right. With the new boundaries, the area previously occupied by the 168th Infantry was now the responsibility of the 32nd Division. When the 83rd Brigade took over the front, most observers expected the offensive to resume shortly. The men of the 165th Infantry and the 166th Infantry "longed to sweep over the wire and trenches still held by the Germans just in front of them, drive them down the rear slope of the ridge through St. George and Landres-St. George up the slope on the other side."[22]

As the 166th assumed its new role and the 165th shifted right to cover the area abandoned by Alabama's 167th, the men settled into a state of chronic boredom punctuated by spasms of terror from enemy shelling. On the left, near where the 166th was positioned, the Young Men's Christian Association established a canteen in Fléville, about two miles southeast of the front line. The canteen was very popular; soldiers who could get there bought whatever items of comfort were for sale. But the Ohioans along the front and so not able to make it to the canteen were, undoubtably, the ones most in need of its stores. Into this situation stepped a man Raymond Cheseldine of the 166th referred to as "one of God's Noblemen." Mac McIlvain, from Cleveland, Ohio, was tall, thin, stooped, very deaf, and too old for active service, but "every inch a man." He saw the YMCA as an agency of mercy and not a commercial entity. He would gather up the regiment's daily allotment of YMCA stock, organize the goods into individual bundles, then take the bundles forward to the front and distribute them free of charge. When soldiers assigned to the rear tried to buy these goods, Mac would say, "No, you fellows out of the line can't buy this from me. You go somewhere else. Those boys up front can't buy it either, but they will get it just the same." Mac's account books were always short and, when challenged about this, he said, "If they want money for every cigarette, I'll pay them myself. Those boys, living their last day on earth, maybe, ain't going to pay for their last cigarette!"[23]

The New Yorkers of the 165th did their best to transcend what Father Duffy called the "dreariest, draggiest days" of the war. The regiment's soldiers spent their days and nights on a bare hillside, living in muddy little pits they had dug. Each man had a blanket, no overcoat, and no fresh underwear or socks. "They were dirty, lousy, thirsty, often hungry; and nearly every last man was sick," Father Duffy wrote.[24]

Captain Herman Bootz, who had served in the Boer War, chronicled the condition of Major Alex Anderson's 2nd Battalion. Bootz, a tough character not given to sympathy, wrote that of the battalion's 405 men, 35 percent were "suffering various illnesses, especially rheumatism, colds, and fevers." Company commanders told Bootz these men were not receiving medical treatment needed to ready them to fight. First aid men could do little, as they were only supplied with bandages. Bootz laid much of the blame for the situation on the fact that the "majority of the men have summer underwear, if any, and no overcoat and only one blanket." This, he added, was completely "inadequate to keep a soldier in fit physical condition for field service in the climate that is found this time of year in France." Bootz finished his report by stating that he deemed it his duty to alert his commanding officers.[25]

For the two regiments pulled off the line, the 167th and 168th, things were slightly better. The Iowans of the 168th moved to the Exmorieux Farm. While lacking real shelter, that setting was out of artillery range, a boon to men badly needing rest and recuperation. Many were so sick that not even hot food could lift their spirits. Eight months of battlefield horror had left them "weak and apathetic." And in a few days they were to be sent "back, always back, to throw themselves under the Juggernaut of inevitable annihilation until the last man was wiped out."[26]   Since February, rumors and promises had dangled the illusion of genuine R&R—a month in a clean rest camp, leaves in Paris—none of which materialized. Morale was seeping away; depression was setting in. John Taber wrote from firsthand experience:

> But this time as the men lay wearily in their fox-holes on the hillside, listening to the artillery and wondering whether it would be two days or two weeks before they would be flung into the line again, they quite naturally felt that they were nothing but puppets in a ghastly farce, helplessly caught in the hand of some angry God who was sweeping them again and again into the consuming fire of battle.[27]

Exmorieux Farm, site of the 168th Infantry's camp. (*National Archives*)

Unexpected succor lifted the 168th Infantry. Besides new clothing and blankets as well as a YMCA cart hauling "longed-for sweets," Chaplain Robb brought a truckload of food and cigarettes. With administrative legerdemain he had secured scarce supplies and transport for them. Renewed, the men did laundry. Whatever of their filthy, verminous clothing they did not throw away was soon boiling in syrup cans over hillside fires. Someone found a German-built bathhouse. One by one, companies hiked two miles to that facility for the men's first hot showers in months. By November 1, the 168th was "on its feet once more, reduced in numbers, but ready to go on with what it had."[28]

The 167th was camping nearby in the Bois de Montrebeau, between Exermont and Apremont. The woods had seen vicious fighting by the 1st Division and showed it, but the Alabamians took heart as clear skies and sunshine replaced rain. The Alabama men, too, itched to clean themselves and their gear. "Buckets, bacon cans, German mess equipment, in fact, all available receptacles were pressed into this service," remembered one Alabama soldier. New clothing and blankets arrived, and another intact German bathhouse came to light. Spirits lifted, they awaited new orders.[29]

Rainbow Division commander Menoher convened infantry brigade commanders Reilly and MacArthur to discuss details of the coming attack and the division's possible role in it. The roster for the assault was undecided. The conclave took place at MacArthur's P.C. at La Neuve-Forge

Farm about half a mile east of Exermont. Apparently worried about leaks, Menoher herded his subordinates upstairs and into MacArthur's bedroom.[30]

Reilly later characterized the space and its furnishings as typical of a French farmhouse: rough plank floor, woodstove, built-in bed, and a small wooden table with three chairs. Two windows' dirty panes filtered the "gloomy light of a wet winter's afternoon" as the men sat.[31]

Menoher summarized the situation along the front, emphasizing Pershing's intense expectations regarding it. He asked MacArthur to comment. As was his habit, MacArthur stood and began to pace, speaking excitedly. His extemporaneous remarks, characteristically, were so comprehensive that Menoher and Reilly "regretted then and afterwards that there was no stenographer present to take it down and preserve it." In sum, MacArthur posited that the Germans were ready to break and that the "Rainbow Division was fully capable of playing its part in such an advance."[32]

Menoher turned to Reilly, who said intelligence from prisoners and observers along the line indicated that the part of the Kriemhilde Stellung facing the 83rd Brigade was no longer the main part of the German defensive line. He advocated an overwhelming barrage of artillery and machine gun fire as the key to a successful infantry attack. He described his brigade as not only ready but eager to make that attack.[33]

Instead, word came from AEF and 1st Army that the better rested 2nd Division was to lead the assault. Reilly persuaded General Summerall to plead his case to higher-ups, but 1st Army and the AEF insisted on using fresh troops, a decision Summerall later mourned.[34]

The Rainbow Division was to be limited to dedicated artillery and machine gun support. For optimum impact, Colonel Reilly asked that the 151st and 149th Machine Gun Battalions be assigned to his command, giving him three machine gun battalions. His request was quickly approved, and Reilly worked with the battalion commanders to place and aim their weapons.[35]

The division's November 1 role fit into a larger plan for using artillery and machine gun fire. Working with Reilly, Colonel William Hughes, division chief of staff, in effect had mapped every German machine gun along the line that confronted the attackers. When orders for the attack came, Hughes and Reilly met with V Corps division commanders and their artillery chiefs at Summerall's headquarters. Hughes explained his and Reilly's methods, and Summerall ordered the artillery commanders

Camp of the 149th Field Artillery near Apremont. (*National Archives*)

to work with Hughes and Reilly to blanket every enemy machine gun with artillery fire. Major Winn of the 151st Machine Gun Battalion was there to answer questions about overhead machine gun fire. Because of Winn's experience at Saint Mihiel and the Côte de Châtillon, Summerall placed him in overall command of the 122 guns.[36]

The artillery barrage began the night of October 31. The machine guns joined in at 3:30 a.m. November 1. The 2nd Battalion of the 166th Infantry had remained in position along the line and watched as the soldiers and Marines of the 2nd Division "leap frogged" at the German lines. One Ohioan waxed jealous of the combined gunnery. "They had us up there S.O.L. [shit out of luck] for two weeks, and now listen to what they're givin' them Marines," he said. "I ain't hankerin' fer no more fight than's necessary, but somebody's always takin' the joy out of life."[37] The fire was extremely effective; the 2nd Division did not suffer a single casualty from German machine gun fire until the men were a mile north of the German lines that ran from Saint Georges to Landres-et-Saint Georges.[38]

As the 2nd Division pushed over the hills beyond the remnants of the Kriemhilde Stellung, the men of the Rainbow Division awaited their imminent turn in pursuit of a now broken enemy toward the Meuse River and the city of Sedan.

12

THE RACE TO SEDAN, NOVEMBER 2–11, 1918

"The Rainbow had entered the line for the last time. It was to make its last forced marches within the next few days. It was to fight its last battle and suffer its last losses in wounded and killed at the hands of the enemy."

—Henry Reilly in *Americans All*

Just after midnight on November 8, Captain Russell Baker, commander of the 166th Infantry's D Company, was called to regimental headquarters at Chémery. He found Colonel Hough waiting. Hough told Baker Colonel Le Comte Denie of the French 40th Division had requested that Colonel Reilly assign one infantry company from the Rainbow Division to accompany the French on their advance to Sedan. Reilly asked Hough to pick a company from the Ohio regiment. D Company was to represent the division in the French advance. Baker quickly returned to his company and got them ready to move out. At 7:00 a.m. on November 8, D Company set out to meet the French.[1]

Baker and his men, accompanied by Captain Harry "Hank" Gowdy and Lieutenant Alison Reppy, arrived in Frenois, where the French division was camped, around noon. They were assigned to the French 252nd Infantry Regiment, reporting to Lieutenant Colonel Ludoric Abel de Ville.

The French, who planned to send patrols toward Sedan that night, had organized a dinner for Baker and the other American officers. The sumptuous meal took place in the high-ceilinged, candle-lit hall of the grandiloquent Château du Nord. Baker asked Lieutenant Reppy to say a few words. Reppy stood, pulling from a pocket a miniature American flag his wife had sent him. Praising France and her army, Reppy turned to the host and explained the symbolism of the stars and stripes, bowed, and presented the flag to the colonel, who clenched the flag, held it high, and shouted, "*Vive l'Amerique!*"[2]

Afterwards, two platoons from D Company accompanied a French patrol into the suburbs of Sedan, reaching the west bank of the Meuse, so close to the city they felt "they could throw pebbles onto the roofs of the silent houses." The pause ended with a burst of Maxim rounds. The patrol withdrew, its D Company participants able to boast that the 166th Infantry had reached "the coveted goal of Sedan."[3]

Orders readying the Rainbow Division infantry regiments to attack were cancelled when the 2nd Division broke through so quickly. Again, hopes for rest bloomed and quickly withered. On November 2, the division moved out on what became an arduous trek in support of the 2nd Division. Chaplain Robb of the 168th Infantry wrote, "Marching all night in the cold, drizzly rain, over muddy and shell torn roads, with but little food and practically no sleep, we moved forward over the roads that were crowded with marching troops, struggling horses, poor and thin from the loss of food, trying to drag their heavy load in pursuit of the rapidly retreating enemy."[4] John Taber concurred: "With cheerless visions of mud, kilometers, and Hell, the 168th left its camp and headed north, a threatening sky overhead and a sloppy road under foot." That night the Iowans bivouacked at a sad-sack former German campsite near Sommerance, most electing to pitch shelter tents rather than sleep in leaky huts.[5]

Alabama's 167th fetched up about a mile south of Sommerance on November 2. The next morning, the regiment marched twelve miles, through Sommerance, Landres-et-Saint Georges, and Imécourt. The men bivouacked on a hillside between Imécourt and Verpel. While moving through Verpel, the soldiers heard a rumor that an armistice had been signed, a phenomenon that dogged their advance. The Alabamians beheld a landscape so riddled by shells that craters overlapped. German corpses, abandoned equipment, and dead horses dotted flattened wheat fields.[6]

The 168th left Sommerance following the 167th's route until reaching Imécourt, where the unit turned northeast and stopped for the night on a hill north of the village, like myriad others nothing but skeletal ruins. The land had been so "completely churned up" by high explosives that a private said, "Well, it might be valuable as a curiosity, but no one but goats and soldiers could ever live on it." Across the road from their bivouac were strewn dead German soldiers and American Marines. Nearly forty abandoned German artillery pieces and mounds of other equipment were nearby. Souvenir hunting broke out. "The American soldier would risk his life for a first-class souvenir, and it had become a common saying in France that the English were fighting for the freedom of the seas, the French for the lost provinces, and the Americans for souvenirs," a soldier said.[7]

The 165th and 166th were in the lead; they had been at the front when orders to move forward arrived. The 166th marched almost ten miles on November 3, reaching Verpel for the night. The men went to bed hungry; supply wagons had stalled in mud and congestion at Champignelles. After several hours, an "officious and bull-headed" M.P. split the supply train, sending the halves by different routes. The wagons did not catch up with the regiment at Verpel until well after midnight.[8]

The 165th reached Brieulles-sur-Bar on November 4, there shifting left to follow the 78th Division's advance. Like other Rainbow Division regiments, the 165th was slowed by supply wagon troubles.[9] The unit had lost more than half its mules and horses, and surviving animals were worn down by hunger, steep muddy roads, and lack of stables, never mind artillery fire and aerial bombing. Many dropped dead in harness.[10]

The morning of November 4 saw the 166th on the march as well. While the night had been wet and without hot food, Sergeant Dana Daniels recorded in his diary that he had scrounged soft, dry straw for the floor of his pup tent, which he had shared with two other soldiers.[11] Amid rumors that the Rainbow Division would soon be passing through the 78th Division to assume the lead in the advance, the regiment made for Brieulles-sur-Bar and Verrières. The Ohioans' lead scouts reached those towns late that afternoon but came under heavy German shelling. At Authe, about two miles southeast of Brieulles-sur-Bar, the 166th made camp for another night without hot food.[12] In the first of many such instances, men saw white flags.[13] The flags, flying from every house, were intended to signal that the Germans had left and as a silent plea not to shell the village.

Lieutenant Alison Reppy greets a French officer at the Château du Nord near Sedan. (*National Archives*)

To the southeast of the 166th, the 167th passed through Sivry-lès-Buzancy and Bar-lès-Buzancy, stopping about a mile north of Bar-lès-Buzancy.[14] The 168th followed on the same route, hiking up and down hills through ankle-deep mud. The men passed a freshly emplaced battery of American ten-inch guns whose crews soon learned that the Germans had retreated out of range. Saint-Pierremont was being shelled, so the Iowans stopped for the night near the 167th campsite.[15]

Rumors about leapfrogging the 78th proved true. Around 9:30 p.m., 42nd Division Headquarters ordered the division to pass through the 78th at noon the next day along a line from Les Petite Armoises to Verrières to Saint Pierre Mont.[16] The division was to take the lead in pursuing the Germans as they retreated toward Sedan and the Meuse River.

That night the skies cleared, and German pilots bombed division campsites, suddenly roaring overhead. Men yelled for smokers to douse cigarettes and "pulled their blankets closer about their necks and prayed." After a long terrible moment, men heard a "breath-taking whish and crash" as a bomb struck the road directly ahead. A second bomb had a mule screaming and men crying out. The pilot banked for another run. "There is nothing so terrifying as to be out in the open under aerial bombardment," wrote one Iowan. "The feeling of absolute impotence and inability to strike back, the strain that in a few moments can eat up the stored vitality of a week—none of this can be translated into words."[17]

There was another whish, another crash, another blinding flash. Bomb racks empty, the aviator strafed the camp before recrossing the Meuse. Another bomber bore in, hitting the Iowans' campsite and the main street of Bar-lès-Buzancy.[18]

The 166th's bivouac near Authe received similar treatment. So did a battalion from the 6th Division, known in the AEF as the "Sight Seeing Sixth" because the unit always seemed to avoid combat. The men from the 6th camped across the road and began to light campfires and fire up field kitchens. Men from the 166th, knowing how close the enemy was, looked on in horror. The regiment's mule drivers urged the newcomers to douse their lights, but no one would listen, and their "lights burned merrily."[19]

Soon bombers came. To no avail, the mule skinners shouted to douse the fires, so they decided to save the 6th's animals, corralling them across the road and taking cover themselves as men from the 6th laughed.[20]

Those devil-may-care lights made fat, tempting targets. At least twelve bombs fell on the 6th's camp, killing several men and destroying equipment. Once the bombers were gone, the mule drivers returned the animals they had saved, barely able to disguise their disgust for the officers and men who refused to listen to experienced front-line soldiers.[21]

Events of the night of November 4 kept the 117th Engineers busy. About midnight, 42nd Division Headquarters learned that the Germans had blown up the causeway across the Bar Valley north of Brieulles-sur-Bar. The 1,000-foot-long, fifteen-foot-high causeway through creeks and marshes was not fit for crossing even on foot. The craters from German explosives yawned every seventy-five feet, some penetrating to the original creek bottom.[22]

The "Fighting Engineers" of the 117th were ordered to repair the causeway. It took them most of the morning of November 5 to assemble their engineering equipment. The engineers worked twenty-four hours a day across the Bar Valley. The 1st Battalion, made up of South Carolinians, completed the main pass at 10:00 p.m. on November 6. Trucks began slowly moving forward, and the engineers jury-rigged a "corduroy" bridge of timbers lashed together and laid to serve as a crude roadway for the infantry on November 5.[23]

The Rainbow Division's leadership had to consider how best to chase and catch the fleeing foe. One factor was the way the enemy was retreating toward the Meuse. After the American breakthrough, the German Supreme Command ordered troops to occupy the Nachhut Stellung by

Men of Ohio's 166th Infantry march along a rail line on November 3, 1918. (*National Archives*)

3:00 a.m. on November 3. This was no fortified position but a line on the map showing natural defensive features.[24]

In the area where the 78th Division had been operating and where the Rainbow Division would now assume responsibility, the Nachhut Stellung ran from north of Ochés to the crossroads west of La Berlière, then to a point on the Pont-Bar to Stonne Highway south of the Nocièves Farm before continuing along the highway to Pont-Bar. This line was defended by the 76th Reserve, the 195th, and the 14th Reserve infantry divisions, who had been ordered to hold their positions until November 4. That afternoon, Third German Army headquarters ordered these troops to begin withdrawing on the night of November 4-5 to the "Brown Line," the next defensive line on the way to Sedan and the Meuse. Like the Nachhut Stellung, the Brown Line was terrain suitable for a delaying action.[25]

The Brown Line began on the Meuse near La Sartelle Farm, running west to the village of Yoncq before hugging hills south of Flaba to the Montgarni Farm and on to the woods below Maisoncelle and a ridge south of Chémery. During the day on November 5, as the Rainbow Division was beginning its advance, the Third German Army ordered the next phase of their withdrawal, a retreat to the Meuse River Stellung. This last line of defense ran from north of the river to a bridgehead position in front of Sedan.[26]

Along these lines, the Germans positioned units to machine-gun pursuing Americans and hold up the American advance, hopscotching groups of gun crews to keep up a murderous rate of fire as the Americans inexorably advanced. German soldiers used all their skill, and, in some cases, made heroic stands and died rather than yield.[27] Given this resistance and the risk of surprise attack, the Rainbow Division elected to not advance via four columns moving along parallel roads with advance guards. Rather, they proceeded with their four infantry regiments advancing abreast and deployed for combat.[28]

By noon on November 5, the 166th were off and, thanks to the 117th Engineers, able to cross the Bar Valley swamp and march through Tannay before arriving in the Bois de Mont Dieu. The unit passed the lines of the 78th Division about 2:30 p.m. The 166th continued into the woods about four miles, throwing out patrols on the advance toward La Neuville-à-Marie. As one patrol approached the village, a German rear guard unit there opened fire. The 1st Battalion and a platoon of the machine gun company, which were in the lead, stopped their advance and spent the night of November 5 in the northern edge of the Bois de Mont Dieu. That evening, the 166th's supply train caught up with the support and reserve battalions. By midnight, those units had arrived at the 1st Battalion's position and were able to provide hot food.[29]

The 165th, with its 1st Battalion in the lead, advanced without resistance through the town of Sy and La Forge Farm. When they reached the château Chartreuse Du Mont-Dieu, German machine gunners slowed them but quickly withdrew when the New Yorkers deployed to attack. Patrols pushed forward into Le Vivier at 4:00 p.m., and thirty minutes later, the patrols and the main battalion reached the Raillère Farm on the northern edge of the Bois du Mont Dieu.[30]

The 168th, up before sunrise, had a hot breakfast and began marching cross-country over the fields around 7:00 a.m. By noon, they had reached a line from Verrières to Saint Pierremont where they were supposed to relieve a unit from the 78th Division. No such unit ever appeared. Colonel Tinley formed the regiment into its usual battle formation with the 3rd Battalion in the lead assault position followed by the 2nd Battalion in support and the 1st Battalion in reserve. K Company, on the left, was able to maintain liaison with the 167th, but no one was able to find the unit from the 77th Division ostensibly advancing on the right. The pace of advance was quick; the German retreat was devolving into a rout. The artillery could not keep up, so lead assault units got extra machine gun

Private Allen Floyd from I Company of the 166th Infantry is greeted by a grateful French couple after their liberation. (*National Archives*)

support. The Iowans had part of the 168th Machine Gun Company and two companies from the 151st Machine Gun Battalion assigned to move forward with the 3rd Battalion.[31]

The terrain the 168th advanced through now stood apart from past settings. Instead of a "hideous, shell-torn" wasteland, the Iowans were traversing smooth, cultivated fields, heavily wooded hills, clear streams, and isolated farms nestled in clearings. Only the occasional shell hole and the distant boom of artillery belied the quietude. Nearing Les Grandes Armoises in the late afternoon the unit ran into light artillery fire. The 3rd Battalion halted for the night about a mile beyond the village on the Les Grandes Armoises to Stonne Road. Downpours and cold winds arrived, accompanied by German artillery fire that fell without injuring a soul.[32] "I never spent a more miserable night," Captain Leon Miesse of the 166th wrote in his diary. "Between the rain and shrapnel, we had a lovely time."[33]

The 167th marched that morning through Fontenois and Saint Pierremont, halting late that morning in a small valley east of Verrières. At noon, the Alabamians moved into combat formation with their 1st Battalion in the lead, encountering light, scattered artillery fire. They moved rapidly through Les Grandes Armoises and into the Bois du Mon Dieu, making about four miles by nightfall and camping near La Grange du Mont Farm.[34]

Residents of Les Grandes Armoises celebrated the unit's arrival. Hundreds of French civilians streamed from their houses, greeting the men with cheers, hugs, kisses, and gifts of bread, apples, and other foods, even commodities in short supply.[35] In one town, the 166th were told young women from area villages all had been kidnapped to Germany to toil as laborers weeks before and that all the men between seventeen and fifty years of age had been taken deep into Germany. Retreating Germans had swiped all the foodstuffs they could carry along with all the livestock.[36]

Despite his armies' success during the first days of November, Pershing, stung by British criticism of their performance in the Meuse-Argonne, yearned to vindicate himself and the AEF. At I Corps Headquarters on the afternoon of November 5, he told I Corps commander General Joseph T. Dickman he wanted American forces to take Sedan.[37]

A few hours later, General Fox Conner, AEF Chief of Staff, called at 1st Army Headquarters, intending to direct General Liggett to see that Pershing's desires were met. Neither Liggett nor his chief of staff, General Drum, was present, so Conner and Colonel George Marshall, the 1st Army planning chief, drafted an order reading, "General Pershing desires that the honor of entering Sedan should fall to the American First Army. He has every confidence that the troops of the I Corps, assisted on their right by the V Corps, will enable him to realize this desire."[38]

Marshall decided to hold the order until Liggett or Drum had approved its contents. Drum was the first to return to headquarters; he approved it—in edited form. "In transmitting the foregoing message, your attention is invited to the favorable opportunity now existing for pressing our advantage throughout the night," he added. "Boundaries will not be considered binding." The revised order went to the I and V Corps commanders.[39]

Erasing divisional boundaries violated every aspect of good military common sense, and the language invited the widest possible interpretation, inspiring contradictory orders and confusion. At V Corps headquarters, General Summerall read the message, focusing on its ending sentence, and decided to "grab additional glory" for his corps and the 1st Division, in particular. He ordered the 1st Division on a forced night march November 5-6 to capture Sedan. Not only were the 77th Division and 42nd Division of I Corps advancing well ahead of the 1st Division—to reach Sedan, but the 1st Division would also have to cut across I Corps boundaries, pushing the other two divisions out of the way.[40]

The 1st Division's grab for glory not only hampered the Rainbow Division; it also slowed everyone. The 1st Division eventually strayed so far west that the troops entered the French Fourth Army's sector. General Liggett was unaware of what Drum had done until November 7 when he received an angry complaint from the French. Liggett exploded, later saying this was "the only occasion in the war when I lost my temper completely." He immediately directed the 1st Division to withdraw. Summerall's bizarre grandstanding embarrassed Pershing, undercutting his campaign to show the French and British that the AEF was a disciplined, mature military organization.[41]

The night of November 5, 42nd Division Headquarters issued Field Order No. 53 which stated:

> 1. The enemy is retreating rapidly across the Meuse. The 40th Div. (French) is in liaison on our left. The 77th Div. is in liaison on our right. The First Army Corps continues the pursuit with the object of defeating the enemy's rear guards and capturing or destroying his troops and transports before a crossing is affected.
> 2. The 42nd Div. will continue the pursuit tomorrow at 530 hrs., will reach the Meuse and secure the bridge head at Sedan.
> 3. The pursuit will be pushed with the utmost vigor. The opportunity presented to the Division is one of the most brilliant of the war. Brigade and regimental commanders will by personal example and leadership, insure the rapid progress of the front line battalions.[42]

The next day, November 6, the Rainbow Division continued its advance. In heavy morning fog, all four infantry regiments moved forward, encountering only light resistance. One regiment characterized the advance as "little more than a walking match."[43]

During the morning, a small group from K Company of the 168th went half a mile ahead to scout a farmhouse the Germans had just abandoned. A woman there, amazed to see American soldiers, excitedly summoned her family to greet these most unexpected but very welcome visitors. After she was joined by her elders, a "sad looking young girl," and three small children bussing the doughboys, she insisted the Americans allow her to pour coffee—roasted barley, she admitted shamefacedly, but served with Relief Commission sugar. The woman said she had not heard from her husband and brother since they left for army service in August 1914. The Germans had taken everything, even chickens, cattle, and horses. After doing their best to answer a plethora of questions, the men of the patrol shook hands and departed with a hearty "*Bonne chance!*"[44]

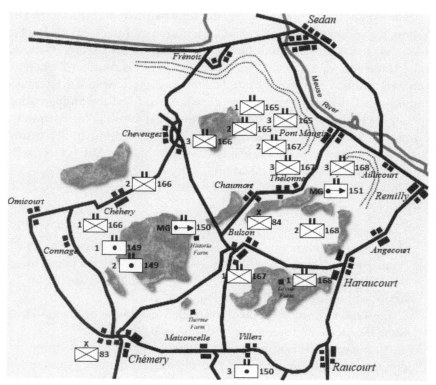

Map 11. The Rainbow Division's final positions opposite Sedan on November 8, 1918. (*Author*)

Later that day, the 168th's scouts reached the outskirts of Haraucourt. As in most area villages and towns, a white flag flew from the church steeple. The scouts nonetheless approached with caution, as did civilians they met, until the officer leading the scouts announced, "*Nous sommes Américains.*" Joy reigned. *Tricoleurs* hidden for four years appeared in the windows of nearly every home.[45]

The Ohioans of the 166th received a similar welcome in Chémery-sur-Bar, where they arrived to cheers, flowers, and embraces. The people provided warm billets for the night in their homes, where Dana Daniels of E Company said the men dried their clothes and blankets and "hunted cooties." They also found one German soldier whom they took prisoner but not before a villager took the opportunity to pummel him. Saved from assault, he was apparently very willing to talk, saying that the Germans were massing to make a stand just south of Sedan.[46]

During the night of November 6, the 166th lost contact with the 165th on their right but did manage to gain liaison with the French 40th Division to their immediate left across the Bar River. The French commanding officer sent word to Colonel Hough via the American liaison officer, Lieutenant Lombardi, that they had received no orders changing sector boundaries, which meant that Sedan was within the French sector. But since the relationship between Hough and the French was so cordial, they agreed that any overlapping would not become a subject of controversy.[47]

At this point, while relations between the 166th and the French were smooth, the American 1st Division was still blundering about in a blind charge to be the first to reach Sedan. General Liggett's change to the orders sent out by General Drum regarding sector boundaries had not yet arrived at the 1st Division. At about 1:00 a.m. on November 7, the 16th Infantry Regiment of the 1st Division appeared out of the dark and marched past the Beauménil Farm in the 168th Infantry's sector. The Iowans' guards from I Company halted the men from the 16th and told their officers that there was nothing but Germans ahead. The officer in command of the 16th's men arrogantly replied, "Hell, this is the 1st Division, Regular Army—forward, march." At Pont-Maugis they thought to spend the night. But a German infantry battalion was still occupying that village, and when the 16th Infantry entered, the Germans laid down a withering fire that drove the Regular Army back in ignominious retreat.[48]

During the night of November 6-7, 42nd Division headquarters issued orders for the following day. Field Order No. 54, which reached most regimental commanders after midnight, said: "1. The enemy is still in retreat. The 1st Army Corps continues the attack. 2. The 42nd Div. will continue the pursuit at once and will continue it day and night without halting. The Meuse will be reached and Sedan will be taken tonight [November 7]."[49] As with most orders issued by the division in recent weeks, this one set almost certainly unattainable goals. It seemed to assume that such an advance could be made without a well-coordinated plan or artillery support. While German resistance was fading, there was little doubt that the foe would put up a fierce fight to hold the bridgehead at Sedan.

The 168th set out at 6:30 a.m. on November 7. The 3rd Battalion remained in the lead. The men advanced easily until, cresting a hill west of Aillicourt and Remilly-Aillicourt near the Meuse, they caught the heaviest machine gun fire they had seen during the advance, along with artillery fire from a height across the river. The lead companies withdrew to the road below the crest and reorganized. The fusillade was such that the men from the 168th could not move. Everyone dug in.[50]

To the left of the 168th, the 167th Infantry had experienced heavy German artillery and machine gun fire throughout the night of November 6-7, and the men could see the sky behind the German lines lit brightly as the enemy burned their last remaining supplies on this side of the Meuse. On the morning of November 7, ordered by I Corps to immediately speed up, the 167th advanced. Lieutenant Colonel Bare would have preferred to wait until more troops were on his flanks. He had the 2nd Battalion move to the lead on the left, and they moved forward in dense fog along the Bulson to Thèlonne road until they reached a steep hill west of Thèlonne. German artillery fire dictated a pause. Once over the hill, the battalion moved on toward the village of Noyers-Pont-Maugis under increasingly heavy machine gun fire. They drove the German gunners back, but a sudden rent in the fog exposed two companies of Alabamians. Germans opened up with machine guns and minenwerfers, inflicting numerous casualties. The battalion withdrew to a ravine southwest of Noyers-Pont-Maugis.[51]

To the 2nd Battalion's right, the 3rd Battalion moved forward about half a mile southwest of Thèlonne, where a high road embankment provided cover. The battalion commander, Captain Fallow, sent a company to advance into Thèlonne, assigned a strong patrol to establish a position along the Meuse River near Pont-Maugis, and had the balance of the battalion remain behind in support. At noon, M Company drove the Germans out of Thèlonne and established outposts north of the town. Then, the patrols pushed on to the river at 2:15 p.m., the first unit in the division to reach the Meuse.[52]

The 165th moved forward around 7:30 a.m., immediately receiving heavy fire from Hills 346 and 252 to their north. The two lead companies, very short of ammunition, took Hill 346 in a bayonet charge, inflicting numerous casualties and taking many prisoners. At 1:30 p.m., the 3rd Battalion advanced past Hill 346 and captured Hill 252. Ninety minutes later, the regiment sent two patrols of about twenty men each to scout toward Wadelincourt. They were a hundred yards away when they encountered strong resistance, so they pulled back and dug in.[53]

On the division's far left, Colonel Hough of the 166th had also ignored the order to move out to take Sedan overnight. He did direct the 3rd Battalion to move out at 2:30 a.m., followed by the 2nd and 1st Battalions

A recent photo of the village of Thèlonne. (*Major William Carraway, Historian, Georgia Army National Guard*)

once the men had a hot meal at 3:00 a.m.[54] Lead patrols from the 3rd Battalion reached Chéhéry by 4:00 a.m. and quickly moved through the town, capturing Germans trying to drive two trucks away.[55] The 3rd Battalion pressed on despite increased German artillery and machine gun fire. As the rest of the regiment moved through Chéhéry, patrols from the 28th Infantry of the 1st Division showed up right behind them. This surprised Colonel Hough, who had not known that the 1st Division had received similar orders to take Sedan.[56]

Shortly, General John Parker, commander of the 1st Division, arrived in Chéhéry. He set up a command post and told Colonels Hough and Reilly he was going to advance on Sedan no matter what orders the 166th had received.[57]

The 28th Infantry marched out of Chéhéry right beside the men from the 2nd Battalion on the highway to Sedan and began to try to overtake the 3rd Battalion in the advance position. Major Haubrich kept the 3rd Battalion in the tragicomic race for Sedan. As enemy resistance increased near Cheveuges around 9:20 a.m., Major Haubrich called for the 2nd Battalion to move forward to his left while the 1st Battalion came forward on his right. He planned to envelop both flanks of the German defenses, but 1st Division troops balked. They moved up on his line of advance and would not withdraw, preventing his attack.[58]

While Haubrich was trying to wrangle the 28th Infantry, K Company of the 166th Infantry's 3rd Battalion moved forward toward Cheveuges along the road from the village of Chéhéry. Despite enemy artillery fire, the company made good progress until heavy machine gun fire brought them to an abrupt halt. The company commander, Captain Reuben Hutchcraft, moved forward to the leading edge of the company to investigate. "Hutch," as he was known to close friends in the regiment, was described by Colonel Hough as "honest, chivalrous, and fearless." Hough saw him as the very epitome of a soldier and an officer and gentleman. Small in stature, he was referred to by his platoon when a new lieutenant as "the Boy Scout."[59] His men soon came to admire and respect him as a leader.

Crouching low to the ground, Hutchcraft could see that the Germans had hidden their Maxims well in a copse of pines atop a knoll north of Cheveuges and about 100 yards away from K Company's position. He ordered his men to stay down and zigzagged up the slope toward the German position. The Germans focused fire on him, but he eluded their aim until, thirty yards from the enemy, he fell, "his body riddled with bullets."[60]

Seeing his captain go down, Private Eli Mutie got up and tried to run to Hutchcraft's aid. He only got a few feet. Corporal John Allen, Private Earl Dempsey, and Private Bobell Purdy each set out, also with fatal results. Private Werner Eich slithered seventy yards to the captain. Eich tried to stem the bleeding, to no avail. Grasping Eich's hands, Hutchcraft said, "They've got me, boys, but don't give up," and died.[61]

Fierce fighting continued along the road and by 2:00 p.m. the situation had deteriorated to the point that no further progress was possible. Haubrich ordered all men on the line of attack to dig in. They were about a half-mile south of Cheveuges and only about four miles from the Meuse and Sedan, with the Germans on a hill two miles below the riverbanks.[62] There was no artillery support, and the units from the two different American divisions refused to cooperate.[63]

Late on the afternoon of November 7, orders from Division Headquarters said all American units within the 42nd Division's boundaries were under the direct command of the 83rd Brigade. The orders also told the 166th to fall back and make camp in La Neuville-á-Maire. The lead position was to go to the French 40th Division. This was intended to show respect for the long-suffering French and was seen by everyone as very appropriate.[64]

Top, the village of Chéhéry. Bottom, members of the 166th Infantry outside Cheveuges. The hill in the distance on the left is where Captain Hutchcraft and the men who tried to rescue him were killed on November 7, 1918. (*National Archives*)

During the day on November 8, the Rainbow Division was relieved, and its regiments began to pull back to rest. Unknown to them, peace negotiations were bearing fruit. By the end of October, the Germans accelerated their peace campaign because of unrest inside Germany and the steady attrition of its allies. Bulgarian support for the Central Powers had collapsed on September 29, the Turks had sued for peace on October 30, and the rapidly deteriorating Austro-Hungarians had made a separate

Recent photo of the view of Sedan from the final positions of the 151st Machine Gun Battalion. (*Major William Carraway, Historian, Georgia Army National Guard*)

peace with the Allies on November 3. The last German senior officer opposed to reaching an armistice and a peace agreement was General Erich Ludendorff, who was dismissed by German chief of staff, Field Marshal Paul von Hindenburg, on October 26. On October 29, sailors in the German High Seas Fleet refused orders to put to sea. Their actions encouraged a civilian peace faction, and civilian strikes and anti-government demonstrations multiplied across Germany.[65]

On the night of November 7, a German delegation crossed the French lines to set terms for an armistice with the Allies. The Kaiser abdicated, and revolution broke out in Germany. Marshal Foch gave the German representatives until 11:00 a.m. on November 11 to sign the agreement. At 5:10 a.m. on November 11, 1918, the Germans signed the armistice agreement, which would take effect at 11:00 a.m.[66] The "war to end all wars" was over, and the Rainbow Division's fighting was done at last.

13

ARMISTICE, NOVEMBER 11, 1918

> Comrades true, born anew, peace to you. Your souls will be where heroes are and your memory shine like the morning star. Brave and dear, shield us here. Farewell!
> —From the poem, "Rouge Bouquet," by Joyce Kilmer, Sergeant, 165th Infantry Regiment, killed in action at the Ourcq River, July 30, 1918

Official word of the armistice began to reach most of the Rainbow Division the afternoon of November 11; the 165th Infantry did not receive the news until the night of November 13.[1] All units were heading south to the rear as the war ended. For the first time since August 1914, a person could not hear artillery rumbling from the direction of the front. Private Roy Baily of the 166th wrote in his diary, "Left Sammouth at 8 a.m. arrived at 2 p.m. in Beffu. Noise stopped at 11a.m."[2]

Reactions varied. In the 166th, there was little outright expression. The only thought in most Ohioans' minds seems to have been going home.[3] Chaplain Robb revealed the news to the men of the 168th from the steps of a shell-torn church in Briquenay. "It really was beyond comprehension, this glorious news—too much to grasp all at once," an Iowan wrote. "No more whizz-bangs, no more bombs, no more mangled, bleeding bodies, no more exposure to terrifying shell fire in the rain and cold and mud!" The regimental band blared George M. Cohan's "Over There" and the Iowans bellowed "We won't come back till it's over, over there." Now, it was over.[4]

Like the Ohioans, the Alabama men of the 167th greeted the news with great reserve. "They received the announcement with a quiet significance," wrote one soldier. "There was no cheering, no outward signs of enthusiasm, for they were glad beyond expression."[5]

On November 13, the 165th Regiment arrived in Landres-et-Saint Georges, the town the New Yorkers had fought so hard and unsuccessfully to capture in mid-October. That night, after the men had pitched their tents on a nearby hillside, the official announcement was made. In celebration, the men liberated signal rockets, lit the night sky with them, and started huge bonfires all over the hillside where they were camped.[6]

The men of the division would not be heading home soon. The Rainbow Division was to be part of the new 3rd Army, or the Army of Occupation, based along the western bank of the Rhine River. The men would sleep in billets that seemed luxurious and have three hot meals per day. Despite the boredom and a deep desire to go home, this duty was far from disagreeable.

News in March of an inspection and review by General Pershing set the 42nd's rumor mill spinning. Men believed pervasively that this was a step on the journey home. The division's regiments began practicing, and, on March 8, Dana Daniels of the 166th recorded that they had "an inspection of short packs, mess gears, bayonets, rifles, helmets, shoes, and clothes" in preparation for the review.[7]

On March 16, 1919, a cloudy day marked by rain and snow flurries, Pershing reviewed and inspected the Rainbow Division at the Ludendorff Bridge in Remagen, Germany.[8] Not long after Pershing and his entourage departed, news came that the Rainbow Division was going home.

The first of the infantry regiments to leave was New York's 165th. The men of the Fightin' 69th boarded trains for the French port of Brest on April 2, 1919. On April 6, they embarked for Hoboken aboard two troopships, one of which was the U.S.S. *Harrisonburg*, a converted liner known as the *City of Paris* before being acquired by the U.S. Navy.[9]

The regiment arrived April 21 in New York harbor, greeted by a flotilla carrying friends and family. As would be the process for all the regiments, men not from New York received their discharges and were sent home individually. A few days later, the rest of the regiment paraded down Fifth

Avenue in Manhattan as thousands cheered.[10]

The Ohioans of the 166th boarded trains to Brest over three days from April 6-8. They boarded the giant passenger ship *Leviathan*, once a German-flagged luxury liner called *Vaterland*.[11] Joining them were the Iowans of the 168th, who had left Germany on April 8.[12] The *Leviathan* was too large to dock at Brest, so the ship anchored in the harbor and small boats ferried the men of the 166th and 168th to the ship, whose coal bunkers needed filling. Told it might take days to recruit a coal gang, hundreds of soldiers volunteered. They donned blue denim overalls and went to work. By April 17, the *Leviathan* was fueled. She hauled anchor and set off across the Atlantic.[13]

Colonel Donovan leads the 165th Infantry through the Victory Arch during their parade down Fifth Avenue. (*National Archives*)

The *Leviathan* arrived in New York on April 25 and docked at Hoboken, New Jersey. The men of the 166th disembarked immediately; the 168th left the ship the following day. The 166th went to Camp Brewer and the 168th went to Camp Upton, both on Long Island. Men not from Ohio or Iowa were discharged and went home.[14]

The 166th left Camp Brewer for Ohio on May 9. The trains pulled out around 10:00 a.m. and, traveling via Syracuse, Buffalo, Dunkirk, Cleveland, Galion, and Delaware, reached Columbus between 3:00 p.m. and 3:45 p.m. on Saturday, May 10, 1919, to participate in a grand parade.[15] Seemingly every newspaper in Ohio had carried the story of the 166th's return as front-page news, and people from the companies' hometowns traveled to the state capital to see the parade. Columbus Mayor George J. Karb directed that all businesses close when the parade began at 4:00 p.m. and that factory whistles greet the men being called the "Gallant Buckeyes."[16] Streets around Union Station in Columbus thrummed with relatives wanting to be the first to welcome their "boys" home. Conservative estimates put the crowd for the parade at 20,000.[17]

The 168th Infantry performed a final pass in review at Camp Upton on May 3 before boarding trains for Iowa on May 11. As their three trains crossed the Mississippi River into Iowa at Dubuque, Davenport, and

K Company of the 166th Infantry parades down the streets of Delaware, Ohio, after their return from France. (*National Archives*)

Keokuk on May 13, each was "vociferously greeted by the townspeople, and by committees of prominent citizens from all over the State." Each town staged a parade, which was accompanied by speeches, flowers, and food. As the regiment's trains continued toward Des Moines, their journey became what John Taber called a "progress of triumph unequalled in the history of Iowa." As the trains passed through smaller towns along their three parallel routes, mobs of citizens cheered. John Taber wrote, "Even at the cross-roads small crowds of country people gathered to shout their welcome as the trains shot by" and "Cedar Rapids, Marshalltown, Waterloo, Ottumwa, and Oskaloosa met them with enormous throngs and rousing receptions."[18]

All three trains finally arrived in the capital city during the wee hours of May 14. Despite the "untimeliness" of their arrival, thousands of Iowans were there to cheer. The men remained on the trains until disembarking for a lunch at the city's coliseum and a massive parade. A holiday had been declared in the city and throngs lined the parade route. "The streets through which the parade was to pass were gay with flags and bunting, and leading up the hill to the State House, where the reviewing stand was placed, a court of honor, culminating in an arch of triumph, had been erected," John Taber wrote. "The sky was blue, the air was clear—it was a perfect day."[19]

The 167th's Alabamians departed by train for Brest on April 6. The U.S. Navy provided three battleships for their journey across the Atlantic: U.S.S. *Minnesota, Montana*, and *North Carolina*. The dreadnoughts departed Brest on April 15 and arrived in New York on April 25. The regiment was sent to Camp Merritt, New Jersey, where the men from outside Alabama were discharged before the rest boarded trains for Camp Shelby, Mississippi. The trains crossed into Alabama on May 9, reaching Montgomery on May 12 for celebrations and a parade before heading to Camp Shelby, where the regiment's men were mustered out by May 18.[20]

Via this process, repeated across all the division's units, the Rainbow Division passed into history. While reactivated in World War II and still referred to as the Rainbow Division, the reconstituted unit comprised regiments created by the draft and enlistment rather than from National Guard forces.

The Rainbow Division's history in the Great War is a story of valor and sacrifice. The 168th's chaplain, Winfred Robb, would later write of this remarkable group of citizen-soldiers:

> We wondered by what process of fate, better men than ourselves had been called upon to pass through the door of death leaving their loved ones and all behind, while ours was to be the privilege of returning to home and friends. We had passed, as our dead had passed, through a long summer of battle, but to us fate had been very kind.[21]

The final chapter of the Saint Mihiel and Meuse-Argonne Offensives concluded in the early 1930s with establishment and construction of American military cemeteries in both regions. Combined, the cemeteries contain the graves of more than 18,000 American soldiers, many from the Rainbow Division. Placed under the care of the American Battle Monuments Commission in 1934, they still enjoy that stewardship. The Saint Mihiel American Cemetery lies west of Thiaucourt. The Meuse-Argonne Cemetery, largest of the American World War I cemeteries, is east of Romagne-sous-Montfaucon. An inscription on a wall of the chapel at the Saint Mihiel American Cemetery reads, "This chapel has been erected by the United States of America in grateful remembrance of her sons who died in the World War." This inscription and all those in the American World War I cemeteries in France seek not to glorify war nor the Allied victory, but simply honor Americans who made the tragic and supreme sacrifice for a cause in which most truly believed.[22]

Perhaps the best tribute for those lost from the Rainbow Division came from Father Duffy: "Men pass away, but institutions survive. In time we shall all go to join our comrades who gave up their lives in France. But in our own generation, when the call came, we accepted the flag of our fathers; we have added to it new glory and renown—and we pass it on."[23]

AFTERWORD

After the war, a few men who were part of the Rainbow Division story continued in military service; most returned to civilian life. Here are brief biographies of those whose experiences or post-war writings influenced this volume:

Walter Bare. The executive officer of the 167th Infantry who played a key role in the final capture of the Côte de Chatillon, Bare returned from France to resume working as a manager at the telephone company in Birmingham, Alabama. He continued to serve in the Alabama National Guard. He passed away on February 5, 1937, at age 44.[1]

Ernest Bennett. Following his demotion to administrative duties as commander of the 168th Infantry, Bennett contracted influenza in September 1918 and was hospitalized in Vittel. He returned home to Des Moines, Iowa, was discharged, and began a career in public service as treasurer and later first district supervisor for Polk County. He died of pneumonia at the Veteran's Administration Hospital in Des Moines in 1950.[2]

Robert Brown. After being relieved as commander of the 84th Brigade, Brown remained in Europe commanding American rest camps in Great Britain and France. In 1919 he was assigned to the 26th Division during that unit's occupation of the west bank of the Rhine River in Germany. He returned to the United States in September 1919 and commanded a variety of units, retiring from active duty in November 1923. He was 77 when he died at the Presidio in San Francisco, California, in September 1937.[3]

Raymond Cheseldine. One of the two chroniclers of the 166th Infantry's history, Cheseldine went into publishing with Madison Press in London,

Ohio. In 1924, he returned to active duty as a lieutenant colonel in his state's militia bureau. Cheseldine resumed civilian life in 1929 and worked on the Federal Reserve Board and for the Federal Trade Commission. Recalled to active duty during World War II, he worked in the industrial division of the Office of the Chief of Ordnance in the War Department. In 1945, he was promoted to colonel and went to occupied Germany as an advisor to General Lucius Clay, commander of American forces there. He later became an executive assistant to the undersecretary of the army, retiring in 1951. He passed away on December 26, 1954, and is buried in Arlington National Cemetery.[4]

Dana Daniels. A soldier who kept a detailed wartime diary, Daniels returned home to Union County, Ohio. He farmed and was very active in veterans organizations. He purchased and operated the White Swan Tavern on State Route 4 between Marysville and Marion, Ohio. Daniels died on June 25, 1953, and was laid to rest at Oakdale Cemetery in Marysville.[5]

William Donovan. Donovan became commander of the 165th Infantry during the fighting near Landres-et-Saint Georges. In 1923, he was awarded the Medal of Honor for valor in that action. During the presentation ceremony, Donovan refused to keep the medal, saying that it belonged not to him but "to the boys who are not here, the boys who are resting under the white crosses in France or in the cemeteries of New York, also to the boys who were lucky enough to come through."[6] He returned to legal work, holding positions in the U.S. Department of Justice before founding his own law firm in 1929. Though a Republican and a harsh critic of Franklin D. Roosevelt, he and FDR became close during the 1930s due to shared concern about a coming second war in Europe. In 1941, Roosevelt named Donovan to lead the Office of Strategic Services, created to further American espionage activities and unconventional warfare operations during World War II. After the war, Donovan returned to his law practice until President Harry S. Truman appointed him to head the new Central Intelligence Agency in 1947. He died on February 8, 1959.[7]

Father Francis P. Duffy. Father Duffy was arguably the epitome of what a military chaplain in combat should be and was greatly admired, loved, and respected by the men of the 165th Infantry. Returning to New York City, his hometown, he served as pastor of Holy Cross Church in Hell's Kitchen, a block from Times Square, and was very active in activities of the regiment's veterans organization. He died on June 27, 1932, and was buried in Old Saint Raymond's Cemetery in the Bronx with full military honors.[8]

Thomas Fallow. The man who flanked the Germans by leading a detachment from the 167th Infantry through a gap built into the barbed wire at the base of the Côte de Chatillon, Fallow returned to his home in Opelika, Alabama. He worked there as a bank clerk until his death on July 21, 1949, at age 58.[9]

Ferdinand Foch. The mercurial chief of the French general staff who sparked several confrontations with John Pershing, Foch served as a military representative to the Paris Peace Conference, where he argued for punitive treatment of Germany including permanent occupation of the west banks of the Rhine by foreign troops. He was deeply critical of the Treaty of Versailles. "This is not peace," he said. "It is an armistice for 20 years."[10] Foch died on March 20, 1929, and was buried in Les Invalides, next to Napoleon.[11]

John Hayes. Company clerk for the 167th Infantry's I Company and author of a wartime memoir, Hayes returned to Tallapoosa, Alabama. In the late 1920s he relocated to Palatka, Florida, where he clerked at the post office. He passed away on September 17, 1971, at age 79.[12]

Martin Hogan. Author of a post-war memoir, Hogan returned home to New York City. He found work as a deckhand on a tugboat, remaining in the 165th Infantry and rising to first lieutenant.[13] He became an auditor, moving briefly to Cleveland, Ohio, before returning to New York City, where he died in April 1961.[14]

Benson Hough. The 166th Infantry's much beloved commanding officer returned to his law practice in Delaware, Ohio, becoming a Justice on the Ohio Supreme Court in 1920. He was promoted to major general in the Ohio National Guard in 1923, the same year he left the state high court to become U.S. Attorney for the Southern District of Ohio. In 1925 he was confirmed by the U.S. Senate as a Judge for the U.S. District Court for the Southern District of Ohio. He remained in office until his sudden death from a heart attack on November 19, 1935.[15]

Michael J. Lenihan. The commander of the 42nd Division's 83rd Brigade who was relieved of command during the Meuse-Argonne Offensive, Lenihan remained in the army and reverted to his peacetime rank of colonel in 1919. He taught at the Naval War College before becoming Chief of Staff of the XII Army Corps in 1924. Lenihan was promoted to brigadier general in 1925. In the last year of his active army service, he commanded the 3rd Infantry Division in 1928-29.[16] He died in Philadelphia, Pennsylvania, on August 13, 1958, at the age of 93.[17]

Douglas MacArthur. MacArthur was named superintendent at the U.S. Military Academy at West Point, New York, which allowed him to retain his wartime rank of brigadier general and not revert to his peacetime rank of major.[18] He left West Point in 1922 and began a series of assignments in the Philippines, Georgia, and Maryland. In November 1930, he was appointed U.S. Army Chief of Staff and promoted to major general. In 1935, he was offered the position of Field Marshal of the Commonwealth of the Philippines by Manuel Quezon, President of the Philippines. With President Roosevelt's approval, MacArthur accepted the assignment, which also included his Regular Army duties as military advisor to the Commonwealth Government of the Philippines.[19] In the summer of 1941, with war looming in the Pacific, Roosevelt federalized the Philippine Army, named MacArthur commander of U.S. Army Forces in the Far East, and promoted him to lieutenant general. In December 1941, MacArthur led the desperate and ill-fated defense of the Philippines until President Roosevelt ordered him evacuated to Australia in February 1942.[20] Two months later, MacArthur was appointed Supreme Commander of Allied Forces in the Southwest Pacific Area of Operations. He led successful campaigns to drive the Japanese from New Guinea in 1943-44 and the Philippines in 1944-45. MacArthur accepted the formal surrender of the Japanese in Tokyo Bay in September 1945, then oversaw the occupation of Japan until the United States returned power to the Japanese government in 1949.[21] When North Korea invaded South Korea in June 1950, MacArthur was assigned to lead all United Nations forces. He remained in that role until relieved by President Truman in April 1951 for his controversial public remarks regarding American military policy in Korea. MacArthur retired and lived quietly in civilian life until his death in April 1964.

Charles MacArthur. The author of *A Bug's-Eye View of the War*, MacArthur initially returned to Chicago, Illinois, where he had made a reputation as a reporter. In the early 1920s, he moved to New York City where he began a highly successful career as a playwright and screenwriter. His works included *The Front Page*, a hit comic play based in part on his own experiences as a journalist and adapted to film in 1931 and 1974, as well as screenplays for *Wuthering Heights* (1939) and *Gunga Din*

(1939). He was a member of the Algonquin Round Table and shared an apartment with author Robert Benchley. In 1928, he married actress Helen Hayes, a match that lasted the rest of his life. MacArthur passed away in New York City on April 21, 1956, at age 61.[22]

William Mann. Mann, who along with Douglas MacArthur was the architect of the 42nd Division and served as the unit's first commander until relieved by General Pershing in December 1917, returned to the United States and was assigned to command the Department of the East in the United States. He retired from the army in July 1918.[23] He became an executive at the Equitable Trust Company of New York, working for Equitable until his death in Washington, D.C., on October 8, 1934, at age 80.[24]

George C. Marshall. The officer responsible for planning the Saint Mihiel and Meuse-Argonne Offensives, Marshall went on to a remarkable career. As the army's Chief of Staff during World War II, he oversaw and directed operations in Europe and the Pacific. President Truman appointed him as Secretary of State in 1947. In that position, he shepherded into being the eponymous Marshall Plan for rebuilding Western Europe, for which in 1953 he received the Nobel Peace Prize. In 1950-51, he was Secretary of Defense. He passed away on October 16, 1959, and is buried in Arlington National Cemetery.[25]

Charles T. Menoher. In November 1918, Menoher was promoted to the permanent rank of brigadier general and left the 42nd Division to command the VI Corps. In December 1918, he was named director of the U.S. Army Air Service. Largely because of friction with his assistant, Colonel William Mitchell, he was relieved of the post at his own request in October 1921. He was promoted to major general in March 1921 and in 1922-24 commanded the U.S. Army's Hawaiian Division, and in 1925-26 the IX Corps Area at San Francisco. He retired from the Army in March 1926 and died in Washington, D.C., on August 11, 1930. He is buried in Section 3 of Arlington National Cemetery.[26]

Leon Miesse. Author of a journal and a prolific correspondent, Miesse returned home to his wife in Lancaster, Ohio. He eventually relocated to Salem, New Jersey, where he became a plant engineer at the Anchor Hocking factory. The men in the plant called him "Cap" for Captain. He never spoke much about his wartime experiences to his children or grandchildren. He passed away in April 1979.[27]

Thomas Neibaur. The diminutive Chauchat gunner who helped stop a German counterattack at the Côte de Chatillon, Neibaur spent several months in field hospitals recovering from his wounds. A German bullet remained in his hip the rest of his life. Awarded the Medal of Honor, Neibaur returned home to a hero's welcome from 10,000 fellow residents of Sugar City, Idaho. He reclaimed his job in a sugar beet factory until 1928 when his arm was severely mangled in an accident involving a cutting machine. Permanently disabled, he struggled to survive during the Great Depression. When the public learned of his plight in 1939, popular pressure resulted in him being hired as a night security officer at the state capitol building in Boise. In 1941, he entered a veterans' hospital in Walla Walla, Washington, for tuberculosis and died there on December 23, 1942, at age 44.[28]

Ravee Norris. One of two key architects of the successful assault on the Côte de Châtillon, Norris returned to Jefferson, Alabama, and was honorably discharged in June 1919. He moved to Richmond, Virginia, where he married and became a real estate broker. He died on November 18, 1972, at 84.[29]

John J. Pershing. Following his return to the United States, the venerable commander of the AEF was promoted to General of the Armies for his distinguished service during World War I. Congress authorized the President to promote Pershing to this rank, the highest possible for any member of the armed forces, which was created especially for him.[30] He became the army's chief of staff in 1921, remaining so until his retirement in 1924 at age 64. In 1938, struck down by heart disease, he took up residence at Washington, D.C.'s Walter Reed Army Hospital, where he resided until his death on July 15, 1948, at age 87. He lay in state at the U.S. Capitol for two days before being interred with full military honors at Arlington National Cemetery.[31]

Henri-Phillipe Pétain. The renowned French general, who became a key ally of John Pershing in the creation of a separate American army in France, remained in the French army. Between the wars, he commanded that force and served twice as a government minister. He was known as *le vieux Maréchal* ("the Old Marshal"). When France fell in June 1940, Pétain elected to negotiate an armistice with Germany and lead the collaborationist government headquartered at Vichy, France. After the war, Pétain was tried, convicted for treason, and sentenced to death. Due to his age and World War I service, his sentence was commuted to life in prison. Pétain died in a private home in Port-Joinville on the Île d'Yeu on July 23, 1951, at age 96.[32]

Henry Reilly. Reilly remained a brigadier general in the reserves and began a career as an author and correspondent while working for the *Chicago Tribune* and as publisher and editor of the *Army-Navy Journal*. He suffered a stroke in 1957 before passing away on December 13, 1963.[33]

Alison Reppy. Reppy was the other recorder of the 166th Infantry's history. After his discharge, he re-enrolled at the University of Chicago, where he received a doctorate in jurisprudence in 1922. He became a member of the St. Louis law firm of Buder & Buder. He wrote numerous legal texts and served as a law professor at the University of Oklahoma, Rutgers University, and New York University. In 1950 he became dean of the New York University Law School, a position he held until his death on August 20, 1958.[34]

Winfred Robb. The beloved chaplain of the 168th Infantry returned to the United States in 1919. He moved to California where he left the ministry and worked as a farmer before becoming postmaster of Riverside, California.[35] He died on August 28, 1963, at age 74.[36]

Lloyd Ross. The other key architect of success on the Côte de Châtillon, Ross remained in the Iowa National Guard, rising to major general and command of the 34th Division, composed of National Guard units from Iowa, Minnesota, North Dakota, and South Dakota. In 1940, he retired from the army and continued to work as Iowa's assistant Secretary of State. He died in Des Moines, Iowa, on August 8, 1958.[37]

William Screws. As commander of Alabama's 167th Infantry, Screws was one of only two regiment commanders in the Rainbow Division to remain in his position throughout the war. Upon returning to Alabama, he went back to work as an inspector and instructor for the Alabama National Guard, serving until 1926. In 1930, Screws retired. In 1940, he received an honorary promotion to brigadier general in the National Guard in recognition of his World War I service. Screws became involved in local politics in Montgomery, Alabama, serving four terms as Commissioner of Public Affairs 1931-47 and on the city's Civil Defense board during World War II, a role he held until 1949. Screws died at the age of 80, on October 26, 1955, of a heart attack.[38]

Claude Stanley. After successfully leading the 168th Infantry's 2nd Battalion at Saint Mihiel and the Meuse-Argonne, Stanley returned to his law practice at Stanley and Stanley in Corning, Iowa. He went into politics and was elected State Senator from the Sixth District, comprising Adams and Taylor Counties, in 1932. Named in 1937 to the Iowa Employment Security Commission, he served on that body until his retirement in 1959 at the age of 87. He died in Muscatine, Iowa, on June 29, 1965, at age 93.[39]

John Taber. The author of a monumental two-volume history of the 158th Infantry, Taber was demobilized on May 12. 1919, two years to the day from when he entered the army. He never married and worked as a writer, living in New York City until passing away in his sleep on September 23, 1986.[40]

Mathew Tinley. Like Lloyd Ross, his comrade from the 168th Infantry, Tinley remained in the Iowa National Guard and commanded the 34th Division. He became vice president of the National Guard Association in 1932 and served as its president in 1933-34. He had returned to his practice as a physician, which he continued until 1951. He passed away in Council Bluffs, Iowa, on March 11, 1956.[41]

Clyde Vaughn. The officer who led 25 valiant men holding one of General Gouraud's "sacrifice posts" at Champagne, France, Vaughn recovered from wounds to his jaw inflicted there and returned to Liberty Hill, Texas. He resumed teaching school in Liberty Hill and nearby Pearsall. He passed away in San Antonio, Texas, on November 17, 1968, at age 76.[42]

Cooper Winn. The officer whose revolutionary machine gun tactics helped secure Hill 288 and the Côte de Châtillon, Winn returned to the United States to become a banker in Port Chester, New York. He died on October 26, 1963, at age 83 and is buried in Macon, Georgia.[43]

NOTES

CHAPTER ONE: A NEW AMERICAN DIVISION IN FRANCE

1. Douglas MacArthur quoted in Henry J. Reilly, *Americans All: The Rainbow at War; Official History of the 42nd Rainbow Division in the World War* (Columbus, OH: The F. J. Heer Printing Co., 1936), 27.
2. Newton Baker in Introduction to Reilly, *Americans All*, 5-6.
3. Douglas MacArthur quoted in Reilly, *Americans All*, 27.
4. Walter B. Wolf, *A Brief Story of the Rainbow Division* (New York: Rand McNally, 1919), 12; Douglas MacArthur quoted in Reilly, *Americans All*, 27.
5. Edward M. Coffman, *The War to End All Wars: The American Military Experience in World War I* (Lexington: University Press of Kentucky, 1998), 19.
6. Douglas MacArthur quoted in Reilly, *Americans All*, 19.
7. James J. Cooke, *The Rainbow Division in the Great War, 1917-1919* (Westport, CT: Praeger, 1994), 8.
8. Wolf, *Brief Story of the Rainbow Division*, 6-7.
9. Ibid.
10. George W. Cullum, *Biographical Register of the Officers and Graduates of the U.S. Military Academy at West Point, N.Y Since its Establishment in 1802, Volume III* (Boston: Houghton, Mifflin, and Company, 1891), 415; George W. Cullum, *Biographical Register of the Officers and Graduates of the U.S. Military Academy at West Point, N.Y Since its Establishment in 1802*, Supplement *Volume IV* (Cambridge, MA: Riverside Press, 1901), 457; George W. Cullum, ed. Lieutenant Charles Braden, *Biographical Register of the Officers and Graduates of the U.S. Military Academy at West Point, N.Y Since its Establishment in 1802*, Supplement *Volume V* (Saginaw, MI: Seemann & Peters, Printers, 1919), 414; George W. Cullum, ed. Lieutenant Charles Braden, *Biographical Register of the Officers and Graduates of the U.S. Military Academy at West Point, N.Y Since its Establishment in 1802*, Supplement *Volume VI* (Saginaw, MI: Seemann & Peters, Printers, 1920), 482.
11. Wolf, *Brief Story of the Rainbow Division*, 6-7.
12. Joyce Kilmer quoted in Francis P. Duffy, *Father Duffy's Story: A Tale of Humor and Heroism, of Life and Death with the Fighting Sixty-Ninth* (New York: George B. Doran Company, 1919), 332.
13. Duffy, *Father Duffy's Story*, 13.
14. Cheseldine, *Ohio in the Rainbow*, 37-41.

15. Ibid., 43.
16. *Marysville Journal-Tribune*, Marysville, Ohio, April 4, 1917, 3.
17. David G. Thompson, "Ohio's Best: The Mobilization of the Fourth Infantry, Ohio National Guard, in 1917," *Ohio History Journal, Volume 101, Winter-Spring 1992* (Columbus, OH: Ohio Historical Society, 1992), 43.
18. Cheseldine, *Ohio in the Rainbow*, 44.
19. Alison Reppy, *Rainbow Memories: Character Sketches and History of the First Battalion, 166th Infantry, 42nd Division, American Expeditionary Force* (Columbus, Ohio: Executive Committee, First Battalion, 166th Infantry, 1919), 7-8.
20. Ibid.
21. Ruth Smith Truss, "The Alabama National Guard's 167th Infantry Regiment in World War I," *Alabama Review 56* (January 2003), 3-34.
22. Nimrod Thompson Frazer, *Send the Alabamians* (Tuscaloosa: University of Alabama Press, 2014), Kindle Edition, 21.
23. Winfred E. Robb, *The Price of Our Heritage: In Memory of the Heroic Dead of the 168 Infantry* (Des Moines, IA: American Lithographing and Printing Co., 1919), 13.
24. Robb, *The Price of Our Heritage*, 15.
25. John H. Taber, *The Story of the 168th Infantry Regiment, Vol. I* (Iowa City: State Historical Society of Iowa, 1925), 3.
26. Taber, *168th Infantry Regiment, Vol. I*, 3.
27. Robb, *The Price of Our Heritage*, 23.
28. Taber, *168th Infantry Regiment, Vol. I*, 6.
29. Ibid., 12.
30. Cooke, *The Rainbow Division*, 13.
31. Taber, *168th Infantry, Vol. I*, 11.
32. Leon Miesse, Robert Laird, ed., *100 Years On: WW I—Leon Miesse, Captain, 166th* (Unknown Location: Zerone Publishing, 2017), Miesse to his wife, September 12, 1917, 11.
33. Leon Miesse to his wife, October 9, 1917. Miesse, *100 Years On*, 26.
34. Cooke, *The Rainbow Division*, 17.
35. Ibid., 18-19.
36. Carl F. Ebert, *A Brief History of Co. D, 166th Infantry* (Marion, OH: Unknown Publisher, 1939), 10.
37. Dana Daniels, *Dana Daniels Diary, 1917-1919* (Columbus, OH: Dana Daniels Collection, Ohio Historical Society, MS 5; Box 1, Folder 6), 2.
38. Ebert, *A Brief History of Co. D*, 10.
39. Reilly, *Americans All*, 111.
40. Robert H. Ferrell, *The Question of MacArthur's Reputation: Cote de Chatillon, October 14-16, 1918* (Columbia: University of Missouri Press, 2008), 15.
41 Virgil Ney, *Evolution of the US Army Infantry Mortar Squad: The Argonne to Pleiku* (Fort Belvoir, Virginia: Technical Operations, Incorporated, Combat Operations Research Group, 1966), 20-30.
42. *History of Machine Guns and Automatic Rifles* (Washington, D.C.: Small Arms Division, Office of the Chief of Ordnance, U.S. Government Printing Office, 1922), 13-14.
43. Tompkins, *The Story of the Rainbow Division*, 23.
44. Cheseldine, *Ohio in the Rainbow*, 88.
45. Ibid.
46. Wolf, *Brief Story of the Rainbow Division*, 10-11.

CHAPTER TWO: FROM THE TRENCHES TO THE AISNE-MARNE

1. Cheseldine, *Ohio in the Rainbow*, 113.
2. Ibid.
3. *Richwood Gazette*, Richwood, Ohio, March 14, 1918, 1; *Marysville Journal-Tribune*, Marysville, Ohio, March 7, 1918, 2.
4. Notes on Photo from U.S. Army Signal Corps. Subject 7659, March 3, 1918, National Archives and Records Administration (NARA).
5. Robb, *The Price of Our Heritage*, 41; Cheseldine, *Ohio in the Rainbow*, 105.
6. Coffman, *War to End All Wars*, 150.
7. Allan R. Millett, *Well Planned, Splendidly Executed: The Battle of Cantigny May 28-31, 1918* (Chicago: Cantigny First Division Foundation, 2010), 154.
8. John J. Pershing, *My Experiences in the World War* (New York: Frederick A. Stokes, 1931; Reprint: Kindle Edition, Trench Press, 2018), 230.
9. Wolf, *Brief Story of the Rainbow Division*, 11.
10. Robb, *Price of Our Heritage*, 41.
11. Taber, *168th Infantry, Vol. I*, 63.
12. Cheseldine, *Ohio in the Rainbow*, 113.
13. Louis L. Collins, *History of the 151st Field Artillery Rainbow Division*, ed. Wayne E. Stevens, vol. 1 (St. Paul: Minnesota War Records Commission, 1924), 36.
14. Martin Hogan, *The Shamrock Battalion of the Rainbow* (New York: D. Appleton and Company, 1919), 89.
15. Cheseldine, *Ohio in the Rainbow*, 113.
16. Taber, *168th Infantry, Vol. I*, 89-90.
17. Wolf, *Brief Story of the Rainbow Division*, 13.
18. Cheseldine, *Ohio in the Rainbow*, 171-174.
19. Ibid., 148-149.
20. Leone Miesse journal entry for June 28, 1918. Miesse, *100 Years On*, 125.
21. Neiberg, *The Second Battle of the Marne*, Kindle Location 160.
22. Patrick Takle, *Nine Divisions in Champagne: The Second Battle of Marne* (Barnsley, UK: Pen & Sword Books Ltd, 2015), Kindle Edition, Kindle Location 171-174.
23. Takle, *Nine Divisions in Champagne*, Kindle Location 622-645.
24. Ibid.
25. Wolf, *Brief Story of the Rainbow Division*, 24-25.
26. Ibid.
27. Reilly, *Americans All*, 246.
28. Ibid., 250.
29. Cheseldine, *Ohio in the Rainbow*, 152.
30. Henry J. Reilly, *America's Part* (New York: Cosmopolitan Book Corporation, 1928), 241.
31. Neiberg, *Second Battle of the Marne*, Kindle Edition, Kindle Locations 1166-1171.
32. Cheseldine, *Ohio in the Rainbow*, 162.
33. Ibid.
34. Neiberg, *The Second Battle of the Marne*, Kindle Edition, Kindle Locations 1260-1265.
35. Amerine, *Alabama's Own*, 123.
36. Tompkins, *The Story of the Rainbow Division*, 56.
37. *American Armies and Battlefields in Europe: A History, Guide, and Reference Book* (Washington, D.C.: U.S. Government Printing Office, 1938), 344; Reilly, *America's Part*, 241; Report of Captain Henry Grave, Commanding Officer, I Company, 166th Infantry Regiment, cited in Cheseldine, *Ohio in the Rainbow*, 167.

38. Hogan, *The Shamrock Battalion*, 126-128.
39. Pershing, *Experiences*, Kindle Edition, 159.
40. Stephen C. McGeorge and Mason W. Watson, *The Marne, 15 July-6 August 1918* (Washington, D.C.: Center of Military History, United States Army, 2018), 36.
41. Cooke, *The Rainbow Division*, 117.
42. French Sixth Army, Special Orders No. 3,543, Trilport, Seine-et-Marne. July 21, 1918—11:15 a.m., *United States Army in the World War, 1917-1919, Military Operations of the American Expeditionary Forces, Volume 5* (Washington, D.C: Center of Military History, United States Army, 1989), 357.
43. Cooke, *The Rainbow Division*, 118-119.
44. 3d Section, General Staff French Sixth Army, No. 2,184/3 Trilport, Seine-et-Marne, July 21, 1918—-6:30 p. m., General Orders No. 3,563 for July 22, *United States Army in the World War, Volume 5*, 358.
45 Reilly, *The Rainbow Division*, 312.
46. NOTE: Henry Reilly was also the colonel in command of the Rainbow Division's artillery and would later serve as commander of the 83rd Brigade.
47. Reilly, *The Rainbow Division*, 312.
48. McGeorge and Watson, *Battle of the Marne*, 58.
49. Ibid., 58-59.
50. Ibid., 61.
51. John H. Taber, Stephen Taber, ed., *A Rainbow Division Lieutenant in France: The World War I Diary of John H. Taber* (Jefferson, NC: McFarland & Co., Inc., 2015), 99.
52. Frazer, *Send the Alabamians*, 167.
53. Taber, *168th Infantry, Vol. I*, 317-318.
54. Ibid., 318-319.
55. Lawrence O. Stewart, *Rainbow Bright* (Philadelphia: Dorrence, 1923), 77-78.
56. Taber, *168th Infantry, Vol. I*, 320.
57. Frazer, *Send the Alabamians*, 167.
58. Reilly, *Americans All*, 347.
59. 2d Section. General Staff, No. 22, July 24 to July 25, 1918 (20 h. to 20 h), I Army Corps, AEF, Buire, Aisne. July 26. 1918, *United States Army in the World War, Volume 5*, 447.
60. 3d Section. General Staff, No. 2.244/3, Plan of Attack, FRENCH SIXTH ARMY, Marigny-en-Orxois, Aisne, July 24, 1918—-7 p.m., General Orders No. 3,592, *United States Army in the World War, Volume 5*, 365.
61. John B. Hayes, *Heroes Among the Brave* (Loachapoka, AL: Lee County Historical Society, 1978), 22; Frazer, *Send the Alabamians*, 169-170.
62. Reilly, *Americans All*, 345.
63. Frazer, *Send the Alabamians*, 174-175; Reilly, *Americans All*, 348.
64. Hayes, *Heroes Among the Brave*, 22.
65. The 37mm was a French-manufactured gun intended to provide fire support at ranges from 1,300 to 4,900 feet, and it was the smallest field gun used by the U.S. Army. It was designed for mobility and could fire up 35 rounds per minute. *Handbook of Artillery Including Mobile, Anti-Aircraft and Trench Materiel* (Washington, D.C.: Office of the Chief of Ordnance, U.S. Government Printing Office, 1920), 51-53.
66. Hayes, *Heroes Among the Brave*, 22.
67. Taber, *168th Infantry, Vol. I*, 328-329.
68. Frazer, *Send the Alabamians*, 177; Walter Bare quoted in Reilly, *Americans All*, 349.
69. Frazer, *Send the Alabamians*, 177-178.

70. Walter Bare quoted in Reilly, *Americans All*, 350.
71. Field Orders, No. 26, I Army Corps, AEF, Buire, Aisne, July 27, 1918, 1:10 a.m., *United States Army in the World War, Vol. 5*, 668.
72. General Orders, No. 51, Plan of Attack, 42nd Division AEF, Trugny, Aisne, July 27. 1918, 9:30 a.m., *United States Army in the World War, Vol. 5*, 551.
73. Reilly, *Americans All*, 328.
74. Supreme Headquarters, Operations Section to Group of Armies German Crown Prince, No. 9536, July 27, 1918, 11:00 p.m., *United States Army in the World War, Volume 5*, 669.
75. American Battle Monuments Commission, *42nd Division Summary of Operations in the World War* (Washington, D.C.: U.S. Government Printing Office,1944), 32.

CHAPTER THREE: THE CALM BEFORE THE STORM
1. Duffy, *Father Duffy's Story*, 207.
2. Hayes, *Heroes Among the Brave*, 32.
3. Ibid., 31.
4. Taber, *A Rainbow Division Lieutenant in France*, Kindle Edition, 97.
5. Duffy, *Father Duffy's Story*, 207.
6. Ibid.
7. Coffman, *War to End All Wars*, 255.
8. Duffy, *Father Duffy's Story*, 207-208.
9. Amerine, *Alabama's Own*, 164.
10. Taber, *A Rainbow Division Lieutenant in France*, Kindle Edition, 98.
11. Duffy, *Father Duffy's Story*, 223-224.
12. Tompkins, *Story of the Rainbow Division*, 95-96.
13. Pierpont J. Stackpole, Ferrell, Robert H., ed., *In the Company of Generals: The World War I Diary of Pierpont L. Stackpole* (Columbia: University of Missouri Press, 2009), 116.
14. National Archives and Records Administration (NARA), Record Group (RG) 200, Index and Case Files relating to Reclassification and Reassignment of Officers, Reclassification of Regular Army Brigadier Generals and Major Generals, Entry NM 1022, Relief History of Brigadier General R. A. Brown, 130-84-2-5, August 21, 1918, 24, cited in Frazer, *Send the Alabamians*, 202-203.
15. National Archives and Records Administration (NARA), Record Group (RG) 200, Index and Case Files Relating to Reclassification and Reassignment of Officers, Reclassification of Regular Army Brigadier Generals and Major Generals, Entry NM 1022, Relief History of Brigadier General R. A. Brown, 130-84-2-5, August 21, 1918, 24, cited in Frazer, *Send the Alabamians*, 202-203.
16. Frazer, *Send the Alabamians*, 202-203.
17. Ibid.
18. Duffy, *Father Duffy's Story*, 229.
19. Ibid.
20. Taber, *168th Infantry, Vol. II*, 48.
21. Ibid., 48-49.
22. Duffy, *Father Duffy's Story*, 225-226.
23. Ibid., 226.
24. Taber, *168th Infantry, Vol. II*, 49-50.
25. Ibid.
26. Cheseldine, *Ohio in the Rainbow*, 218.

27. Taber, *A Rainbow Division Lieutenant in France*, 99.
28. Taber, *168th Infantry, Vol. II*, 50.
29. Cheseldine, *Ohio in the Rainbow*, 219-220.
30. Ibid.
31. Cooke, *The Rainbow Division*, 138.
32. Taber, *168th Infantry, Vol II*, 53-54.
33. Reilly, *Americans All*, 525.
34. Frazer, *Send the Alabamians*, Kindle Edition, 210-211.
35. Charles MacArthur, *War Bugs* (New York: Doubleday, Doran & Company,1929), 124.
36. William Donovan quoted in Reilly, *Americans All*, 390-391.
37. Ravee Norris quoted in Reilly, *Americans All*, 522-523.
38. Ibid.
39. Taber, *168th Infantry, Vol II*, 55; Amerine, *Alabama's Own*, 168-169.
40. William Donovan quoted in Reilly, *Americans All*, 390-391.
41. Lloyd Ross quoted in Reilly, *Americans All*, 518.
42. Reilly, *Americans All*, 532.
43. Taber, *168th Infantry, Vol. II*, 58-59.
44. Ibid., 59-60.
45. Ibid., 61.

CHAPTER FOUR: PREPARING FOR THE SAINT MIHIEL OFFENSIVE

1. Taber, *168th Infantry, Vol II*, 69.
2. Ibid., 69-70.
3. Ibid.
4. Ibid.
5. Pershing, *Experiences*, Kindle Edition, 475.
6. Reilly, *Americans All*, 536.
7. Ibid., 533.
8. Ibid.
9. Ibid.
10. Ibid., 533-534.
11. Ibid., 534.
12. David Bonk, *St. Mihiel, 1918: The American Expeditionary Force's Trial by Fire* (Oxford, UK: Osprey Publishing, 2011), Kindle Edition, Kindle Location 492; Eisenhower, *Yanks*, Kindle Location 3215-3223.
13. Taber, *168th Infantry, Vol II*, 74.
14. Reilly, *Americans All*, 534-535.
15. Ibid., 535.
16. Pershing, *Experiences*, Kindle Edition, 474-475.
17. *United States Army in the Great War, 1917-1919, Military Operations of the American Expeditionary Forces, Vol 8* (Washington, D.C.: Center of Military History, United States Army, 1990), 4.
18. Donald A. Carter, *St. Mihiel, 12–16 September 1918* (Washington, D.C.: Center of Military History, U.S. Army, 2018), 14-17.
19. Ibid., 14.
20. Ibid., 13.
21. Coffman, *War to End All Wars*, 268.
22. Carter, *St. Mihiel*, 15.

23. Bonk, *St. Mihiel, 1918*, Kindle Edition, Kindle Location 514.
24. Ibid., 528.
25. Ibid., 528.
26. Ibid.
27. Coffman, *War to End All Wars*, 269-270; Carter, *St. Mihiel*, 31-32.
28. Carter, *St. Mihiel*, 31-32.
29. Coffman, *War to End All Wars*, 270-271; Pershing, *Experiences*, Kindle Edition, 557-558.
30. Pershing, *Experiences*, Kindle Edition, 558; Bonk, *St. Mihiel*, 1918, Kindle Edition, Kindle Location 542.
31. Pershing, *Experiences*, Kindle Edition, 558.
32. 1st Army, AEF, Ligny-en-Barrois, August 30, 1918, Notes on Conversation Between General Pershing and Marshal Foch at Ligny-En-Barrois, *United States Army in the World War, Vol. 8*, 39.
33. Coffman, *War to End All Wars*, 270-271; Bonk, *St. Mihiel*, Kindle Location 542.
34. 1st Army, AEF, Ligny-en-Barrois, August 30, 1918, Notes on Conversation Between General Pershing and Marshal Foch at Ligny-En-Barrois, *United States Army in the World War, Vol. 8*, 39.
35. Pershing, *Experiences*, Kindle Edition, 564-656; Coffman, *War to End All Wars*, 271-272; 1st Subsection, 3d Section, G.S., No. 3528, Headquarters, Allied Armies, Bombon, September 2, 1918, Conference of September 2, *United States Army in the World War, Vol. 8*, 47-48.
36. Carter, *St. Mihiel*, 20.
37. Coffman, *War to End All Wars*, 273-274.
38. Amerine, *Alabama's Own*, 170-171.
39. Cheseldine, *Ohio in the Rainbow*, 225.
40. Taber, *168th Infantry, Vol. II*, 62-63.
41. Frazer, *Send the Alabamians*, Kindle Edition, 215.
42. Ibid.
43. Cheseldine, *Ohio in the Rainbow*, 225.
44. Taber, *168th Infantry, Vol. II*, 64-65.
45. Hogan, *The Shamrock Battalion*, 200.
46. Taber, *168th Infantry, Vol. II*, 66.
47. Cheseldine, *Ohio in the Rainbow*, 226-227.
48. Cheseldine, *Ohio in the Rainbow*, 226; Hogan, *The Shamrock Battalion*, 202.
49. Cheseldine, *Ohio in the Rainbow*, 227.
50. Taber, *168th Infantry, Vol. II*, 70-73.
51. Amerine, *Alabama's Own*, 173.
52. Cheseldine, *Ohio in the Rainbow*, 227.
53. Wolf, *Brief History of the Rainbow Division*, 37.
54. Taber, *168th Infantry, Vol. II*, 73.

CHAPTER FIVE: INTO THE SALIENT

1. Cheseldine, *Ohio in the Rainbow*, 235.
2. Taber, *168th Infantry, Vol. II*, 75-76.
3. Cooke, *The Rainbow Division*, 150.
4. Reilly, *Americans All*, 544-545; Taber, *168th Infantry, Vol. II*, 77-78.
5. Cooke, *The Rainbow Division*, 150.

6. Ibid.
7. Reilly, *Americans All*, 551.
8. Frazer, *Send the* Alabamians, Kindle Edition, 221; Taber, *168th Infantry*, Vol. II, 78.
9. Taber, *168th Infantry*, Vol. II, 80.
10. Taber, *168th Infantry*, Vol. II, 78-79.
11. Wolf, *Brief Story of the Rainbow Division*, 40.
12. Ibid.
13. Wolf, *Brief Story of the Rainbow Division*, 40; Taber, *168th Infantry*, Vol. II, 78-79.
14. Coffman, *War to End All Wars*, 278.
15. Conrad H. Lanza, "The Artillery Support of Infantry in the A.E.F.," *Field Artillery Journal 26, January-March 1936* (Washington D.C.: The United States Field Artillery Association, 1936), 62.
16. Coffman, *War to End All Wars*, 278; Reilly, *Americans All*, 540.
17. Taber, *168th Infantry*, Vol. II, 88-89.
18. Reilly, *Americans All*, 542-544.
19. Amerine, *Alabama's Own*, 173-174.
20. Reilly, *Americans All*, 543-544, 548; Cheseldine, *Ohio in the Rainbow*, 228.
21. Cheseldine, *Ohio in the Rainbow*, 228.
22. William Donovan quoted in Reilly, *Americans All*, 561.
23. Duffy, *Father Duffy's Story*, 233.
24. Reilly, *Americans All*, 543; Cooke, *The Rainbow Division*, 150.
25. William Donovan quoted in Reilly, *Americans All*, 562.
26. Taber, *168th Infantry*, Vol. II, 87.
27. Taber, *168th Infantry*, Vol II, 88.
28. Frazer, *Send the Alabamians*, Kindle Edition, 224.
29. William Donovan quoted in Reilly, *Americans All*, 562.
30. Amerine, *Alabama's Own*, 174-175.
31. Taber, *168th Infantry*, Vol. II, 88-89; Cheseldine, *Ohio in the Rainbow*, 229; Coffman, *War to End All Wars*, 279.
32. MacArthur, *War Bugs*, 135-136.
33. William Donovan quoted in Reilly, *Americans All*, 563.
34. Operations Section, Group of Armies Von Gallwitz, No. 3322, September 3. 1918, *U.S. Army in the World War*, Vol. 8, 289-290.
35. Operations Section German Supreme Headquarters No. 10204. Addendum No.1, September 10. 1918, *U.S. Army in the World War*, Vol. 8, 294; Operations Section, Group of Armies von Gallwitz, No. 222, September 10, 1918; 4:18 p.m., *U.S. Army in the World War*, Vol. 8, 295-296.
36. Foreign Armies Section, German Supreme Headquarters, September 11, 1918, *U.S. Army in the World War*, Vol. 8, 299.
37. Coffman, *War to End All Wars*, 279.
38. Battle Notes of the Chief of the General Staff of Army Detachment C, September 12, 1918, *U.S. Army in the World War*, Vol. 8, 302.
39. Duffy, *Father Duffy's Story*, 235.
40. Taber, *168th Infantry*, Vol. II, 91.
41. Hugh S. Thompson, *Trench Knives and Mustard Gas: With the 42nd Rainbow Division in France* (College Station: Texas A&M University Press, 2004), 169-170.
42. Duffy, *Father Duffy's Story*, 236.
43. William Donovan quoted in Reilly, *Americans All*, 563.
44. Carter, *St. Mihiel*, 35; Amerine, *Alabama's Own*, 177.

45. Reppy, *Rainbow Memories*, 17.
46. Duffy, *Father Duffy's Story*, 236-237.
47. Duffy, *Father Duffy's Story*, 237; Hogan, *The Shamrock Battalion*, 211.
48. Amerine, *Alabama's Own*, 166-167, 175-176.
49. Frazer, *Send the Alabamians*, 226-227.
50. Wolf, *Brief Story of the Rainbow Division*, 40.
51. Taber, *168th Infantry, Vol. II*, 79.
52. Ibid., 91.
53. Ibid., 89-90.
54. Major Lloyd Ross quoted in Reilly, *Americans All*, 558-559.
55. Taber, *168th Infantry, Vol. II*, 92.
56. Ibid.
57. Thompson, *Trench Knives and Mustard Gas*, 170.
58. Taber, *168th Infantry, Vol. II*, 92-95.
59. Ibid.
60. Ibid.
61. Thompson, *Trench Knives and Mustard Gas*, 173-179.
62. Taber, *168th Infantry, Vol. II*, 96.
63. Ibid., 97.
64. Ibid., 98.
65. Cheseldine, *Ohio in the Rainbow*, 231.
66. Ibid., 241.
67. Coffman, *War to End All Wars*, 279-280.
68. Ibid.
69. Leon Miesse letter to his wife entry for September 16, 1918. Miesse, *100 years On*, 156-157.
70. Austin Dewitt "Dusty" Boyd to his family, September 23, 1918. *Austin Dewitt "Dusty" Boyd in WWI*, 11.
71. Cheseldine, *Ohio in the Rainbow*, 232
72. William Donovan quoted in Reilly, *Americans All*, 563.
73. Cheseldine, *Ohio in the Rainbow*, 232-233.
74. Duffy, *Father Duffy's Story*, 242.
75. Taber, *168th Infantry, Vol. II*, 105.
76. Claude Stanley quoted in Reilly, *Americans All*, 555.
77. Frazer, *Send the Alabamians*, Kindle Edition, 228; Cheseldine, *Ohio in the Rainbow*, 233.
78. Cheseldine, *Ohio in the Rainbow*, 233.
79. Van Santvoord Merle-Smith quoted in Reilly, *Americans All*, 565.
80. Taber, *168th Infantry, Vol. II*, 102.
81. Cheseldine, *Ohio in the Rainbow*, 234.
82. Frazer, *Send the Alabamians*, Kindle Edition, 228.

CHAPTER SIX: TAKING AND HOLDING THE SALIENT

1. Vincent Fleckenstein quoted in Reilly, *Americans All*, 583.
2. Ibid., 583-584.
3. Ibid., 584.
4. Ibid.
5. Ibid., 584-585.

6. Taber, *168th Infantry, Vol. II*, 114.
7. 42nd Division Intelligence Report cited in Taber, *168th Infantry, Vol. II*, 117.
8. Reilly, *Americans All*, 546-547.
9. Cheseldine, *Ohio in the Rainbow*, 234; Leon Miesse journal entry for September 13, 1918. Miesse, *100 Years On*, 155-156.
10. Wolf, *Brief Story of the Rainbow Division*, 42.
11. Duffy, *Father Duffy's Story*, 240, 247-248.
12. Ibid., 240.
13. William Donovan quoted in Reilly, *Americans All*, 564.
14. Amerine, *Alabama's Own*, 178.
15. Taber, *168th Infantry, Vol. II*, 109; Claude Stanley quoted in Reilly, *Americans All*, 555.
16. Taber, *168th Infantry, Vol. II*, 110-111.
17. Claude Stanley quoted in Reilly, *Americans All*, 556; Taber, *168th Infantry, Vol. II*, 111.
18. Taber, *168th Infantry, Vol. II*, 111-112.
19. Taber, *168th Infantry, Vol. II*, 111-112; Reilly, *Americans All*, 557-558.
20. Van Santvoord Merle-Smith quoted in Reilly, *Americans All*, 566.
21. Claude Stanley quoted in Reilly, *Americans All*, 557.
22. Taber, *168th Infantry, Vol. II*, 113.
23. Cheseldine, *Ohio in the Rainbow*, 236.
24. Ibid., 236-237.
25. Reilly, *Americans All*, 547.
26. Douglas MacArthur quoted in Reilly, *Americans All*, 577.
27. Ibid.
28. Taber, *168th Infantry, Vol. II*, 119-120.
29. Ibid., 120.
30. Ibid.
31. Ibid., 118-119.
32. Ibid., 135.
33. Reilly, *Americans All*, 578.
34. Taber, *168th Infantry, Vol. II*, 130.
35. Ibid., 132.
36. Taber, *168th Infantry, Vol. II*, 131-132.
37. Claude Stanley quoted in Reilly, *Americans All*, 579.
38. Taber, *168th Infantry, Vol. II*, 141-143.
39. Reilly, *Americans All*, 581-582.
40. Ibid., 583-585.
41. Amerine, *Alabama's Own*, 180.
42. Vincent Fleckenstein quoted in Reilly, *Americans All*, 583-585.
43. Vincent Fleckenstein quoted in Reilly, *Americans All*, 583-585; Amerine, *Alabama's Own*, 180.
44. Taber, *168th Infantry, Vol. II*, 140.
45. Ibid., 141-142.
46. Ibid., 142-143.
47. Amerine, *Alabama's Own*, 181.
48. Cheseldine, *Ohio in the Rainbow*, 239; Reppy, *Rainbow Memories*, 17.
49. Reppy, *Rainbow Memories*, 17.
50. Official Report of Lieutenant Aubrey DeLacy cited in Cheseldine, *Ohio in the Rainbow*, 239.

51. Ibid.
52. Ibid., 237.
53. Ibid.
54. Ibid., 237-238.
55. Ibid., 238.
56. Ibid.
57. Ibid.
58. Hogan, *The Shamrock Battalion*, 225.
59. Taber, *A Rainbow Division Lieutenant in France*, 119.

CHAPTER SEVEN: TO THE MEUSE-ARGONNE
1. Reppy, 17.
2. Ibid., 17.
3. Daniels, *Diary*, 49-50.
4. Hayes, *Heroes Among the Brave*, 37.
5. Matthew Tinsley quoted in Reilly, *Americans All*, 666.
6. Reilly, *Americans All*, 713.
7. Taber, *168th Infantry Regiment, Vol. II*, 160-161.
8. Leon Miesse journal entry, October 11, 1918, Miesse, *100 Years On*, Kindle Edition, 177.
9. Richard S. Faulkner, *Meuse Argonne, 26 September-November 11, 1918* (Washington, D.C.: Center of Military History, United States Army, 2018), 7.
10. Faulkner, *Meuse-Argonne*, 9.
11. Maarten Otte, *The Meuse Argonne 1918: Breaking the Line* (Barnsley, United Kingdom: Pen & Sword Books, Ltd., 2018), Kindle Edition, Kindle Location 303.
12. Faulkner, *Meuse-Argonne*, 10.
13. Faulkner, *Meuse*-Argonne, 16; Eisenhower, *Yanks*, Kindle Edition, Kindle Location 3466.
14. Eisenhower, *Yanks*, Kindle Edition, Kindle Location 3472.
15. Ibid. Kindle Location 3480.
16. Faulkner, *Meuse*-Argonne, 17-18.
17. Ibid., 18-20.
18. Eisenhower, *Yanks*, Kindle Edition, Kindle Location 3493.
19. Coffman, *War to End All Wars*, 300.
20. Faulkner, *Meuse-Argonne*, 14.
21. Faulkner, *Meuse*-Argonne, 13-14; Eisenhower, *Yanks*, Kindle Edition, Kindle Location 3493.
22. Faulkner, *Meuse-Argonne,* 12.
23. Faulkner, *Meuse-Argonne,* 14-16.
24. Ibid., 14-16.
25. Ibid.
26. Ibid., 18-20.
27. Tompkins, *Story of the Rainbow Division*, 129.
28. Operations Section, No. 10,436, Supreme Headquarters in the Field, Office Chief of Staff, September 22, 1918, *United States Army in the World War, Vol. 9* (Washington, D.C.: Center of Military History, United States Army, 1990), 509.
29. Intelligence Officer, Supreme Headquarters, at Headquarters, Group of Armies German Crown Prince, No. 12698, September 27, 1918, *United States Army in the World War, Vol. 9*, 514-516.

30. Operations Section, Foreign Armies, No. 10, 553, Supreme Headquarters in the Field, Office Chief of Staff, September 29, 1918, *United States Army in the World War, Vol. 9,* 523.
31. Pershing, *Experiences,* Kindle Edition, 597.
32. Donald Smythe, *Pershing: General of the Armies* (Bloomington: Indiana University Press, 1986), 195.
33. James Harbord, *An American Army in France* (Boston: Little, Brown and Co., 1936), 436.
34. Harry S. Truman to Bess Wallace, November 23, 1918, *Papers of Harry S. Truman Pertaining to Family, Business, and Personal Affairs,* Truman Library and Museum, Independence, Missouri.
35. Faulkner, *Meuse-Argonne,* 22-23.
36. Cooke, *The Rainbow Division,* 164; Faulkner, *Meuse-Argonne,* 24, 26.
37. Faulkner, *Meuse-Argonne,* 26.
38. Ferrell, *MacArthur's Reputation,* 11.
39. Ibid., 26-27.
40. Coffman, *War to End All Wars,* 335; Faulkner, *Meuse-Argonne,* 28-29.
41. Frazer, *Send the Alabamians,* Kindle Edition, 231.
42. Roy Bailey, *Roy Bailey Diary, 1917-1919* (Unpublished. Accessed at www.markboyd.info/MarionsOwn/Sgt_Bailey), 67.
43. Cheseldine, *Ohio in the Rainbow,* 240; Daniels, *Dana Daniels Diary, 1917-1919,* 47.
44. Cheseldine, *Ohio in the Rainbow,* 241.
45. Duffy, *Father Duffy's Story,* 253; Amerine, *Alabama's Own,* 189.
46. Cheseldine, *Ohio in the Rainbow,* 241; Daniels, *Diary,* 47-48.
47. Cheseldine, *Ohio in the Rainbow,* 241, 244; Daniels, *Diary,* 48.
48. Duffy, *Father Duffy's Story,* 253; Hogan, *The Shamrock Battalion,* 227-228.
49. Hogan, *The Shamrock Battalion,* 227-228, 230; Duffy, *Father Duffy's Story,* 253.
50. Amerine, *Alabama's Own,* 189-190; Frazer, *Send the Alabamians,* Kindle Edition, 233.
51. Taber, *168th Infantry Regiment, Vol. II,* 151.
52. Stewart, *Rainbow Bright,* 117.
53. Taber, *168th Infantry Regiment, Vol. II,* 151-152; Taber, *Diary,* 120.
54. Taber, *168th Infantry Regiment, Vol. II,* 152-153; Taber, *A Rainbow Division Lieutenant in France,* Kindle Edition, 121-122.
55. Taber, *168th Infantry Regiment, Vol. II,* 153.
56. MacArthur, *War Bugs,* 173.
57. Faulkner, *Meuse-Argonne,* 32-33.
58. Frazer, *Send the Alabamians,* Kindle Edition, 232.
59. Duffy, *Father Duffy's Story,* 254-255.
60. Cheseldine, *Ohio in the Rainbow,* 248.
61. Cooke, *The Rainbow Division,* 168.
62. 191-33.1: Operations Report, First Army, AEF, Souilly, Meuse, October 12, 1918, From Noon, October 10 to Noon, October 11, 1918, *United States Army in the World War, Vol. 9,* 252.
63. Taber, *168th Infantry Regiment, Vol. II,* 156.
64. Ibid., 156-157.
65. Ibid., 157.
66. Ibid., 158.
67. Ibid., 159.

68. Ibid., 159-160.
69. Amerine, *Send the Alabamians*, 190-191.
70. Hayes, *Heroes Among the Brave*, 37.
71. Duffy, *Father Duffy's Story*, 162; Hogan, *The Shamrock Battalion*, 233-234.
72. Cheseldine, *Ohio in the Rainbow*, 248-249; Wolf, *Brief History of the Rainbow Division*, 45.
73. Wolf, *Brief History of the Rainbow Division*, 45.
74. Faulkner, *Meuse-Argonne*, 41-42.
75. Ibid., 45-46.

CHAPTER EIGHT: THE ASSAULT ON THE KRIEMHILDE STELLUNG BEGINS

1. Hogan, *The Shamrock Battalion*, 6.
2. Hogan, *The Shamrock Battalion*, 246.
3. Ibid., 235.
4. Ibid., 242-243.
5. Ibid., 244.
6. Ibid., 245.
7. Ibid.
8. Ibid., 246.
9. Ibid., 246-247.
10. Ibid., 248.
11. Ibid., 248-249.
12. Ibid., 249-250.
13. Eisenhower, *Yanks*, Kindle Edition, Kindle Location 4465.
14. Ibid.
15. Eisenhower, *Yanks*, Kindle Edition, Kindle Location 4474; Coffman, *War to End All Wars*, 327.
16. Faulkner, *Meuse-Argonne*, 48.
17. Wolf, *Brief Story of the Rainbow Division*, 46; Duffy, *Father Duffy's Story*, 265-266.
18. Wolf, *Brief Story of the Rainbow Division*, 46; Duffy, *Father Duffy's Story*, 265-266.
19. Duffy, *Father Duffy's Story*, 265-266.
20. Ibid.
21. Reilly, *Americans All*, 643.
22. Ibid., 644.
23. Reilly, *Americans All*, 645; Lloyd Ross quoted in Reilly, *Americans All*, 668.
24. Reilly, *Americans All*, 645.
25. Ibid., 645-646.
26. Ibid., 646.
27. Ibid.
28. Ibid., 648.
29. Ibid., 649.
30. Taber, *168th Infantry, Vol. II*, 167.
31. Ferrell, *MacArthur's Reputation*, 17.
32. Raymond Turner quoted in Reilly, *Americans All*, 673-674; Lloyd Ross quoted in Reilly, *Americans All*, 669.
33. Raymond Turner quoted in Reilly, *Americans All*, 674.
34. Ibid., 674-675.
35. Ibid., 675.

36. Lloyd Ross quoted in Reilly, *Americans All*, 668-669.
37. Taber, *168th Infantry, Vol. II*, 168.
38. Frazer, *Send the Alabamians*, Kindle Edition, 262; Amerine, *Alabama's Own*, 193.
39. Reilly, *Americans All*, 711; Frazer, *Send the Alabamians*, Kindle Edition, 262.
40. Cooper Winn quoted in Reilly, *Americans All*, 711-712; Frazer, *Send the Alabamians*, Kindle Edition, 262.
41. Duffy, *Father Duffy's Story*, 268.
42. Ibid., 267.
43. William Donovan quoted in Reilly, *Americans All*, 691.
44. Ibid., 690.
45. Duffy, *Father Duffy's Story*, 266.
46. George Geran quoted in Reilly, *Americans All*, 704; Daniels, *Diary*, 50.
47. Taber, *168th Infantry, Vol. II*, 168.
48. Ibid., 168-169.
49. Ibid., 169.
50. Ibid., 169-170.
51. Ibid., 170.
52. Amerine, *Alabama's Own*, 193.
53. Amerine, *Alabama's Own*, 193-194; Frazer, *Send the Alabamians*, Kindle Edition, 264-265.
54. Walter Bare quoted in Reilly, *Americans All*, 677; Amerine, *Alabama's Own*, 194.
55. Duffy, *Father Duffy's Story*, 268; William Donovan, Van Merle-Smith, and John Rowley quoted in Reilly, *Americans All*, 691-692.
56. William Donovan quoted in Reilly, *Americans All*, 692.
57. Hogan, *The Shamrock Battalion*, 237-238.
58. Ibid., 238.
59. Ibid., 240-241.
60. Cheseldine, *Ohio in the Rainbow*, 250; George Geran quoted in Reilly, *Americans All*, 704-705.
61. George Geran and R.R. Gowdy quoted in Reilly, *Americans All*, 704-705, 707-708.
62. George Geran quoted in Reilly, *Americans All*, 704-705.
63. Taber, *168th Infantry, Vol. II*, 172.
64. M.A. Means quoted in Reilly, *Americans All*, 717.
65. Taber, *168th Infantry, Vol. II*, 173.
66. Ibid., 174-176.

CHAPTER NINE: TAKING HILL 288 AND HILL 242

1. Duffy, *Father Duffy's Story*, 270.
2. Thomas Reilley and James Finn quoted in Reilly, *Americans All*, 697-698.
3. Ibid., 697.
4. Ibid.
5. Thomas Reilley quoted in Reilly, *Americans All*, 698.
6. Ibid.
7. Thomas Reilley quoted in Reilly, *Americans All*, 698; Duffy, *Father Duffy's Story*, 270.
8. Thomas Reilley quoted in Reilly, *Americans All*, 698.
9. Thomas Reilley quoted in Reilly, *Americans All*, 698.
10. Ibid., 699.
11. Thomas Reilley quoted in Reilly, *Americans All*, 699; Duffy, *Father Duffy's Story*, 270.

12. *Cemetery Records*, Records of the American Battle Monuments Commission, Arlington, Virginia, 1918-1995.
13. Frazer, *Send the Alabamians*, Kindle Edition, 267; Lloyd Ross quoted in Reilly, *Americans All*, 672.
14. Lloyd Ross quoted in Reilly, *Americans All*, 672; Taber, *168th Infantry, Vol. II*, 176.
15. Ravee Norris quoted in Reilly, *Americans All*, 681.
16. Ibid., 681-682.
17. Ibid., 682.
18. Ravee Norris quoted in Reilly, *Americans All*, 682; Frazer, *Send the Alabamians*, Kindle Edition, 268.
19. Ravee Norris quoted in Reilly, *Americans All*, 682.
20. Reilly, *Americans All*, 654.
21. Ibid.
22. *Official War Diary of the 166th Infantry Regiment* for October 15, 1918, cited in Cheseldine, *Ohio in the Rainbow*, 252.
23. Faulkner, *Meuse-Argonne*, 20, 44.
24. *Official War Diary of the 166th Infantry Regiment* for October 15, 1918, cited in Cheseldine, *Ohio in the Rainbow*, 252.
25. Ibid., 253.
26. Ibid., 252.
27. Ibid., 253.
28. Cheseldine, *Ohio in the Rainbow*, 255-256.
29. Cheseldine, *Ohio in the Rainbow*, 262; *The Official Roster of Ohio Soldiers, Sailors, and Marines in the World War, 1917-18* (Columbus, OH: F. J. Heer Printing Co., 1926).
30. William Donovan quoted in Reilly, *Americans All*, 695; Duffy, *Father Duffy's Story*, 273.
31. William Donovan quoted in Reilly, *Americans All*, 695-696.
32. Ibid., 696.
33. Alex Anderson and Henry Fecheimer quoted in Reilly, *Americans All*, 696.
34. Duffy, *Father Duffy's Story*, 274.
35. Reilly, *Americans All*, 655-656, 696.
36. Amerine, *Alabama's Own*, 195-196.
37. Ibid., 195-196.
38. Reilly, *Americans All*, 655.
39. Taber, *168th Infantry, Vol. II*, 176-177.
40. Ibid., 177.
41. Ibid., 177-178.
42. Ibid., 178.
43. Ibid., 179-180.
44. Ibid.
45. Ibid., 181-182.
46. Ibid., 182.
47. Ibid., 182-183.
48. Ibid., 183-184.

CHAPTER TEN: THE CÔTE DE CHÂTILLON

1. Nimrod T. Frazer, *The Best World War I Story I Know: On the Point in the Argonne, September 26-October 16, 1918* (Tuscaloosa: University of Alabama Press, 2018), Kindle Edition, Kindle Location 2465.

2. Frazer, *Best World War I Story*, Kindle Edition, Kindle Location 2749.
3. NOTE: The accounts of the events that occurred related to the plans for the attack on October 16 differ widely in some cases, and the veracity of some statements cannot be verified. The story presented here focuses on those that appear to be the most reliable, and a sequence of events that seems to be the one most likely to have occurred.
4. William Hughes quoted in Reilly, *Americans All*, 658.
5. Ibid.
6. Reilly, *Americans All*, 663.
7. Reilly, *Americans All*, 664.
8. Ibid., 682.
9. Ravee Norris quoted in Reilly, *Americans All*, 682.
10. Ibid., 684.
11. Ibid.
12. Walter Bare quoted in Reilly, *Americans All*, 678.
13. Ibid., 678-679.
14. Taber, *168th Infantry, Vol. II*, 187.
15. Ibid.
16. Harold Denny quoted in Taber, *168th Infantry, Vol. II*, 187-188.
17. Taber, *168th Infantry, Vol. II*, 189.
18. Cooper Winn quoted in Reilly, *Americans All*, 711-712.
19. Taber, *168th Infantry, Vol. II*, 189.
20. Ibid., 189-190.
21. Ibid., 190-191.
22. Amerine, *Alabama's Own*, 196; Ravee Norris quoted in Reilly, *Americans All*, 684.
23. Ravee Norris quoted in Reilly, *Americans All*, 685.
24. Ibid.
25. Taber, *168th Infantry, Vol. II*, 191.
26. Ibid.
27. Ibid., 191-192.
28. Ibid., 193.
29. Ibid., 193-194.
30. Reilly, *Americans All*, 664.
31. Taber, *168th Infantry, Vol. II*, 195-196.
32. Ibid.
33. Ravee Norris quoted in Reilly, *Americans All*, 685.
34. Sherman L. Fleek, *Place the Headstones Where They Belong* (Logan: Utah State University Press, 2008), xvii.
35. Fleek, *Place the Headstones*, 70-72.
36. Fleek, *Place the Headstones*, 120-124; *Medal of Honor, 1863-1968: In the Name of the Congress of the United States* (Washington, D.C.: U.S. Government Printing Office, 1968), 455-456.
37. Fleek, *Place the Headstones*, 124-125; *Medal of Honor*, 455-456.
38. Fleek, *Place the Headstones*, 126; *Medal of Honor*, 456.
39. *Medal of Honor*, 456.
40. Ravee Norris quoted in Reilly, *Americans All*, 685; Taber, *168th Infantry, Vol. II*, 196-198.
41. Ravee Norris quoted in Reilly, *Americans All*, 685-686.
42. *Official War Diary of the 166th Infantry Regiment* for October 16, 1918, cited in Cheseldine, *Ohio in the Rainbow*, 254.

43. Ibid.
44. Duffy, *Father Duffy's Story*, 276.
45. Ibid., 276-277.
46. Ibid., 277.
47. Ibid.
48. Cheseldine, *Ohio in the Rainbow*, 256.
49. Ibid.
50. Duffy, *Father Duffy's Story*, 278.
51. Daniels, *Diary*, 50-51.

CHAPTER ELEVEN: EXPLOITING THE BREAKTHROUGH
1. Reilly, *Americans All*, 751-753.
2. Ibid.
3. Taber, *168th Infantry, Vol II*, 212.
4. Thomas Reilly quoted in Reilly, *Americans All*, 756.
5. George Geran quoted in Reilly, *Americans All*, 756.
6. Reilly, *Americans All*, 754.
7. Duffy, *Father Duffy's Story*, 269.
8. Cheseldine, *Ohio in the Rainbow*, 256-257.
9. Ibid., 257.
10. Taber, *168th Infantry, Vol. II*, 201.
11. Ibid., 202.
12. Ibid.
13. Ibid., 202-203.
14. Ibid., 203.
15. Ibid.
16. Cheseldine, *Ohio in the Rainbow*, 257.
17. Ibid., 258.
18. Bailey, *Roy Bailey Diary, 1917-1919*, 69.
19. Enoch Williams to his mother, October 27, 1918. Enoch Williams, *Letters Home*, 123-124.
20. Reilly, *Americans All*, 736.
21. Pershing, *Experiences*, Kindle Edition, 646.
22. Reilly, *Americans All*, 737.
23. Cheseldine, *Ohio in the Rainbow*, 259-260.
24. Duffy, *Father Duffy's Story*, 290-291.
25. Ibid.
26. Taber, *168th Infantry, Vol. II*, 209.
27. Ibid., 209-210.
28. Ibid., 210-212.
29. Amerine, *Alabama's Own*, 201-203.
30. Reilly, *Americans All*, 746.
31. Ibid. Note: The author was one of the three officers present at this meeting and was able to describe it in detail.
32. Ibid., 746-747.
33. Ibid., 747.
34. Ibid.
35. Ibid., 743-744.

36. William Hughes quoted in Reilly, *Americans All*, 745.
37. Cheseldine, *Ohio in the Rainbow*, 260.
38. Reilly, *Americans All*, 745.

CHAPTER TWELVE: THE RACE TO SEDAN
1. Cheseldine, *Ohio in the Rainbow*, 276.
2. Ibid., 277.
3. Cheseldine, *Ohio in the Rainbow*, 276; Reppy, *Rainbow Memories*, 19.
4. Robb, *Price of Our Heritage*, 393.
5. Taber, *168th Infantry, Vol. II*, 212-213.
6. Amerine, *Alabama's Own*, 203.
7. Taber, *168th Infantry, Vol. II*, 214-215.
8. Cheseldine, *Ohio in the Rainbow*, 265-266.
9. Duffy, *Father Duffy's Story*, 297.
10. Reilly, *Americans All*, 776-777.
11. Daniels, *Diary*, 52.
12. Cheseldine, *Ohio in the Rainbow*, 266.
13. Daniels, *Diary*, 53.
14. Amerine, *Alabama's Own*, 204.
15. Taber, *168th Infantry, Vol. II*, 215-216.
16. Reilly, *Americans All*, 776.
17. Taber, *168th Infantry, Vol. II*, 216-217.
18. Ibid., 217.
19. Cheseldine, *Ohio in the Rainbow*, 266.
20. Ibid., 267.
21. Ibid.
22. Cheseldine, *Ohio in the Rainbow*, 267; Tompkins, *Story of the Rainbow Division*, 139-140.
23. Tompkins, *Story of the Rainbow Division*, 140-141; Cheseldine, *Ohio in the Rainbow*, 267.
24. Reilly, *Americans All*, 781.
25. Ibid., 782.
26. Ibid., 783.
27. Ibid., 778-779.
28. Ibid., 778.
29. Cheseldine, *Ohio in the Rainbow*, 267-268.
30. Reilly, *Americans All*, 779-780.
31. Taber, *168th Infantry, Vol. II*, 217-218.
32. Ibid., 218-219.
33. Leon Miesse journal entry for November 5, 1918. Miesse, *100 Years On*, 187.
34. Amerine, *Alabama's Own*, 204-205.
35. Ibid., 206.
36. Cheseldine, *Ohio in the Rainbow*, 268.
37. Faulkner, *Meuse-Argonne*, 66-68.
38. Ibid., 68.
39. Ibid.
40. Ibid.
41. Ibid., 68-69.

42. Cheseldine, *Ohio in the Rainbow*, 268-269.
43. Taber, *168th Infantry, Vol. II*, 220.
44. Ibid., 220-221.
45. Ibid., 222-223.
46. Leon Miesse journal entry for November 6, 1918. Miesse, *100 Years On*, 187; Daniels, *Diary*, 55.
47. Reilly, *Americans All*,
48. Taber, *168th Infantry, Vol. II*, 223-224.
49. Cheseldine, *Ohio in the Rainbow*, 270.
50. Taber, *168th Infantry, Vol. II*, 225-226.
51. Amerine, *Alabama's Own*, 209-210.
52. Ibid., 211.
53. Reilly, *Americans All*, 799.
54. Cheseldine, *Ohio in the Rainbow*, 270.
55. Daniels, *Diary*, 56.
56. Cheseldine, *Ohio in the Rainbow*, 270-271.
57. Coffman, *War to End All Wars*, 351.
58. Cheseldine, *Ohio in the Rainbow*, 273.
59. Cheseldine, *Ohio in the Rainbow*, 272.
60. Ibid.
61. Ibid., 273.
62. Daniels, *Diary*, 56.
63. Cheseldine, *Ohio in the Rainbow*, 273.
64. Ibid., 275-276.
65. Faulkner, *Meuse-Argonne*, 69.
66. Coffman, *American Experience in World War I*, 355.

CHAPTER THIRTEEN: ARMISTICE
1. Duffy, *Father Duffy's Story*, 305.
2. Bailey, *Roy Bailey Diary, 1917-1919*, 71.
3. Cheseldine, *Ohio in the Rainbow*, 278.
4. Taber, *168th Infantry, Vol. II*, 231-232.
5. Amerine, *Alabama's Own*, 218.
6. Duffy, *Father Duffy's Story*, 305.
7. Daniels, *Dana Daniels Diary, 1917-1919*, 64-65.
8. Reppy, *Rainbow Memories*, 22.
9. Duffy, *Father Duffy's Story*, 327.
10. Duffy, *Father Duffy's Story*, 327-328.
11. Cheseldine, *Ohio in the Rainbow*, 324; Daniels, *Dana Daniels Diary, 1917-1919*, 69-70.
12. Taber, *168th Infantry, Vol. II*, 275.
13. Cheseldine, *Ohio in the Rainbow*, 325.
14. Daniels, *Dana Daniels Diary, 1917-1919*, 71-72; Taber, *168th Infantry, Vol. II*, 277-278.
15. Daniels, *Dana Daniels Diary, 1917-1919*, 71-72; *Chillicothe Gazette*, May 11, 1919.
16. *Mansfield News-Journal*, May 10, 1919.
17. *Chillicothe Gazette*, May 11, 1919.
18. Taber, *168th Infantry Regiment, Vol. II*, 279-280.
19. Ibid.

20. Amerine, *Alabama's Own*, 260-267.
21. Robb, *Price of Our Heritage*, 349.
22. American Battle Monuments Commission, *American Armies and Battlefields in Europe* (Washington, D.C.: U.S. Government Printing Office, 1938), 147-149, 247-248.
23. Duffy, *Father Duffy's Story*, 330.

AFTERWORD

1. 1920 *U.S. Federal Census*, Census Place: Montgomery Ward 3, Montgomery, Alabama; Roll: T625_36; Page: 8A; Enumeration District: 101; *U.S., Veterans Administration Master Index, 1917-1940* [database on-line]. Lehi, UT. USA: Ancestry.com Operations, Inc., 2019.
2. Taber, *168th Infantry, Vol. II*, 65; *Des Moines Tribune*, Des Moines, Iowa, August 24, 1950.
3. *Cullum's Register, Supplement, Vol. VIII*, https://penelope.uchicago.edu/Thayer/E/Gazetteer/Places/America/United_States/Army/USMA/Cullums_Register/3068*.html.
4. *Times Recorder*, Zanesville, Ohio, December 27, 1954.
5. Biographical data accompanying archived copy of diary, Ohio History Connection, Columbus, Ohio, MS 5; Box 1, Folder 6.
6. Thomas A. Rumer, *The American Legion: An Official History, 1919–1989* (New York: M. Evans and Co., 1990), 107.
7. Douglas Waller, *Wild Bill Donovan: The Spymaster Who Created the OSS and Modern American Espionage* (New York: Free Press, 2011), 93, 111.
8. "Beloved Chaplain of Fighting 69th Dies," *Chronicle-Telegram*. June 27, 1932.
9. *1920 U.S. Federal Census*, Records of the Bureau of the Census, Record Group 29. National Archives, Washington, D.C.; *U.S., Find a Grave Index, 1600s-Current* [database on-line]. Lehi, UT, USA: Ancestry.com Operations, Inc., 2012.
10. Ruth Henig, *Versailles and After, 1919–33* (London and New York: Routledge, 1995), 52.
11. Find a Grave, database and images (https://www.findagrave.com/memorial/5607/ferdinand-foch: accessed 18 April 2023), memorial page for Ferdinand Foch (2 Oct 1851–20 Mar 1929), Find a Grave Memorial ID 5607, citing Les Invalides, Paris, City of Paris, Île-de-France, France; Maintained by Find a Grave.
12. United States of America, Bureau of the Census. *Fifteenth Census of the United States, 1930* (Washington, D.C.: National Archives and Records Administration, 1930); *U.S., Find a Grave Index, 1600s-Current* [database on-line]. Lehi, UT, USA: Ancestry.com Operations, Inc., 2012.
13. 1920 U.S. Federal Census, Manhattan Assembly District 16, New York, New York, Roll T625-1216, page 11A; New York, U.S. Military Service Cards, New York State Military Museum.
14. 1920 U.S. Federal Census, Cleveland, Ohio, Enumeration District 0256, page 16; New York, New York Death Index, 1949-1965.
15. *Biographical Directory of Federal Judges*, Federal Judicial Center, accessed online at https://www.fjc.gov/node/1382421; *Lancaster Eagle-Gazette*, Lancaster, Ohio, November 20, 1935.
16. Bill Thayer, "Michael Joseph Lenihan," penelope.uchicago.edu, 2016.
17. *Philadelphia Inquirer*, Philadelphia, Pennsylvania, August 15, 1958.
18. MacArthur, *Reminiscences*, 85.
19. William Manchester, *American Caesar: Douglas MacArthur 1880–1964* (Boston: Little, Brown, 1978), 130-132; D. Clayton James, *The Years of MacArthur, Volume 1, 1880–1941* (Boston: Houghton Mifflin, 1970), 295-347.

20. Louis Morton, *The Fall of the Philippines, United States Army in World War II* (Washington, D.C.: U.S. Army Center of Military History. CMH Pub 5-2, 1953), 19; James, *The Years of MacArthur*, 98.
21. James, *The Years of MacArthur*, 336-354.
22. *New York Daily News*, April 22, 1956.
23. *Evening Star*, Washington, D.C., July 29, 1918; *Meriden Morning Record*, Meriden, Connecticut, January 3, 1918.
24. *New York Times*, October 9, 1934
25. David W. Del Testa, Florence Lemoine, and John Strickland, *Government Leaders, Military Rulers, and Political Activists* (London and New York: Routledge, 2001), 120.
26. Michael Robert Patterson, *Charles Thomas Menoher—Major General, United States Army*, https://www.arlingtoncemetery.net/cmenoher.htm, April 9, 2023.
27. Miesse, *100 Years On*, 53.
28. Fleek, *Place the Headstones*, 167, 184-186.
29. Georgia Adjutant General's Office, *World War I Statements of Service Cards*, Georgia State Archives, Morrow, Georgia; *Richmond Times-Dispatch*, Richmond, Virginia, November 21, 1972.
30. J. R. McCarl, *Decisions of the Comptroller General of the United States. Vol. 4* (Washington, D.C.: U.S. Government Printing Office, 1925), 317.
31. *Coshocton Daily Tribune*, Coshocton, Ohio, July 15, 1948.
32. *The Reader's Companion to Military History*, Eds. Robert Cowley and Geoffrey Parker, www.history.com.
33. *Chicago Tribune*, Chicago, Illinois, December 14, 1963.
34. *New York Times*, New York, August 21, 1958.
35. *1930 United States Federal Census*, Census Place: West Riverside, Riverside, California; Page: 1A; Enumeration District: 0087; 1940; Census Place: Riverside, Riverside, California; Roll: m-t0627-00278; Page: 2A; Enumeration District: 33-54.
36. National Archives at St. Louis, MO; *Applications for Headstones, 1/1/1925 - 6/30/1970*; NAID: NAID 596118; Record Group Number: 92; Record Group Title: Records of the Office of the Quartermaster General.
37. *Des Moines Register*, Des Moines, Iowa, August 10, 1958.
38. Ruth Smith Truss, *William P. Screws*, March 8, 2017, Encyclopedia of Alabama, www. https://encyclopediaofalabama.org/article/william-p-screws.
39. "Senator Claude Stanley," *The Iowa Legislature*, https://www.legis.iowa.gov/legislators.
40. Taber, *A Rainbow Division Lieutenant in France*, Kindle Edition, 1-2; *Danville News*, Danville, Pennsylvania, July 17, 1987.
41. *New York Times*, March 12, 1956.
42. *Austin-American Statesman*, Austin, Texas, November 22, 1968.
43. *1930 U.S. Federal Census*, Census Place: Port Chester, Westchester, New York; Roll: 1665; Page: 6A; Enumeration District: 0318; *U.S., Find a Grave Index, 1600s-Current* [database on-line]. Lehi, UT, USA: Ancestry.com Operations, Inc., 2012.

BIBLIOGRAPHY

American Armies and Battlefields in Europe: A History, Guide, and Reference Book. U.S. Government Printing Office, Washington, D.C., 1938.

American Battle Monuments Commission. *42nd Division Summary of Operations in the World War.* U.S. Government Printing Office, Washington, D.C., 1944.

Amerine, William H. *Alabama's Own in France.* Eaton & Gettinger, New York, 1919.

Armstrong, David A. *Bullets and Bureaucrats: The Machine Gun and the United States Army, 1861-1916.* Greenwood Press, Westport, Connecticut, 1982.

The Army Lineage Book, Volume II: Infantry. Washington, D.C., U.S. Government Printing Office, 1953.

Asprey, Robert B. *The German High Command at War: Hindenburg and Ludendorff Conduct World War I.* Quill House, Fort Mill, South Carolina, 1993.

Austin-American Statesman, Austin, Texas.

Bailey, Roy. *Roy Bailey Diary, 1917-1918.* Unpublished. Accessed at www.markboyd.info/MarionsOwn/Sgt_Bailey/pages_62-70.html.

Biographical Directory of Federal Judges, Federal Judicial Center, accessed online at https://www.fjc.gov.

Biographical Register of the Officers and Graduates of the U.S. Military Academy at West Point, N.Y. Since its Establishment in 1802. Volume IV. Riverside Press, Cambridge, Massachusetts, 1901.

Biographical Register of the Officers and Graduates of the U.S. Military Academy at West Point, N.Y. Since its Establishment in 1802. Supplement

Volume V. Lieutenant Charles Braden, ed. Seeman & Peters, Printers, Saginaw, Michigan, 1919.

Biographical Register of the Officers and Graduates of the U.S. Military Academy at West Point, N.Y. Since its Establishment in 1802. Supplement Volume VI. Seeman & Peters, Printers, Saginaw, Michigan, 1920.

Biographical Register of the Officers and Graduates of the U.S. Military Academy at West Point, N.Y. Since its Establishment in 1802. Supplement Volume VI-A. Colonel Wirt Robinson, ed. Seeman & Peters, Printers, Saginaw, Michigan, 1920.

Bonk, David. *St. Mihiel, 1918: The American Expeditionary Force's Trial by Fire.* Osprey Publishing, Oxford, United Kingdom, 2011.

Boyd, Austin Dewitt. *Austin Dewitt "Dusty" Boyd in WWI: Service in France and Germany*, Mark Boyd, ed. Unpublished. Accessed at www.markboyd.info/adboyd/war.html#mar-15-1919.

Carter, Donald A. *St. Mihiel, 12–16 September 1918.* Center of Military History, U.S. Army, Washington, D.C., 2018.

Cheseldine, R.M. *Ohio in the Rainbow: Official Story of the 166th Infantry, 42nd Division, in the World War.* F.J. Heer Printing Company, Columbus, Ohio, 1924.

Chicago Tribune, Chicago, Illinois.

Chinn, George M. *The Machine Gun: History, Evolution and Development of Manual, Automatic, and Airborne Repeating Weapons, Volume I.* U.S Government Printing Office, Washington, D.C., 1951.

The Chronicle-Telegram, New York.

Coffman, Edward M. *The War to End All Wars: The American Military Experience in World War I.* The University Press of Kentucky, Lexington, Kentucky, 1998.

Collins, Louis L. *History of the 151st Field Artillery Rainbow Division*, ed. Wayne E. Stevens, vol. 1. Minnesota War Records Commission, St. Paul, Minnesota, 1924.

Cooke, James J. *The Rainbow Division in the Great War, 1917-1919.* Praeger, Westport, Connecticut, 1994.

The Coshocton Daily Tribune, Coshocton, Ohio.

Cowley, Robert and Geoffrey Parker, editors. *The Reader's Companion to Military History*, www.history.com.

Crowell, Benedict and Robert Forrest Wilson. *The Road to France: The Transportation of Troops and Military Supplies, 1917–1918—How America Went to War: An Account from Official Sources of the Nation's War Activities, 1917–1920.* Yale University Press, New Haven, Connecticut, 1921.

Cullum, George W. *Biographical Register of the Officers and Graduates of the U.S. Military Academy at West Point, N.Y. Since its Establishment in 1802, Volume III*. Houghton, Mifflin, and Company, Boston, Massachusetts, 1891.

Daniels, Dana. *Dana Daniels Diary, 1917-1919*. Dana Daniels Collection, Ohio Historical Society (MS 5; Box 1, Folder 6), Columbus, Ohio.

Danville News, Danville, Pennsylvania.

Del Testa, David W., Florence Lemoine, and John Strickland, *Government Leaders, Military Rulers, and Political Activists*. Routledge, London and New York, 2001.

Des Moines Register, Des Moines, Iowa.

Duffy, Francis P. *Father Duffy's Story: A Tale of Humor and Heroism, of Life and Death with the Fighting Sixty-Ninth*. George B. Doran Company, New York, 1919.

Ebert, Carl F. *A Brief History of Co. D, 166th Infantry*. Unknown Publisher, Marion. Ohio, 1939.

Eisenhower, John S.D. *Yanks: The Epic Story of the American Army in World War I*. Simon and Schuster, New York, Kindle Edition, 2001.

Ettinger, Albert M. and A. Churchill. *A Doughboy with the Fighting 69th*. New York: Pocket Books, a division of Simon & Schuster, New York, New York, 1992.

Evening Star, Washington, D.C.

Faulkner, Richard S. *Meuse Argonne, 26 September-November 11, 1918*. Center of Military History, U.S. Army, Washington, D.C., 2018.

Ferrell Robert H. *The Question of MacArthur's Reputation: Cote de Chatillon, October 14-16, 1918*. University of Missouri Press, Columbia, Missouri, 2008.

Fleek, Sherman L. *Place the Headstones Where They Belong*. Utah State University Press, Logan, Utah, 2008.

Frazer, Nimrod Thompson. *Send the Alabamians*. University of Alabama Press, Tuscaloosa, Alabama, Kindle Edition, 2014.

Georgia Adjutant General's Office, *World War I Statements of Service Cards*, Georgia State Archives, Morrow, Georgia.

Green, Chris Newton. *From Blue to a Gold Star: The Story of 1st Lt. C.R. Green and Company A, First Battalion, 168th Infantry*. Self-Published, San Dimas, California, 2018.

Grotelueschen, Mark Ethan. "The AEF Way of War: The American Army and Combat in the First World War." PhD dissertation, Texas A&M University, 2003.

Guild, George R. and Frederick C. Test. *Pocket Field Manual: A Manual Designed for Use of Troops in the Field*. George Banta Publishing Company, Menasha, Wisconsin, 1917.

Haig, Douglas, eds. Gary Sheffield and John Bourne. *War Diaries and Letters, 1914–1918*. Weidenfeld & Nicolson, London, 2005.

Handbook of Artillery Including Mobile, Anti-Aircraft and Trench Materiel. Office of the Chief of Ordnance, U.S. Government Printing Office, Washington, D.C., 1920.

Handbook of the Hotchkiss Machine Gun, Model of 1914. U.S. War Department, Office of the Chief of Ordnance, Washington, D.C., 1917

Harbord, James. *An American Army in France*. Little, Brown, and Co., Boston, 1936.

Hayes, John B. *Heroes Among the Brave*. Lee County Historical Society, Loachapoka, Alabama, 1973.

Henig, Ruth. *Versailles and After, 1919–33*. Routledge, London and New York, 1995.

History of Machine Guns and Automatic Rifles. Small Arms Division, Office of the Chief of Ordnance, U.S. Government Printing Office, Washington, D.C., 1922.

Hochschild, Adam. *To End All Wars: A Story of Loyalty and Rebellion, 1914-1918*. Houghton Mifflin Harcourt Books, New York, 2011.

Hogan, Martin. *The Shamrock Battalion of the Rainbow*. D. Appleton and Company, New York, 1919.

Into the Fight, April–June 1918. Center of Military History, U.S. Army, Washington, D.C., 2018.

James, D. Clayton. *The Years of MacArthur, Volume 1, 1880–1941*. Houghton Mifflin, Boston, 1970.

Joffre, Joseph Jacques Césaire. *The Personal Memoirs of Joffre: Field Marshal of the French Army, Volume II*. Harper and Brothers, New York, 1932.

Lancaster Eagle-Gazette, Lancaster, Ohio.

Lanza, Conrad H. "The Artillery Support of Infantry in the A.E.F.," *Field Artillery Journal 26*, January-March 1936, The United States Field Artillery Association, Washington, D.C., 1936.

MacArthur, Charles. *War Bugs*. Doubleday, Doran & Company. New York, 1929.

MacArthur, Douglas. *Reminiscences*. McGraw-Hill, New York, 1964.

Mahon, John. *New York's Fighting 69th: A Regimental History of Service in the Civil War's Irish Brigade and the Great War's Rainbow Division.* McFarland & Company, Inc., Jefferson, North Carolina, 2004.

Manchester, William. *American Caesar: Douglas MacArthur, 1880–1964.* 1978; reprint, Back Bay Books, New York, 2008.

Marysville Journal-Tribune, Marysville, Ohio.

McCarl, J. R. *Decisions of the Comptroller General of the United States. Vol. 4.* U.S. Government Printing Office, Washington, D.C., 1925

McGeorge, Stephen C. and Mason W. Watson. *The Marne, 15 July-6 August 1918.* Center of Military History, United States Army, Washington, D.C., 2018.

Medal of Honor, 1863-1968: In the Name of the Congress of the United States. U.S. Government Printing Office, Washington, D.C., 1968.

Meriden Morning Record, Meriden, Connecticut.

Miesse, Leon, *100 Years On: WW I – Leon Miesse, Captain, 166th*, Robert Laird, ed. Zerone Publishing, Location Unknown, Kindle Edition, 2017.

Millett, Allan R. *Well Planned, Splendidly Executed: The Battle of Cantigny May 28-31, 1918.* Cantigny First Division Foundation, Chicago, Illinois, 2010.

Moffett, Burt. *Burt Moffett Diary, January 1, 1918–September 7, 1918.* Burt J. Moffett World War I Diaries Collection, Ohio Historical Society (Vol. 1425), Columbus, Ohio.

Morton, Louis. *The Fall of the Philippines, United States Army in World War II.* U.S. Army Center of Military History, Washington, D.C., 1953.

Moss, James A. *Field Service.* George Banta Publishing Company, Menasha, Wisconsin, 1917.

Neiberg, Michael S. *The Second Battle of the Marne.* University of Indiana Press, Bloomington, Indiana, Kindle Edition, 2008.

New York Daily News, New York.

New York Times, New York.

Ney, Virgil. *Evolution of the US Army Infantry Mortar Squad: The Argonne to Pleiku.* Technical Operations, Incorporated, Combat Operations Research Group, Fort Belvoir, Virginia, 1966.

Official Roster of the Soldiers of the State of Ohio in the War with Mexico, 1846–1848. (Reprint Edition). Mansfield, Ohio, Ohio Genealogical Society, 1991.

Otte, Maarten. *The Meuse Argonne 1918: Breaking the Line.* Pen & Sword Books, Ltd., Barnsley, United Kingdom, 2018.

Ottoson, Peter. *Trench Artillery AEF*. Lothrop, Lee, and Shepard, Boston, Massachusetts, 1931.

Papers of Harry S. Truman Pertaining to Family, Business, and Personal Affairs. Truman Library and Museum, Independence, Missouri.

Patterson, Michael Robert. *Charles Thomas Menoher – Major General, United States Army*, https://www.arlingtoncemetery.net/cmenoher.htm, 2023.

Pershing, John J. *My Experiences in the World War*. Frederick Stokes, New York, 1931, Kindle 2-Volume Edition.

Philadelphia Inquirer, Philadelphia, Pennsylvania.

Reilly, Henry J. *Americans All: The Rainbow at War; Official History of the 42nd Rainbow Division in the World War*. The F. J. Heer Printing Co., Columbus, Ohio, 1936.

———. *America's Part*. Cosmopolitan Book Corporation, New York, 1928.

Reppy, Alison. *Rainbow Memories: Character Sketches and History of the First Battalion, 166th Infantry, 42nd Division, American Expeditionary Force*. Executive Committee, First Battalion, 166th Infantry, Columbus, Ohio, 1919.

Richmond Times-Dispatch, Richmond, Virginia.

Richwood Gazette, Richwood, Ohio.

Robb, Winfred E. *The Price of Our Heritage: In Memory of the Heroic Dead of the 168 Infantry*. American Lithographing and Printing Co., Des Moines, Iowa, 1919.

Rumer, Thomas A. *The American Legion: An Official History, 1919–1989*. M. Evans and Co., New York, 1990.

Setzekorn, Eric B. *Joining the Great War, April 1917-April 1918*. Center of Military History, U.S. Army, Washington, D.C., 2017.

Smythe, Donald. *Pershing: General of the Armies*. Indiana University Press, Bloomington, Indiana, 1986.

Sondhaus, Lawrence. *World War I: The Global Revolution*. Cambridge University Press, New York, 2011.

Stackpole, Pierpont J., ed. Robert H. Ferrell. *In the Company of Generals: The World War I Diary of Pierpont L. Stackpole*. University of Missouri Press, Columbia, Missouri, 2009.

Stewart, Lawrence O. *Rainbow Bright*. Dorrence, Philadelphia, Pennsylvania, 1923.

Taber, John H. *The Story of the 168th Infantry Regiment, Volume I and II*. State Historical Society of Iowa, Iowa City, Iowa, 1925.

Taber, Stephen H., ed. *A Rainbow Division Lieutenant in France: The World War I Diary of John H. Taber*. McFarland & Co., Jefferson, North Carolina, 2015.

Takle, Patrick. *Nine Divisions in Champagne: The Second Battle of Marne*. Pen & Sword Books Ltd, Barnsley, United Kingdom, Kindle Edition, 2015.

Taylor, Emerson Gifford. *New England in France, 1917-1919: A History of the Twenty-Sixth Division U.S.A.* Houghton-Mifflin Company, Boston, Massachusetts, 1920.

Thomas, Shipley. *The History of the A.E.F.* George B. Doran, New York, 1920.

Thompson, David G. "Ohio's Best: The Mobilization of the Fourth Infantry, Ohio National Guard, in 1917," *Ohio History Journal, Volume 101, Winter-Spring 1992*. Ohio Historical Society, Columbus, Ohio, 1992.

Thompson, Hugh S. *Trench Knives and Mustard Gas: With the 42nd Rainbow Division in France*. Texas A&M University Press, College Station, Texas, 2004.

Times Recorder, Zanesville, Ohio.

Tompkins, Raymond S. *The Story of the Rainbow Division*. Boni and Liveright, New York, 1919.

Truss, Ruth Smith. "The Alabama National Guard's 167th Infantry Regiment in World War I." *Alabama Review 56 (January 2003)*, Alabama Historical Society in cooperation with The University of Mobile, Mobile, Alabama, 2003.

United States Army in the World War, 1917-1919, Volume 3: Training and Use of American Units with the British and French. Center of Military History, United States Army, Washington, D.C., 1989.

United States Army in the World War, 1917-1919: Military Operations of the American Expeditionary Forces, Volume 5. Center of Military History, United States Army, Washington, D.C., 1989.

United States Army in the World War, 1917-1919: Military Operations of the American Expeditionary Forces, Volume 8. Center of Military History, United States Army, Washington, D.C., 1990.

United States Army in the World War, 1917-1919: Military Operations of the American Expeditionary Forces, Volume 9. Center of Military History, United States Army, Washington, D.C., 1990.

U.S. Federal Census. Bureau of the Census, Washington D.C., 1920, 1930, 1940.

Waller, Douglas. *Wild Bill Donovan: The Spymaster Who Created the OSS and Modern American Espionage*. Free Press, New York, 2011.

Williams, Enoch. *Letters Home from Somewhere in France (P.S. Send cigarettes & chocolate)*, Gary Williams, ed. Unpublished. Accessed at https://archive.org/details/EnochWilliamsWwiLettersHome1917-1919.

Wilson, Woodrow. *War Messages, 65th Cong., 1st Sess. Senate Doc. No. 5, Serial No. 7264*. Washington, D.C., 1917.

Wolf, Walter B. *A Brief History of the Rainbow Division*. Rand, McNally & Co., New York, 1919.

INDEX

A Company, 116, 134, 148-149, 153, 158, 169-170, 176, 182
Aire River, 124-125, 141
Aisne-Marne, ix-x, 17, 24, 32-34, 37, 41, 47, 49-54, 56, 64-66, 72, 77-80, 97, 121, 130, 157
Aisne River, 33, 124
Alabama National Guard, 227
Algonquin Round Table, 225
Allen, John, 212
American Battle Monuments Commission, 219
American Expeditionary Forces (AEF), x-xi, 3, 10-14, 19-20, 30, 32, 50-51, 56, 58, 63-68, 72, 74, 81, 110, 120-126, 133, 136-137, 140-141, 144, 157, 173, 182, 184, 192-193, 196, 202, 206-207, 226
Americans All (Reilly), 198
Anderson, Alex, 167, 194
Andon Creek, 141
Apremont, 63, 131, 195, 197
Aquinas College High School, 84
Argonne Forest, xii, 69-70, 124-125, 128, 130
Arlington National Cemetery, 222, 225-226
Armistice, ix, 16, 133, 199, 214-215, 217, 219, 223, 226
Army Detachment C, 65
Army Group Gallwitz, 79, 86-87
Army-Navy Journal, 227
Army Signal Corps, xiii, 68, 115, 175
Army War College, 4, 20

Austro-Hungarian Divisions, 65, 103, 213

B Company, 39, 116-117, 134, 149-150, 153, 158, 169-170, 176, 178, 181-182
Baccarat, viii, 16, 19-20, 23-25, 54, 82
Baden, Max von, 133
Bailey, Roy, 130, 192, 215
Baker, Newton, 2, 4, 12
Baker, Russell, 198-199
Baltimore Sun, 126
Banks, Harley, 101-102
Bantheville, 142
Bar Valley, 202, 204
Bare, Walter, 149, 154, 163, 174-176, 210, 221
Base Hospital No. 48, 93
Bavarian Divisions, 29, 65
Bell, Ernest, 39
Benchley, Robert, 225
Bennett, Ernest, 38, 49-50, 221
Betsworth, Walter, 112
Betty, Harold, 185
Bird, Dyer, 18-19, 22
Bly, Robert, 169
Bois de Beney, 103-106
Bois de Charey, 108, 111
Bois de Dampvitoux, 77, 106, 108, 112
Bois de la Grande Souche, 108
Bois de la Sonnard, 79, 90-94
Bois des Haudronvilles, 108
Bombon, 64
Bootz, Herman, 194

Bourmont, 54-57
Boyd, Dusty, 96
Brandt, Arthur, 191
Brest, 216-217, 219
Brewer, Guy, 91, 93, 97, 217
A Brief Story of the Rainbow Division (Wolf), 138
Brown, Robert A., 4, 7, 38, 49-51, 221
Brunhild Stellung, 124
Buder & Buder, 227
A Bug's Eye View of War (MacArthur), 224
Bullard, Robert, 136
Bundy, Omar, 33, 68

C Company, 91, 135, 149, 153, 158, 170, 176, 178-182, 190
Camp Brewer, 217
Camp Merritt, 219
Camp Mills, 3, 5, 8-10, 15, 52, 172, 182
Camp Shelby, 219
Camp Upton, 217
Carpentier, George, 84
Carraway, William, xiii, 151, 178-179, 211, 214
Central Intelligence Agency, 222
Champagne, 24, 26, 29-31, 64, 121, 182, 228
Charly-sur-Marne, 53-54
Chateau-Thierry, 30, 32, 34, 52-54
Chateau du Nord, 199, 201
Chauvoncourt, 63
Chehery, 211-213
Chemery, 198, 203, 208
Cheseldine, Raymond, xiii, 18, 23, 53, 73, 76, 82, 101, 109, 193, 221-222
Chicago Tribune, 227
Church of Christ, 131
Citadel, 87
City of Paris, 216
Clark, Merl, 181
Clay, Lucius, 222
Cohan, George M., 216
Collins, Louis, 21
Combres Group, 65
Composite Army C, 86

Conger, Arthur, 68-69
Conner, Fox, 68, 206
Cote Dame Marie, 125, 142
Cote de Chatillon, xii, 142-146, 149-155, 158-159, 162, 164, 170-186, 188-192, 197
Cote de Maldah, 134, 142, 151
Cuba, 5, 80

D Company, 39, 130, 135, 148-150, 152-153, 158, 170, 176, 182, 198-199
Daniels, Dana, 120, 186, 200, 208, 216, 222
Degoutte, Jean Marie Joseph, 32-34, 37
Dempsey, Earl, 212
Denie, Le Comte, 198
Dennis, George, 94-95
Dickman, Joseph T., 206
Donovan, William "Wild Bill", 51, 56, 58, 84-87, 90, 96, 99, 105-106, 133, 150-155, 166-167, 217, 222
Dravo, Charles, 185
Dresbach, Irvin, 166
Drum, Hugh, 124, 141-142, 173, 206-209
Duffy, Francis P., xiii, 46-48, 51-52, 84, 133, 150, 160, 162, 167, 184, 188-189, 194, 220, 222

E Company, 106, 108, 152, 156, 176, 182, 190, 208
Eben, Johannes von, 32
Eich, Werner, 212
8th Landwehr Division, 65
18th Howitzer Field Artillery, 81-82
80th Division, 126
84th Infantry Brigade, xi, 4, 7, 35, 38, 40, 49-50, 60, 77-81, 90-91, 103, 110-111, 115, 138, 142-145, 163, 174-175, 184-185, 191-193, 221
82nd Division, 144, 152, 156, 166, 184
83rd Infantry Brigade, 4-6, 9, 40, 50, 53, 77-78, 81, 91, 103, 112, 117, 142-146, 164, 167, 174, 184-185, 187-188, 193, 196, 212, 223
89th Division, 72, 82, 85, 91, 111, 118,

129, 187-189, 193
Eisenhower, John, 122
Equitable Trust Company, 225
Espy, Robert, 39
Essey-et-Maizerais, 96-98
Exermont, 135-136, 150, 169, 184, 195-196
Exmorieux Farm, 195

F Company, 91, 97, 106, 152, 156, 168, 176, 178, 180-181, 183
Fallow, Thomas, 163, 172-173, 179-180, 210, 223
Fecheimer, Henry, 167
Federal Reserve Board, 222
Federal Trade Commission, 222
Field Order No. 36, 144
5th Landwehr Division, 65
51st Iowa Infantry, 49
52nd Jaeger Division, 129
Field Order No. 37, 160, 164
Field Order No. 38, 174
Field Order No. 53, 207
Field Order No. 54, 209
1st Army, xi, 64-72, 77, 80, 82, 101, 110, 120-129, 132-137, 140-146, 164, 173, 175, 184, 186, 192-193, 196, 206-207, 209
1st Battalion, 17, 38-39, 51, 58-59, 78, 84, 86, 88-91, 103, 105, 107-108, 111, 115, 135-136, 147-149, 152, 162, 166-169, 174, 176-177, 190, 202, 204-205, 210-211
First Battle of the Marne, 33
1st Guards Division, 125
Fleckenstein, Vincent, 101-102, 114
Fleming, William, 148-149
Floyd, Allen, 205
Foch, Ferdinand, 30, 32, 62, 64-73, 110, 120-122, 141, 214, 223
Forest of the Lovely Willow, 117
Foret-de-Fere, 35-36, 40, 44, 46, 48, 52, 54
Foret-de-la-Reine, 74-75, 82
4th Alabama, 7, 172
4th Division, 32, 43, 54, 64, 126-127

14th French Division, 20
14th Reserve infantry division, 203
14th Sturm Battalion, 103, 112
40th Division (US), 59
41st Division (US), 59, 182
41st French Division, 20
42nd Division, ix, 3-4, 11, 14, 21, 30, 33-34, 47, 50-51, 60, 64, 72, 81, 84, 99, 111, 118, 132, 134, 142, 144, 160, 164, 173-174, 185, 187, 192-193, 201-202, 206-207, 209, 212, 216, 223, 225
Franco-Prussian War, 121
French Fourth Army, 24, 26-27, 121, 124-125, 128, 193, 207
French 40th Division, 198, 207, 209, 212
French 164th Division, 20, 40
French Sixth Army, 32-37, 40, 43
French 252nd Infantry Regiment, 198
Friedensturm (Peace Offensive), 24, 30
The Front Page (MacArthur), 224
Fuchs, George, 65-67, 79, 87

G Company, 91, 97, 106-107, 152, 156, 176, 182
G-2 Intelligence, 124
Gatley, George, 146
General Order 51, 40
Geran, (Major), 136, 152, 157, 188
German Fifth Party, 125
German High Seas Fleet, 214
German Supreme Headquarters, 43, 86-87, 126-127, 202
German Third Party, 125
German 201st Division, 34
Gorz Group, 65, 68
Gouraud, Henri, 24-30, 228
Gowdy, Harry "Hank", 198
Grant, Ulysses, 123-124
Grave, Henry, 27, 76-77, 96, 166
Greene, Douglas, 48
Greulach, William, 94
Gunga Din (MacArthur), 224

H Company, 60, 91, 97, 106-107, 152, 154, 156, 168, 170, 176, 178-182
Hagen Stellung, 65

INDEX

Hanley, James, 84
Harbord, James, 127
Harrisonburg, 216
Hassavant Farm, 108-109
Hatch, Roscoe, 120
Haubrich, Roger, 26, 166, 211-212
Haumont-les-Lachaussee, 101-102, 107-108, 111-114, 117
Hawaiian Division, 225
Hayes, Helen, 225
Hayes, John, 38, 45-46, 120, 135-136, 223
Healy, Edward, 161-162
Hemphill, Edward, 102
Heroes Among the Brave (Hayes), 45
Hill 212, 40, 42, 58, 91
Hill 230, 156, 190
Hill 240, 136
Hill 242, 143, 146, 149, 162, 165, 169-170, 176-177, 190-191
Hill 252, 210
Hill 262, 145
Hill 263, 135-136, 149-150, 154, 158
Hill 269, 136, 168
Hill 286, 148, 153, 158
Hill 288, 143, 145-146, 148-149, 151, 153-154, 158, 162, 165, 168-169, 172, 190-191, 228
Hill 346, 210
Hindenburg, Paul von, 24, 125, 214
Hogan, Martin, 22, 30, 61, 73, 90, 131, 138-141, 156, 223
Holy Cross Church, 222
Hotchkiss machine gun, 13, 16, 22, 35, 150, 177
Hough, Benson W., 6-7, 52, 82, 99-100, 146, 185, 198, 209-212, 223
Hughes, William, 173, 196-197
Hutchcraft, Reuben, 184, 212-213

I Company, 26-27, 46, 76, 91, 94-96, 103, 135-136, 150, 154-156, 160-161, 163-164, 166-168, 181, 190-191, 205, 223
I Corps, 32, 34, 37, 40, 43, 47, 67-68, 72, 127-129, 141, 206, 210
Idaho National Guard, 182

Imecourt, 199-200
Iowa Employment Security Commission, 228
Iowa National Guard, 5, 50, 227-228

Janis, Elsie, 48-49
Jones, Teddy, 48
Joerg, Robert, 179

K Company, 91, 93, 103, 136, 150, 154, 156-157, 164, 168, 181, 183-184, 204, 207, 212, 218
Karb, George J., 217
Kelley, William, 176
Kelly, Michael, 166-167
Kilmer, Joyce, 215
Kriemhilde Stellung, 65, 100, 125, 134, 139, 142-143, 158-159, 184, 186-188, 192, 196-197

L Company, 91-93, 103, 110, 136, 150, 154-156, 164, 167-168
La Croix Rouge Farm, 37-38, 40, 45-46, 49-50, 56, 81, 91, 182
La Forge Farm, 204
La Grange du Mont Farm, 205
La Tuilerie Farm, 143-144, 149, 164, 169-170, 174, 178-181
Lamarche, 77, 104-105
Lanza, Conrad H., 80
Le Tuilerie Farm, 143-144, 149, 164, 169-170, 178-181
Lee, Robert E., 123-124
Lenihan, Michael J., 4-5, 50, 117, 146, 185, 223
Leviathan, 217
Liggett, Hunter, 47-50, 66, 124, 136, 140-141, 206-209
logistics, 20, 66, 123, 125
Lorraine, 16, 18-24, 63
Louiseville Farm, 106-107
Ludendorff, Erich, 24, 28, 214, 216
Luneville, 16-17, 19-20, 82, 182

M Company, 91-93, 101, 103, 114, 136, 150, 154-156, 164-166, 168, 181-182,

184
MacArthur, Charles, 86, 132, 224-225
MacArthur, Douglas, xi, 1-5, 9, 12, 17, 49-51, 56, 60, 91, 109-110, 117, 148, 150, 154, 162-163, 172-176, 195-196, 224-225
Madine Lager, 99
Maizerais, 72, 79, 95-100
Mann, William, 2, 4-5, 9, 12-13, 225
Marimbois Farm, 107, 111-112, 150
Marne Salient, 32, 34, 64-66, 72, 77, 79-80, 97
Marshall, George C., xi, 66, 69, 122, 206, 225
Maxims, 92-94, 107, 112, 126, 137, 152-153, 156, 162, 166, 178-179, 182, 199, 212
McAndrew, James, 50
McCoy, Frank, 51-52
McIlvain, Mac, 193
Medal of Honor, 183, 222, 226
Menoher, Charles T., 12-13, 49-52, 117-118, 162, 173, 185, 195-196, 225
Merle-Smith, (Captain), 150, 184-185
Metz, 63-67, 70-71, 76, 81, 103, 109-110, 127-128
Meurcy Farm, 40-43, 58
Meuse-Argonne, x-xii, 70-71, 102, 118-123, 125-131, 133-135, 141, 144, 162, 219, 223, 225, 227
Meuse-Argonne American Cemetery, 162
Meuse River, 63, 69, 77, 121-127, 131, 188, 192, 197, 201-203, 209-212
Michel Zone, 65
Miesse, Leon, 1, 9, 24, 120, 205, 225
Militia Bureau, 2, 222
Minenwerfers, 92, 103, 210
Minnesota, 219
Mississippi River, 217
Mitchell, Harry, 51, 133, 146, 150, 184-185, 225
Mont Sec, 79-80, 86, 92
Montana, 219
Montfaucon, 124, 127-128, 130-134, 141-142, 151, 219
Montgarni Farm, 203

Montrebeau, 136, 195
morale, 30, 36, 50, 52, 60, 74, 129, 133, 185-186, 191-194
Moselle River, 63-64, 67, 77
Mueller, Rudolph, 112
Musarde Farm, 143-144, 149, 154, 162, 174-175, 178-179
Mutie, Eli, 212

Nachlut Stellung, 202-203
Napoleon III, 122
National Guard Association, 228
Naval War College, 223
Neibaur, Thomas, 182-183, 226
Nelson, Bernard, 152
Nelson, Oscar, 181
New York University, 227
Ninth Army, 32
91st Division, 126-128
no man's land, 17-18, 22, 26, 82, 86, 88, 91-92, 102, 116, 135, 164, 168, 188
Noble, George B., 48
Nocieves Farm, 203
North Carolina, 219
Norris, Ravee, xii, 56-57, 163, 173-175, 179-184, 226
Notes on Recent Operations No. 3, 137
Noyers-Pont-Maugis, 210

Oakdale Cemetery, 222
Office of Strategic Services, 222
Ohio in the Rainbow (Cheseldine), 76, 101
Ohio National Guard, ix, xiii, 4, 6-7, 18, 99, 223
Ohio Supreme Court, 223
Oklahoma National Guard, 59
Old Saint Raymond's Cemetery, 223
151st Field Artillery, 4, 20-21, 81, 173
151st Machine Gun Battalion, 149, 151, 175, 195, 205, 213
150th Field Artillery, 4, 20, 81-82
150th Machine Gun Battalion, 43, 120
149th Field Artillery, 4, 20, 56, 81, 86, 197
195th Saxon Division, 65

INDEX

102nd Infantry, 36
117th Engineering Regiment, 4, 45, 77, 84, 111, 145, 154, 202, 204
117th Field Signal Battalion, 4, 14
117th Trench Mortar Battery, 4, 20
117th Virginia Military Police Battery, 82
168th Infantry Regiment, xii-xiii, 4-9, 20-22, 27, 35-42, 47-53, 58-61, 73, 78-79, 84, 87, 90-94, 97, 99, 106-114, 120, 131, 135, 144-154, 157-158, 162-164, 168, 170, 175-182, 190-195, 199-201, 204-210, 215-221, 227-228
168th Machine Gun Company, 205
165th Infantry Regiment, xiii, 4-6, 20, 22-23, 30, 42, 46-47, 51-53, 58, 61, 73, 78, 84-87, 98, 100, 105-109, 118, 130, 133, 136, 142-146, 150-160, 164, 168, 184-185, 188, 193, 204, 209-210, 215-217, 222-223
164th French Division, 20, 40
167th Infantry Regiment, 5, 7, 10, 20, 29, 35-39, 42-56, 75, 78, 90-91, 94-98, 101, 106, 108, 112-115, 120, 130-131, 135-136, 144-146, 149-155, 158, 162-164, 167-168, 172-174, 181-183, 193-195, 199-201, 204-205, 210, 216, 219, 221, 223, 227
166th Infantry Regiment, ix, xiii, 1, 4-7, 17-20, 23, 26-27, 30, 42, 52-53, 73, 76, 78, 82, 88, 98-101, 109, 115-120, 129-130, 136, 142-146, 152-155, 158, 164, 184-185, 188-193, 198-205, 209-218, 221, 223, 227
166th Regimental Headquarters, 100
128th French Division, 20
129th Field Artillery, 127
123rd Division, 65
Operation Loki, 67, 86-87
Ourcq River, 32, 35, 37, 40-46, 49, 52, 54, 56-58, 78, 81, 84, 91, 151, 182, 215
"Over There" (Cohan), 216

Pannes, 76, 96-100, 111, 130-131
Paris Peace Conference, 223
Parker, John, 211

Pershing, John J., x-xi, 10-15, 20, 30, 63-73, 80-81, 110, 120-129, 132-137, 140-142, 185, 192, 206-207, 216, 223-226
Petain, Philippe, 67, 70-71, 226-227
Philippines, 4-5, 8, 49-50, 58, 80, 148, 224
The Plan for the Employment of Artillery, 145
prostitutes, 55-56
Pruette, Joseph, 180
Purdy, Bobell, 212
Py River, 25-26, 28

Quezon, Manuel, 224

Rainbow Division, ix-xiii, 2-6, 10-26, 31-35, 40-44, 49, 53-58, 72-73, 76-89, 97, 101-104, 107-110, 113, 117-120, 129, 133-147, 162-167, 173-174, 177, 184-204, 207-208, 213-216, 219-221, 227
Reilley, Thomas, 155, 160-162
Reilly, Henry, xiii, 34, 113-114, 146, 164, 167, 185, 187-188, 195-198, 211, 227
Reminiscences (MacArthur), 17, 172
Renault PT light tanks, 164
Reppy, Alison, 6, 119, 190, 198-199, 201, 227
Rhine River, 63-64, 216, 221, 223
Robb, Winfred, 8, 120, 131, 195, 199, 215, 219, 227
Romagne, 124-125, 134-135, 141-145, 149, 151, 154-155, 168, 171, 192
Roosevelt, Franklin D., 222, 224
Ross, Lloyd, xii, 58-59, 147-149, 163, 169-172, 176-177, 227-228
Rouge Bouquet (Kilmer), 215
Rupt de Mad, 79, 95-97
Russell, David, 117
Rutgers University, 227

Saint Baussant, 79, 94-95, 99-100
Saint-Benoit, 77, 101-108, 112-118, 130
Saint Clement, 16, 19-20, 23, 82
Saint Georges, 141-144, 152-160, 164-167, 174, 185-192, 197, 199, 216, 222
Saint Mihiel, x-xi, 63-72, 74-75, 77, 89,

95, 101, 103, 105, 120-131, 143-144, 149-151, 157, 197, 219, 225, 227
Saint Mihiel American Cemetery, 219
Sartelle Farm, 203
Schroeter Zone, 65
Screws, William, 7, 38, 52, 56, 149, 227
Sebastopol Farm, 105
2nd Battalion, 48, 59, 78, 90-91, 94-95, 97, 104, 106, 108, 110, 116, 135-136, 149, 152, 156-157, 167-168, 174, 188, 190, 194, 197, 204, 210-211
2nd Landwehr Division, 125
Sedan, 63, 121, 124, 188-189, 197-199, 201, 203, 205-214
Seeley, Charles, 181
Services of Supply (SOS), 123, 127, 146
Seventh Training Area, 14-16
78th Division, 184, 200-204
79th Division, 126-128, 132
77th Division, 65, 103, 126, 128-129, 204-207
76th Reserve Division, 125, 203
The Shamrock Battalion (Hogan), 61
Siecheprey, 88, 99
16th Infantry Regiment, 209
67th Field Artillery Brigade, 145-146, 185
Smith, Howard, 170
Sommerance, 136, 151-152, 156, 164, 184, 188-189, 199-200
Souilly, 140-141
Southwick, Charles, 134
Spanish-American War, 2, 5, 8
Spaulding, Roger, 152
Springfield rifle, 13, 23, 102, 139, 161, 178
Stack, Thomas, 110
Stackpole, Pierpont, 49
Stambach, Ernest, 157
Stanley, Claude, 91, 94, 97, 106-108, 110-112, 154, 227-228
Stewart, Lawrence, 36
Stonne Highway, 203, 205
Strickland, Henry, 120
The Story of the 168th Infantry (Taber), 119, 187

Suippe River, 121
Summerall, Pelot, 141, 145-146, 173, 175, 184-188, 196-197, 206-207

Taber, John, xiii, 9, 21, 35-36, 39, 47-49, 52-54, 59-60, 73-75, 78, 84-85, 91-93, 118-120, 132, 169, 176-177, 187-188, 191, 194, 199, 218, 228
tanks, 75, 78, 88164-166
Texas National Guard, 59
Thelonne, 210-211
Thiaucourt, 71, 77, 99-100, 103-105, 219
3rd Battalion, 38-39, 88-89, 93-95, 97-98, 100, 103, 111, 130-131, 135, 138-139, 149, 154, 156, 160, 164, 166, 184, 190, 204, 209-212
3rd Iowa Infantry Regiment, 8, 49
3rd Trench Mortar Battery, 81
13th Landwehr Division, 65
35th Austro-Hungarian Division, 65
35th Division, 119, 126-129, 144
39th Division, 59
32nd Division, 120, 129, 142, 144-145, 149, 153, 168, 193
37th Division, 126-130
33rd Division, 126
Thompson, Hugh, 87, 92-93
356th Infantry, 91, 93, 108
Tinley, Mathew A., 50, 97, 106, 147-148, 154, 163, 175-176, 191-192, 204, 228
Tompkins, Raymond, 126
Toul, 14, 60-63, 67, 73-74, 84
Treaty of Versailles, 223
Truman, Harry, 127, 222-225
28th Division, 126, 128, 211-212
21st French Army Corps, 26
26th Division, 3, 32-35, 64, 103, 107-108, 221
26th Infantry Regiment, 135

University of Chicago, 227
University of Oklahoma, 227
US Department of Justice, 222

V Corps, 67, 72, 126-129, 140-142, 145-146, 173-175, 184-185, 187, 196, 206

Van Hof, Bernard, 48
Vaterland, 217
Vaughn, Clyde, 27-28, 30, 228
Vauquois, 124, 128
Verdun, 63, 65, 125, 130-132
Verpel, 199-200
Vesle River, 32, 35, 43, 46, 54, 67-68
Ville, Ludoric Abel de, 198
Voie Sacree, 130
Volker Stellung, 65

Waggoman, Red, 118
Walsh, Mike, 160-162
Walter Reed Army Hospital, 226
War Department, ix, 1-4, 222, 225
West Point, xii, 4, 12, 224
Weygand, Maxim, 69
Wilhelm I, 122
Wilhelm Zone, 65
Williams, Enoch, 192
Wilson, Woodrow, xi, 1, 12, 49, 133, 149, 186
Winn, Cooper, 149-150, 158, 173-177, 197, 228
Witherell, William, 180-181
Wolf, Walter, 22, 138
Woevre Plain, 63, 67, 77, 103-108, 112
Woods 199, 167
Wren, Edward "Shorty", 39
Wuthering Heights (MacArthur), 224

Yankee Division, 3, 32, 36
YMCA, 192-193, 195